I0488839

Other Books by Joseph Pluta

Economics:

An Evolutionary Alternative to Mainstream Microeconomics
A Micro View of Industry (with Hilal Yilmaz)
Human Progress Amid Resistance to Change
The Marginal Gospel
The Story of Economics
From Adam and Eve to Adam Smith
The Elusive Quest for Efficiency in an Inefficient World (with James Willis)
The Market: Mainstream and Evolutionary Views
Consumers, Competition, and Corporations
Regional Change in the U. S. Brewing Industry
The Imperfect Microscope (with James Willis and Michael Fabritius)
Small Trees in the Large Forest
The Art of Making Choices (with James Willis and Martin Primack)
Markets, Merchants, and Monopolies (with James Willis)
The Energy Picture: Problems and Prospects
Microeconomic Horizons (with James Willis and Martin Primack)
Explorations in Microeconomics (with James Willis and Martin Primack)
Economic and Business Issues of the 1980s

Fiction:

Whatever Happened to Our Dreams?
21 Yesterdays
Small Town Michigan Tales
Two Peninsulas

From Human Evolution To Evolutionary Economics

Joseph E. Pluta

CreateSpace Publishers
North Charleston, South Carolina

Printed in the United States of America

ISBN - 13: 978-1519315816
ISBN - 10: 1519315813

webpage: josephepluta.com

The important thing is not to stop questioning. Curiosity has its own reason for existing.

Albert Einstein

History is who we are and why we are the way we are.

David McCullough

Men think epilepsy divine, merely because they do not understand it....We will one day understand what causes it, and then cease to call it divine. And so it is with everything in the universe.

Hippocrates

It is not the strongest of the species that survive, nor the most intelligent, but the one most responsive to change.

Charles Darwin

TABLE OF CONTENTS

Preface

This book presents a brief survey of economic thought since prehistoric times. Its premise is that all intelligent life has evolved in the midst of two conflicting forces. On the one hand, the accumulation of knowledge and technological advance have been the sources of human progress. Rooted in past binding tradition and custom, the opposing force has been a resistance to change that has slowed that progress. This dichotomy has been a major theme in the writing of Thorstein Veblen, founder of the evolutionary school of economics, and Clarence Ayres, who more explicitly developed the concept.

Ancient Greece and Rome, feudal Europe and Asia, the ongoing industrial ascent that began during the eighteenth century, and other chapters in world history can be addressed and analyzed within this framework. This is their story.

Some evolutionary economists understandably might prefer a different approach or combination of approaches. Especially during the early to mid twentieth century, the University of Wisconsin, Columbia University, and other reputable institutions produced significant scholarship with an evolutionary emphasis. This combined body of work is hereby acknowledged with appreciation for its influence on contemporary scholars.

My own educational experiences include the privilege of having been a student of Ayres at the conclusion of his career at the University of Texas. While insights from a number of evolutionary economists may be found in this book, its primary focus stems from the scholarship of Ayres and from his recollections of conversations with Veblen.

The book is intended for the general audience. No similar survey of the subject currently exists. Before retiring, I used drafts of these chapters in three different undergraduate courses: evolutionary economics, history of economic thought, and microeconomic principles. During my final ten years in the classroom, I found students and colleagues quite receptive to the ideas presented in the pages that follow.

Portions of this book have previously appeared under the title *Human Progress Amid Resistance to Change* published by Friesen Press of Victoria, British Columbia and copyrighted under my name. Substantial updating and rewriting has occurred before the present version has gone to press.

My sincere thanks go to those evolutionary economists with whom I have had several conversations over the years. Their insights have taught me much about this perceptive yet far too often overlooked school of thought. This group includes Wendell Gordon, Kenneth Boulding, Charles Leathers, James Peach, William Dugger, Ray Marshall, Warren Samuels, Clifton Grubbs, Edythe Miller, and Lewis Hill. Many others (especially John Kenneth Galbraith, Gunnar Myrdal, Rick Tilman, and Malcolm Rutherford) have influenced me through their numerous books and professional articles.

Any errors contained herein are mine alone.

Joseph E. Pluta
Austin, Texas
November 2015

Chapter One

History From an Evolutionary Perspective

History is the synthesis of all social sciences turned towards the past.

Emmanuel Le Roy Ladurie

Every true history must force us to remember that the past was once as real as the present and as uncertain as the future.

George Macaulay Trevelyan

Veblen's fundamental distinction is between technology and ceremonialism. This distinction is the basis of a general theory which is implicit in all of his work.

Clarence Ayres

Only a small percentage of professional economists today have more than a passing interest in the history of their discipline. Most are content to mention quite casually in their teaching or research the name of a person responsible for a concept now in popular use. Adam Smith,[1] for example, might dutifully be noted as the "father of economics", division of labor proponent, or limited government advocate. His 1776 classic, *The Wealth of Nations,* might be identified as "the first book in the field" or accorded some other equally inaccurate, obligatory dismissal before something else commands center stage. Similar token recognition might be given to other early economists.

What constitutes the *mainstream* of today's economics is something vastly different than its history. The current emphasis on enhanced analytical rigor and mathematical model building is widely documented,[2] generally accepted, and often praised. The impression offered by this approach implicitly suggests a certain timelessness in economic principles and theories. According to this line of reasoning, Smith and his early followers made us aware of an "Economics" that was more or less "always there". Once discovered, that initial collection of rudimentary economic concepts now merely needs to be reinforced by proofs similar to those offered in the physical sciences, engineering, and (advanced) mathematics.

In fact, much has happened in the evolution of economic ideas both long before and since the eighteenth century insights of Smith. That history is rich in its content, fascinating in its development, and far more global in its origins than the European centered account currently accepted before being largely ignored.

To those scholars interested in the history of ideas, some obvious questions arise: Were the path breaking contributions of Smith, and the next generation of economists he influenced, original? If not, who inspired *them?*

Humans have inhabited this planet for over three million years. How were major economic problems faced from the dawn of the human race until the 1770s? In what ways might writings of the ancient Greeks and early religious texts, for example, be relevant to economic thought throughout history? The problem is compounded by the fact that some of the ideas commonly attributed to Smith and others actually existed several centuries before their time! Evidently, economic thought is much older than many economists are willing to admit. To many contemporaries, age of origin is irrelevant for their purposes anyway, especially if the concepts are not quantifiable.

The Only Constant is Change[3]

There is nothing magical, official, or even necessarily

unique about economic principles offered by widely recognized early members of the profession. One can learn as much about economics from the fables of Aesop, poems of Homer, treatises of Plato and Aristotle, biographies of Plutarch, selected biblical passages, early non-Christian religious sources, the scientific work of Isaac Newton and Charles Darwin, epics of Renaissance humanists, novels of Charles Dickens, and the literature of Chaucer and Dante as from the writings of Adam Smith and later economists.

Specific economic episodes have also involved insights from such notable and diverse figures as Confucius, Socrates, Martin Luther, Herbert Spencer, Andrew Carnegie, J. P. Morgan, and the recently convicted criminal executives of Enron. Economic ideas have been inspired by both the great inventions of the Industrial Revolution and the catastrophe of the Great Depression. Important economic principles may be found in sources ranging from the oldest known Sumerian clay tablets to the novel that was published last week. Economic ideas may even be observed in cartoons and heard in the lyrics of popular music.

The conventional wisdom of the profession has always been in a state of flux. The decline of feudalism during the late Middle Ages paved the way for the rebirth of the market system. The eighteenth-century Industrial Revolution resulted in a body of ideas called *classical economics* (with Smith as its major figure) replacing something known as *mercantilism.* The excessive optimism of some of the classicals and the negative effects of industrialization fueled the dissents of social critics like Karl Marx and Thorstein Veblen. The Great Depression of the 1930s prompted the economic revolution of the Englishman John Maynard Keynes. Finally, post–World War II prosperity and recession ignited macroeconomic controversy among those who call themselves monetarists, new classical economists, post Keynesians, and even new Keynesians.

New theories, therefore, attempt to discard the

weaknesses while retaining the strengths of existing doctrine. The relative success of a new approach is judged by its ability to explain over time a series of economic events, including some which may not have been foreseen when the theory was advanced. Many "new" explanations draw heavily on "old" ideas. The views of influential contemporary economists on the right, left, and center as well as of the politicians who "borrow" these views for their own purposes may be profoundly and eloquently articulated but, in many cases, are not original.

A broadly based survey of early economic ideas will reveal some links between economics and other disciplines like literature, history, political science, philosophy, and the physical sciences. It might even help bring together some of the seemingly disjointed fragments of the educational experience. The story of how economics has evolved since ancient times reveals much about the close scrutiny given to the discipline today.

What makes this history especially intriguing is that the economics profession has been blessed with more than its share of gifted intellects and unusual personalities. These include not only the absent-minded Smith, the pessimistic Thomas Malthus, and the eccentric Jeremy Bentham but also the unorthodox Karl Marx, the dapper Victorian Alfred Marshall, the colorful yet pragmatic Thorstein Veblen, the sophisticated and influential John Maynard Keynes, the tirelessly pro-market anti-government Milton Friedman, and the witty corporate critic John Kenneth Galbraith.

When addressing current controversies, it is entirely appropriate to ask: What motivated some of the most profound thinkers in human history to devise new ways of confronting critical issues? The more these insightful thought processes are understood and appreciated, the easier the current application or criticism of economic principles becomes. Many of the issues the great minds faced were neither unique in their day nor in our own. As a result, the best of their ideas, if studied critically and modified appropriately, can guide the problem solvers of today and tomorrow.

Critique of the Mainstream

Despite its wide acceptance, the mainstream has always had its critics who have also drawn a sympathetic and sizable following. Several schools of thought that have opposed mainstream positions offer valuable perspectives and devastating rebuttals to prevailing doctrine. One school will receive particular attention in the following chapters, primarily because its methods adapt well to changing circumstances and its critique is becoming increasingly relevant today. This broad dissent has come to be known as *evolutionary economics.* Because much of its focus is on institutions, that is, groupings of people with common behavior patterns, members of this group are also frequently called *institutionalists* or institutional economists. *For our purposes, evolutionary economics and institutionalism will be considered one and the same.*

Evolutionary economics is a dissent against a number of the principles popularized by Smith, Marshall, and their followers. It argues that, at best, the mainstream gives an incomplete picture and, at worst, a highly inaccurate one. Its reluctant founder, Thorstein Veblen (1857-1929), argued for a more broadly based economics that paid closer attention to principles advanced in other disciplines.[4] He rejected the idea of building a discipline on a metaphor like the invisible hand[5] that was merely asserted and never proven. According to this metaphor, each individual pursuing his or her own self-interest automatically guaranteed that the public good was served. Ethically dubious and sometimes outright illegal practices of late 19th century corporate managers proved to Veblen that, by pursuing their own self-interest, such respected captains of industry were automatically guaranteeing *only* their self-interest, at the direct expense of everyone else.

While publicly singing the praises of competition and limited government, corporate leaders in Veblen's day did whatever they could to eliminate competition in pursuit of monopoly power while benefitting from federal government favors, both financial and otherwise. The closer such firms got to becoming monopolies, the more they were able to withhold their output from the market in order to charge a higher price for it. Veblen called this artificially contrived scarcity *industrial sabotage*. Its practice, he warned, meant that making money and making goods could sometimes be distinctly different business strategies capable of producing vastly different results.

An Evolutionary Framework

Veblen also argued that the satisfaction maximizing consumers of mainstream economics[6] were based on theories of human behavior that had long since been discredited by the psychology profession. People were not always rational, he maintained, and did not always make purchases based on hard calculations of how much the acquired goods contributed to personal gratification. The person who bought things on impulse amply demonstrated this fact. In place of such a human caricature, Veblen drew upon advances made in Freudian psychology that said human beings behave according to underlying traits or motivational forces called *instincts*.

Such instincts, he argued, involved conscious effort toward some purposeful end result. While many existed, he focused primarily on four such instincts. The *parental bent* is a concern for family and others, broadly speaking, the human race. The *instinct of workmanship* is the pride one takes in ones work, the satisfaction one feels when creating something of quality, and the admiration one has for the skills of others.

Idle curiosity is the quest for knowledge simply for the sake of knowing, not because of the financial reward a specific skill might bring. The *acquisitive drive*, or pursuit of profit, negates the parental bent because it is solely self-seeking and is not motivated by a desire to address the needs of the human family. To Veblen, throughout history the first three instincts worked together and contributed to human progress while being restrained and opposed by the institutions and traditions that fourth instinct and others like it created.

One of Veblen's students, Clarence Ayres (1891-1972), deciphered some of his teacher's obscure prose to formulate what has become an important part of evolutionary economic theory. To Veblen and Ayres, all societies and cultures have been influenced by two opposing forces. The first is *technology*, which is defined broadly as *tools plus human knowledge*. This force is dynamic, progressive, accepting of change, cumulative (one invention leads to another), continuous, and forward looking. It is the primary force in economic growth and human progress. It is the result, not of the profit motive, but of the combined effect of the parental bent, instinct of workmanship, and idle curiosity.

The second force has been called both *institutions* and *ceremonialism*. Institutions, as defined above, are groupings of people with similar behavior patterns. Ceremonialism is concerned with strict attention to prescribed procedures and established ways of doing things. This second force is static, past-binding, resistant to change, authoritative, and past-glorifying. It includes all customs, habits, myths, rituals, traditions, mores, taboos, and superstitions that result in conformity of behavior.[7]

To contemporary evolutionary economists, a "model" of this sort is far more valuable than anything devised by the mainstream. Over time, this approach has come to be known as the *Veblen-Ayres dichotomy.*[8] It will be used throughout this book to evaluate each historical episode presented.

During its own evolution of new methods, the psychology profession would eventually reject its emphasis on instincts as championed by Freud and others. In recent years, however, there is evidence within that profession of a renewed interest in the role of instinct-like properties in cognitive processes. The newly named "modules" bear a distinct similarity to their Freudian and Veblenian predecessors. I have discussed this development in some detail elsewhere.[9]

Major Participants in the Controversy

Mainstream economics may be interpreted as based on *selected* writings of Adam Smith and his classical disciples, including David Ricardo, Thomas Malthus, J. B. Say, Jeremy Bentham, John Stuart Mill, and others. Several decades later, *some* of their ideas were supported, refined, and made more precise by such neoclassical writers as Leon Walras, William Stanley Jevons, Carl Menger, Hermann Gossen, John Bates Clark, and especially Alfred Marshall.[10] Together, their nineteenth-century thinking fit nicely with the views of then notable non-economists. This group included *Social Darwinists* Herbert Spencer and William Graham Sumner, some prominent literary figures including Jane Austen and Robert Browning, more mediocre writers such as Horatio Alger, and prosperous business tycoons such as John D. Rockefeller, Cornelius Vanderbilt, Jay Gould, and J. P. Morgan. The overall success of the American economy in the late nineteenth century offered general support for these optimistic observations, as well as hope that those who had not yet attained the American Dream would one day get there, if they persevered.

The criticism of Karl Marx, in some areas more perceptive than in others, has been rather flippantly dismissed by mainstream observers as naïve, politically extreme, and generally discredited by world events. The dissent of Thorstein Veblen, by contrast, has in a number of cases proven to be more insightful and more accurate than anything that the more analytically precise mainstream has offered the discipline. And yet, the work of Veblen and his numerous followers has been largely ignored by, and considered irrelevant to, mainstream thinking.

Evolutionary economics may be viewed as based on the writings of Veblen, John R. Commons, Wesley C. Mitchell, Clarence E. Ayres, Gunnar Myrdal, John Kenneth Galbraith, and others. Although diverse and not always in agreement with each other, their approaches are in opposition to the mainstream tradition as exemplified by narrowly selected interpretations of Smith and Marshall. The rise of corporate giants near the end of the nineteenth century and their dominance today have provided a model of business that was different from those offered by the mainstream. The observed behavior of consumers then and now has provided patterns that were not accurately explained by the mainstream.

In these areas and in others, the evolutionary position directly challenged established doctrines within the discipline. Growing evidence is emerging that these evolutionary ideas are more relevant today than ever and more accurate in explaining reality than long accepted (or at least long taught) mainstream ideas.

Some professional economists may object to the division of its members into two camps, *mainstream (neoclassical)* vs. *evolutionary (institutionalist)* as imprecise or even misleading. Those in the mainstream might point to several differences between their contemporary views and those of the neoclassicals. The modern version, however, is deeply rooted in the thought of nineteenth-century neoclassical economists, many of whose ideas are accepted by mainstreamers today.

Similarly, there are different groups who now call

themselves evolutionary economists, including some who do not trace their origins to Veblen. Most contemporary followers of Veblen call themselves institutionalists even though Veblen would have preferred the term evolutionary economics. Two recently formed groups, one called the *new institutional economics* and the other *contemporary evolutionary economics,* have little or nothing to do with either Veblen or the original "old" institutionalists. Such squabbling over names aside, the distinction offered here appears justified based on the arguments made in the following pages, the historical origin of these terms, and the intellectual influences on both traditions.

History Matters

The economics discipline has evolved over several centuries in response to specific economic and social problems across the globe. In many cases, when crises surfaced, they were vastly different from anything then known. A previously decreed economic "law" would have been of little value in addressing a new crisis. Instead, proposed solutions were often heavily debated with input from groups of people who possessed conflicting interests in the outcome. As a result, various schools of thought have contributed to a constantly changing body of knowledge that, therefore, must be viewed as a continually evolving process. Understanding how and why economics has altered its focus over time is crucial in knowing how it got to where it is now. Key events in world economic history and the history of economic thought are essential in providing a more complete picture of the discipline's relevance.

Embraced by evolutionary economists, a concept called path dependency[11] may be especially relevant in their analysis. *Path dependency* is sometimes broadly interpreted as simply meaning that history matters. What has occurred before, perhaps by design but more likely by chance, has set in motion a sequence of events that has followed a given direction or path. To most observers, this outlook is too broad and merely states the obvious. A more specific view emphasizes the self-reinforcing nature of institutions. Feedback provided to the existing path often guarantees that it proceeds without modification. A chance experiment, for example, may lead to the development of a given technology that prompts additional applications without adequately surveying viable alternatives.

For almost a century, steel manufacturing in the United States was based on the Bessemer and open hearth processes developed in the 1890s. Even after Japanese and European manufacturers adopted more modern techniques after World War II, American producers stuck with the old way until nearly the twenty-first century.

All cars were powered by gasoline until very recently. Once the technology was established, a general reluctance to change dictated that change did not occur. Hybrid and entirely electric powered cars have finally entered the market long after their performance and efficiency had been demonstrated.

For many years, all movies were made in Hollywood, all cars were made in Michigan, most books were published in New York, and most computer chips were made in California's Silicon Valley. There may have been advantageous reasons for locating at each sight originally but businesses remained there long after those initial advantages had vanished.

The two most commonly cited examples of path dependency are the keyboard and the gauge of railroads. Early typewriters began with the sequence of letters Q-W-E-R-T-Y. This placement was designed to eliminate jamming of keys while other letter groupings allowed for faster, more efficient typing. Even though the early mechanical glitches were quickly resolved, the QWERTY set-up remained and was soon reinforced by typing manuals and instruction kits based on this early line-up of letters. Such positive feedbacks enthroned QWERTY as the standard keyboard.[12] Changing from it now would require not only a technological adjustment but also the retraining of millions of users.

On railroads, gauge is simply the distance between the rails. Back in the 1820s, horses pulled metal carts carrying coal and other materials from mines. The rails on which the wheels of these carts rested were built 4 feet, 8 1/2 inches apart. With his typical wit, Veblen noted how these "silly little bobtailed carriages" (still in use in 1915) slowed the development of superior technology by "the restraining dead hand of . . . past achievement."[13] Today, passenger trains that reach nearly 200 mph roll on the exact same gauge of rails. Different gauges have been shown to be more efficient, especially when long railroad cars must negotiate tight curves. Making those changes on millions of miles of track worldwide and on millions of existing railroad cars, however, simply is no longer feasible primarily due to cost issues.

While these and other examples emphasize path dependency due to established technology preferences, similar lock-in may also occur because of long-held behavior patterns.[14] The accepted path may be moving toward either a beneficial or harmful outcome. Throughout much of human history, the latter situation has predominated.

Reluctance to experiment among members of nomadic tribes during prehistory, among feudal era agricultural workers, and among members of medieval guilds are all examples of path dependency. In each of these cases, progress was slowed. In the first two, the delay lasted for centuries.

Many corporate strategies and government programs today are still implemented according to path dependencies inaugurated when conditions may have justified such patterns but no longer do.[15] Evolutionary economics, with its emphasis on studying past binding institutional resistance to change, appears especially well equipped to focus on needed prerequisites for economic progress centuries ago and for more efficient ways of doing things today.

Footnotes:

1. Some of the more recent readable works on Adam Smith include Maria Pia Paganelli, "Recent Engagement With Adam Smith and the Scottish Enlightenment", *History of Political Economy*, 47, 4 (September 2015), pp. 363-394; Samuel Hollander, *The Economics of Adam Smith,* (Toronto: University of Toronto Press, 1973) and Mark Blaug, ed., *Adam Smith,* (Brookfield, VT: Edward Elgar, 1991).

2. Joseph E. Pluta, *An Evolutionary Alternative to Mainstream Microeconomics*, (North Charleston, South Carolina: CreateSpace Publishers, 2016).

3. While it has become something of a cliche, the phrase is originally attributed to Heraclitus (c 535- c 475 BCE) of Ephesus, a pre-Socratic Greek philosopher.

4. Reading Veblen in the original is not an easy task. For the best summary of his ideas in readable form, see Ken McCormick, *Veblen in Plain English: A Complete Introduction to Thorstein Veblen's Economics,* (Youngstown, New York: Cambria Press, 2006).

5. Smith used the metaphor of the *invisible hand* to allege the widespread benefit of self-interest. He believed the unseen hand of competition regulated the economy much better than the strong, visible hand of mercantilist government. To enhance their own economic well being by producing goods that people needed, producers were made better off while consumers were as well. This tied in nicely with *consumer sovereignty*, the notion that the consumer was king. Those businesses that produced what consumers wanted were successful while those that did not were not. The consumer, in other words, allegedly called the shots.

6. The claim that consumers attempt to maximize satisfaction when purchasing goods was first advanced by Jeremy Bentham (1748-1832). Although controversial from the beginning, the claim quickly became a cornerstone of mainstream thought and a generally accepted maxim in the theory of consumer behavior.

7. David Dequech, "The Institutions of Economics: A First Approximation", *Journal of Economic Issues,* 48, 2 (June 2014), pp. 523-531.

8. This dichotomy has been modified by several researchers since first formally presented by Ayres in 1962 (*The Theory of Economic Progress*, 2nd ed., New York: Schocken Books) and utilized more extensively by Wendell Gordon in 1980 (*Institutional Economics: The Changing System,* Austin, University of Texas Press). Most of this work involved various "updates" so that more recent issues could be analyzed within this framework. One study (Igor Matutinovic, "An Institutional Approach to Sustainability: Historical Interplay of Worldviews, Institutions, and Technology", *Journal of Economic Issues*, 41, 4 (December 2007), pp. 1109-1137), for example, has broadened the approach to include the concept of "worldview" and its potential impact on sustainability. Such updates, while valuable for current research, are not relevant in studying the localized environments that prevailed, say, until the end of the Middle Ages.

9. Pluta, chapter 4.

10. Peter Groenenwegen, *A Soaring Eagle: Alfred Marshall, 1842–1924,* (Brookfield, VT: Edward Elgar, 1995). This nearly 900 page work is *the* authoritative biography on the life and contributions of Marshall. For more recent perspectives, see: Patrik Aspers, "Alfred Marshall and the Concept of

Class", *American Journal of Economics and Sociology,* 69, 1 (January 2010), pp. 151-165 and Jaques Kerstenetzky, "Alfred Marshall on Big Business", *Cambridge Journal of Economics*, 34, 3 (May 2010), pp. 569-586.

11. Richard R. Nelson and Sidney G. Winter, *An Evolutionary Theory of Economic Change*, (Cambridge, MA: Harvard University Press, 1982). While these authors are part of the group called "contemporary evolutionary economics" that does not claim Veblen as its founder, they do provide a thorough discussion of the path dependency concept in this book.

12. Tanjim Hossain and John Morgan, "The Quest for QWERTY", *American Economic Review*, 99, 2 (May 2009): pp. 435-440.

13. Thorstein Veblen, *Imperial Germany and the Industrial Revolution,* (New York: Macmillan, 1915), pp. 125–128.

14. William Barnes, Myles Gartland, and Martin Stack, "Old Habits Die Hard: Path Dependency and Behavioral Lock-in," *Journal of Economic Issues,* 38, 2 (June 2004), pp. 371–377.

15. As the following sources indicate, the concept is widely used in several disciplines besides economics. See Raghu Garud, Arun Kumaraswamy, and Peter Karnoe, "Path Dependence or Path Creation?" *Journal of Management Studies*, 47, 2 (June 2010), pp. 760-774; Taylor C. Boas, "Conceptualizing Continuity and Change: The Composite-Standard Model of Path Dependence", *Journal of Theoretical Politics*, 19, 1 (January 2007), pp. 33-54; and James Mahoney, "Path Dependence in Historical Sociology", *Theory and Society*, 29, 4 (August 2000), pp. 507-548.

Chapter Two

Prehistory and its Legacy

In every island of the Aegean Sea are found abundant traces of a vast prehistoric empire.
James Theodore Bent

We must learn, and we are gradually learning, how to write history with the help of archeology.
Michael Rostovtzeff

Warfare has been an integral part of the human existence since long before we were humans.
Steven A. LeBlanc

Prehistoric humans lived in a world that must have appeared enormous in its dimensions, without known boundaries, and beyond comprehension. Because knowledge of this world was limited, established ways of doing things were not easily discarded. Once some pattern of behavior could be shown to assist in the quest for survival, members of a small tribe embraced it with a reverence that persisted almost indefinitely. Primitive habits, traditions, customs, and rituals governed daily life because they seemed to work. New ideas were shunned and new technology was slow to develop because of the limited time for and the risk involved in any experimentation. The primary human motivation of early nomadic people was neither adventure, nor the quest for profit, nor the accumulation of property. Rather, it was staying alive.

An Approximate Time Frame

Although life was at times almost terrifyingly challenging, the earth's population prior to, say, 5,000 years ago was fairly small. The land mass and resource base provided basic amenities for all who worked diligently and who escaped random misfortune, including accident and illness. Pursuit of game (animals, fish, and birds) along with edible plants and fruit enabled prehistoric humans to survive and generally coexist with nature. The latter, in turn, dictated seasonal variations in migration patterns of animal herds and the people who followed them. The wilderness was large enough that, once a given region saw its animal and fishing resources depleted, people moved on to a seemingly endless frontier where they found new sources of nourishment and temporary shelter.

Prehistory is generally regarded as the period of human existence before the written word. What is known about this period today is the result of archaeological discoveries and careful piecing together of scientific facts. While scientists and archaeologists are cautious about precise dating, prehistory generally comprises two historical and geological periods.[1] The Paleolithic Age (also called the Old Stone Age) begins about three million years ago when humans in East Africa presumably first began making tools and ends about 10,000 years ago when farming first began in parts of the Near East. The Neolithic Age (New Stone Age) immediately follows and concludes about 5,000 years ago with the "birth of civilization" in Mesopotamia and Egypt.

The Myth of a Peaceful Prehistory

Veblen[2] called this approximate time frame the "era of peaceable savagery" because he believed that, based on archaeological evidence available in his day, conflict between tribes was rare and perhaps even non-existent. In support of this claim, he argued that pottery and cave art from Paleolithic times contained peaceful images, such as rites of fertility and small, maternal god-like creatures, *but no weapons*. Proof of abundant weaponry from similar sources in the barbaric predatory stage that followed, however, was displayed in its art, which depicted male deities, violence attributed to religious beliefs, and a god towering above subjects in a master-servant hierarchy.[3] Veblen reasoned that it was not until this predatory period that wealth discrepancies surfaced due to formal ownership. When a surplus above subsistence emerged, greed-inspired violence finally became worth the effort. He stated further that early agriculture with its small settlements and cultivated fields could not have been pursued under warlike conditions.[4]

The myth of the "noble savage" not yet prone to violence and the hope that the human race originated with natural peaceful tendencies has been kept alive by individual archaeological discoveries that do not explicitly show violence. Peaceful Paleolithic cave art and human remains that do not contain evidence of violent death have offered some semblance of assurance to those who cling to such beliefs. Even a thorough history of weaponry[5] begins in late prehistory (3500 BCE) suggesting that no weapons existed prior to this time.

The evidence, however, that the human race has always possessed violent tendencies is overwhelming.[6] "Defleshed" human bones, instances of cannibalism, and proof of ancient warfare as long as 750,000 and even 2 million years ago are all part of the archaeological record.[7] There is also indisputable documentation of violent behavior among possible chimpanzee ancestors, hominoids, protohumans, Neandertals, and other evolutionary forerunners of the human race. In later prehistory, say, 10,000 to 15,000 years ago, there is evidence of arrowheads embedded in skeletons, decapitation, skull fractures caused by stone tools striking the cranium, and intentional dismemberment. Clearly, *prehistory was not free from violence.* If Veblen's era of peaceable savagery ever existed, it must have been much earlier than he hypothesized and even that hopeful assertion has yet to be proven.

The Microscopic Pace of Progress

Many reputable scientists and archaeologists believe that humans walked the earth as early as three million, or even six million, years ago. Some time during early human existence, prehistoric people at various locations across the globe began using crude tools such as clubs and scrapers made of wood, bone, or stone. Over time, stones were eventually chipped to make sharp-edged cutters, sticks were made into spears, and the bow and arrow became a hunting implement, which soon evolved into a weapon.[8] With the discovery of fire, spears could be hardened, cooking became possible, and thus diets expanded to include previously hard to digest foods. Caves could also be freed from animals and made warmer. Fire increased meat consumption, which enhanced protein intake, energy, and productivity in work. Precise or even approximate dates of these important achievements are unknown. Despite these advances, our early ancestors still lived close to subsistence. Famine often decimated almost entire tribes, except its strongest members.

Geologists tell us that there have been more than 20 Ice Ages over the past three million years. During these periods, perhaps as much as one-third of Earth's surface was covered with ice sheets called *glaciers,* some of which may have been several thousand feet (more than a mile) thick. Early humans sometimes migrated great distances on foot in search of food and protection from the elements. Harsh weather, of course, both encouraged and assisted human migration. During the last Ice Age (between roughly 30,000 and 10,000 BCE), for example, people from Asia walked across the ice-covered Bering Strait into what is now Alaska and British Columbia. Eventually, they moved south and east to populate much of both North and South America.[9] Whether or not this was the first migration of people onto the American continents is still being debated. That this path was taken by many early migrants, however, is not in dispute.

Anthropologists, historians, and psychologists still have many unanswered questions about human activity during prehistory. One of the most basic certainly must be: What thought processes inspired the behavior of our earliest ancestors? Of course, survival, often considered the most basic of human instincts, provided ample motivation. More specifically, however, why were some courses of action chosen over others? Although we are still learning about early cognitive development (i.e., use of human brain power) and many theories exist, a modern evolutionary perspective offers a plausible explanation.

In their quest to survive, early humans no doubt took pride in their work and desired to do things as efficiently as they possibly could, given the enormous obstacles they faced. In battling weather and combating hunger, the margin for error was often prohibitively small. Rooted in early human experience, thoughtful motivational direction was likely provided by instinctive behavior aimed at achieving specific purposes.

This pride in even the most basic of early accomplishments may be one of the first manifestations of the instinct of workmanship. According to this evolutionary view, workmanship and other instincts that the mind uses to plot a course of action interacted with established ways of doing things through a process of natural selection.[10] "The instinct of workmanship brought the life of mankind from the brute to the human plane. . . ."[11] It created a positive and progressive force that began whittling away at both established methods of doing things and relatively passive acceptance of nature's benevolence and wrath. Along with other instincts, workmanship eventually produced more complex thought patterns or habits from which reasoning, calculation, judgment, and learning[12] all became possible. What followed over several centuries was a gradual transformation in the way economic activity was organized and lives were lived.

Relative isolation reduced possibilities for advances in technological know-how or what might be called the community of knowledge. Existing tools were, by any modern measure, crude and limited in their capacity to deliver food and other necessities of life. Indeed, the term Stone Age refers to that time frame when tools were, in fact, made of stone. The Copper, Bronze, and Iron Ages that followed were similarly named to reflect advances in tool production. Stone tools were probably not the first tools but earlier versions made of wood likely perished thousands of years ago and therefore have left no record of their existence.

Stone hand-axes existed about 1.3 million years ago in Africa, Asia, and Europe. It was not until 100,000 or so years ago that sharper stones were made by chipping flakes from a naturally pointed stone. Over 11,000 years ago, First Nations people (in what is now the western hemisphere) improved this chipping technique to create pointed arrows which they used to hunt large animals. Such early pieces of chert and flint have come to be known as clovis points because they were first discovered near Clovis, New Mexico. The sickle or reaping knife appears in Europe about this time while various types of blade technology existed in Siberia over 30,000 years ago.[13] Fishhooks, harpoons, needles, pottery, and woven fabric were known to exist at various times during the Paleolithic period.

Early in prehistory, the technology vs. institutions dichotomy was already very much in evidence. On the one hand, concern for other members of the group, proven workmanship, and cautious idle curiosity resulted in rudimentary tools and limited, yet effective, human knowledge. These in turn enabled little more than survival of the species. The pace of economic advance was somewhere between very slow and nonexistent. Reluctance to change, the opposing and restraining force, was dictated by established ways of doing things that were cherished over several generations. Nature's uncertainties discouraged experimentation. Economic progress simply was not a viable concept in a world where merely staying alive occupied human intuition from dawn until dusk.

The Dominance of Superstition

In this pre-scientific era, superstition and ceremonialism held an enormous influence over the thought patterns people possessed. Superstition was rampant as primitive humans sought to understand that which they could not explain in practical terms. Various gods were invented to account for the inexplicable; the sun god, for example, was somewhat logically worshipped as the source of life. Wind, water, and thunder were similarly judged to possess divine attributes. In place of critical or scientific reasoning, prehistoric humans often resorted to imaginary explanation and false belief rooted in lack of understanding (or, put more bluntly, ignorance).

When knowledge increases and ignorance decreases, then superstition decreases. Every increase in knowledge is at the expense of some superstition. This is a necessary first step in scientific and technological advance.[14] Fortunately, the human race over time has proceeded in this general direction. The ceremonial rituals of early humans included specific burial rites that often suggested hope of an afterlife, initiation procedures, group dancing, and music. All of these rituals were more than either a show of respect, an innocent release of energy, or a filler of free time. Rather, they possessed a mystical quality rooted in myth, legend, and supernatural beliefs. Since science in effect did not exist, how else could the majesty of the universe, not to mention the predictability of the seasons, be comprehended?

Historically, this obsession with ceremonial behavior has resisted change and glorified past-binding tradition. Early human cultures embraced such practices as witchcraft, human sacrifice, animal sacrifice, worship of dubious deities, and other rituals that could be justified only by custom and reverence for ancestral behavior.[15] Oral tradition, folklore, cults, reverence for sacred places, shamanistic trances, symbolism, signs from above and other forms of ceremonialism were all rampant throughout prehistory. Indeed, the shaman held a respect that often bordered on reverence. Whatever positive defense of such practices may be offered, their one common feature has been fear of and resistance to new patterns of thought. Economic progress, technological innovation, and cultural advancement have inevitably been slowed by this misplaced respect for previous ways of doing things.

It would not be unreasonable to hypothesize that, when early Paleolithic hominoids first learned to create fire by rubbing flint stones together, this represented one of the first, if not the first, challenges of technology including human know how to established ceremonial beliefs. Prior to this understanding of how fire might be initiated and controlled, early humans likely experienced fire created by lightning, volcanoes, or sun-parched prairie grasses, all of which they probably attributed to a mystical deity or supernatural force. Precise dating of the first human use of fire is impossible. It is, however, generally believed to have occurred during the early Paleolithic Era sometime, say, before 250,000 BCE.

Similarly, archaeologists have shown that the introduction of the potter's wheel in Late Bronze Age Greece met with resistance because making pots by hand was embedded in earlier Greek culture.[16] When births occurred in prehistory, the event was shrouded in mystic ritual, symbolism, socio/cultural mores, and companionship while technology and medical treatment were limited to keeping mother and infant warm.[17] Diets were based on custom and tradition more than nutritional value, even when availability of protein-rich food was not a problem.[18] Postponement of change was the rule. When some hunter-gatherers first encountered agricultural settlements, as many as 1000 years passed before their tribes were willing to try these new methods of obtaining food.[19] Such reluctance has been described as a resistance phenomenon, due to possible challenges to existing power relationships and social organization, rather than backwardness.

The Birth of Civilization

The most recent Ice Age ended about 10,000 BCE. Over the next six to seven thousand years, the human race eventually evolved from a nomadic existence based on hunting and gathering to a more settled lifestyle dependent on agriculture. This change became possible because of cultivation of previously wild vegetation and domestication of animals. Early cultivation of plants included wheat and barley in south Asia (present-day Pakistan), rice and millet in East Asia (China), and maize in Mesoamerica (especially from what is now south central Mexico to Panama). Domestication of animals eventually provided sources not only of power to pull plows but also of meat, milk, hides, and wool to people who began settling in villages.

Because of their required mobility, hunters and gatherers had few permanent possessions. In village communities, however, more tools and pottery could be produced and accumulated, people could become more specialized in their work, and more complex economic and social relationships, including basic manufacturing and trade, could be developed.

The invention of agriculture made possible the

accumulation of a food surplus that allowed people to do other things besides search for food.[20] Herein lie the roots of early economic progress and of leisure time, which, through art and literature, were destined to become the basis of culture. In a hunting/gathering economy, thousands of acres are needed to support a single family. In even a rudimentary agricultural economy, however, perhaps two dozen acres are sufficient. Land, therefore, is used more efficiently and considerable population growth becomes possible. The result is villages and the appearance of workers with skills unrelated to agriculture.

The first civilizations emerged along four major river basins:[21] the Tigris and Euphrates in Sumer (later known as Mesopotamia, today called Iraq), the Nile in Egypt, the Indus in India, and the Yellow River in China. It is one of the great ironies of world history that human civilization began in the same place (Sumer) where some of the most inhumane and uncivilized behavior has occurred in recent years (Iraq).[22]

The Sumerians built a relatively sophisticated society, an important component of which was its uniquely advanced economic system. Its commerce, for example, involved contracts, credit, loans with interest, and business partnerships. To construct their cities and irrigation networks, fairly precise architecture and engineering skills were required. Techniques of mathematics, including formal weights and measures, had to be devised. Sumerian mathematicians developed a notation based on the number 60, from which the 60-second minute, 60-minute hour, 360-degree circle, and concept of a dozen have all survived to the present. Tools, many made of bronze, became a vital part of construction and manufacturing efforts.

The Sumerians opened schools, created the lunar calendar, developed government institutions and laws, and used an early form of money. Perhaps most importantly, the need to keep records required the invention of writing. In this ancient culture, both literature and art thrived. Sumer gave the world its oldest known written story, the *Epic of Gilgamesh,*[23] on clay tablets perhaps as early as 2600 BCE. Although Gilgamesh was an actual king in the city of Uruk on the Euphrates River, the classic poem is a fictional account about the human fear of death and dream of immortality. It also touches on somewhat less-cosmic matters pertinent to economics.

The story describes the production process of building a raft and giant gate for a city after two of its heroes chop down a forest of cedar trees. The heroes later admit how inefficient they were in destroying so many trees for so little output. The text also discusses profits, wages, and skills of workers in various occupations, including trappers, butchers, blacksmiths, jewelers, farmers, craftsmen, a tavern keeper, and a ferryman. Tools such as hatchets, axes, and swords are described in intricate detail.

The most dramatic part of the epic is the sudden appearance of a great flood that destroys the human race, except for a privileged family who survives by building and inhabiting an ark. The storyline is embellished centuries later in the biblical account of Noah's Ark familiar to generations of Christians. Other biblical stories including the Creation, the Garden of Eden, the rivalry between Cain and Abel, and the Tower of Babel are also "borrowed" from similar accounts in Mesopotamian literature. When the Gilgamesh tablets were discovered by archeologists in the 1870s, their contents thoroughly enraged religious fundamentalists, many of whom still downplay their authenticity and significance.

Technology vs. Institutions in Prehistory

Ceremonial behavior clearly dominated any effort to increase knowledge throughout prehistory. For this reason, technological advance proceeded at a microscopic pace. When crude tools first appeared, they were adapted to useful ends only slowly. Basic instincts like workmanship, idle curiosity, and the parental bent, however, did eventually produce changes in established ways of doing things. Long after agricultural techniques were first invented, nomadic hunter/gatherer tribes eventually adopted these methods and joined or formed their own sedentary villages.

Despite their continuing reverence for myth and legend, the ancient Sumerians were among the first cultures in which the pace of technological advance and expanding human knowledge began to challenge past binding institutions and ceremonialism. In their cities and rural enclaves, workmanship was much in evidence as was concern for the well being of other citizens and a curiosity that inspired discovery of new concepts and methods. The changing strength of these forces enabled some amount of sustained economic progress to occur possibly for the first time in the already long history of the human race.

Footnotes:

1. Marvin Perry, *Western Civilization: A Brief History*. 5th ed., (Boston: Houghton Mifflin, 2004), pp. 4-6.

2. Thorstein Veblen, *The Instinct of Workmanship and the State of the Industrial Arts,* (New York: Macmillan, 1914), especially chapters 3 and 4.

3. Veblen, p. 126.

4. Veblen , pp. 100-101.

5. R. Ewart Oakeshott, *The Archaeology of Weapons: Arms and Armour From Prehistory to the Age of Chivalry,* (Mineola, New York: Dover Publications, 1996).

6. Joseph E. Pluta, "Technology vs. Institutions in Prehistory", *Journal of Economic Issues,* 46, 1 (March 2012),

pp. 209-226. See also John Henry, "The Hobbesian Individual in Prehistory: Joseph Pluta vs. Thorstein Veblen: A Comment", *Journal of Economic Issues,* 47, 1 (March 2013), pp. 269-272 and Joseph E. Pluta, "Veblen and the Study of Prehistoric Humans: A Reply to Henry", *Journal of Economic Issues,* 47, 1 (March 2013), pp. 272-275.

7. Juan L. Arsuaga, "The First Europeans: Spanish Caves Paint a New Picture of Evolution on the Continent," *Discovering Archaeology,* 2, 5 (2000), pp. 48-65; Lawrence Keeley, *War Before Civilization: The Myth of the Peaceful Savage,* (Oxford: Oxford University Press, 1996); Raymond C. Kelly, "The Evolution of Lethal Intergroup Violence," *Proceedings of the National Academy of Sciences,* 102, 43 (2005), pp.15294-15298; Steven A. LeBlanc and Katherine E. Register, *Constant Battles: The Myth of the Peaceful, Noble Savage, (*New York: St. Martin's Press, 2004); and Keith F. Otterbein, *How War Began,* (College Station: Texas A&M University Press, 2004).

8. Rondo Cameron and Larry Neal, *A Concise Economic History of the World: From Paleolithic Times to the Present,* 4th ed., (New York: Oxford University Press, 2003), p. 20.

9. Robert J. Muckle, *The First Nations of British Columbia: An Anthropological Survey,* (Vancouver: University of British Columbia Press, 1998), pp. 12–22. A specific prehistoric migration pattern is described in Jenneth E. Curtis, "Migration and Cultural Change: The Northern Iroquoian Case in South-Central Ontario", *Journal of World Prehistory*, 27, 2 (August 2014), pp. 145-195. For economic ideas in First Nations America, see James Cicarelli, "Economic Thought Among American Aboriginals Prior to 1492", *American Journal of Economics and Sociology*, 71, 1 (January 2012), pp. 77-125.

10. Christian Cordes, "Veblen's 'Instinct of Workmanship', Its

Cognitive Foundations, and Some Implications for Economic Theory," *Journal of Economic Issues,* 39, 1 (March 2005), pp. 1–20, especially pp. 4–7.

11. Veblen, p. 37.

12. See Chapter 11 for a more thorough description of this psychological process. A number of contemporary psychologists support this explanation of cognitive development. See, for example, Howard Margolis, *Patterns, Thinking and Cognition: A Theory of Judgment,* (Chicago: University of Chicago Press, 1987). See also Paul Twomey, "Reviving Veblenian Economic Psychology," *Cambridge Journal of Economics,* 22, 4 (July 1998), pp. 433–448 and Tony Lawson, "Process, Order and Stability in Veblen", *Cambridge Journal of Economics*, 39, 4 (July 2015), pp. 993-1030.

13. Vitality Larichev, Uriv Khol'ushkin and Inna Laricheva, "The Upper Paleolithic of Northern Asia: Achievements, Problems, and Perspectives, III. Northeastern Siberia and the Russian Far East." *Journal of World Prehistory,* 6, 4 (1992), pp. 441-476.

14. This argument was often made by Clarence Ayres. See, for example, his *The Theory of Economic Progress,* 2nd ed., (New York: Schocken Books, 1962), especially chapter 8. See also Joseph E. Pluta, "The Last Course on Institutionalism Taught by Clarence E. Ayres," *Research in the History of Economic Thought and Methodology,* 26, B (2008), pp. 309-336.

15. Katrinka Reinhart, "Religion, Violence, and Emotion: Modes of Religiosity in the Neolithic and Bronze Age of Northern China", *Journal of World Prehistory*, 28, 2 (June 2015), pp. 113-177.

16. Ina Berg, "Meaning in the Making: The Potter's Wheel at Phylakopi, Melos (Greece)," *Journal of Anthropological Archaeology,* 26, 2 (2007), pp. 234-252. See also Patrick Roberts, Nicole Boivin, and Michael Petraglia, "The Sri Lankan 'Microlithic' Tradition c. 38,000 to 3,000 Years Ago: Tropical Technologies and Adaptations of *Homo Sapiens* at the Southern Edge of Asia", *Journal of World Prehistory*, 28, 2 (June 2015), pp. 69-112 and Brian M. Fagan, ed. *The Seventy Great Inventions of the Ancient World,* (London: Thames and Hudson, 2004).

17. Emer O'Donnell, "Birthing in Prehistory." *Journal of Anthropological Archaeology,* 23, 2 (2004), pp. 163-171.

18. Elrinl I. Petroutsa and Sotiris K. Manolis. "Reconstructing Late Bronze Age Diet in Mainland Greece Using Stable Isotope Analysis." *Journal of Archaeological Science,* 37, 3 (2010), pp. 614-620.

19. Pablo Arias, "The Origins of the Neolithic Along the Atlantic Coast of Continental Europe: A Survey." *Journal of World Prehistory,* 13, 4 (1999), pp. 403-464.

20. It has recently been argued, however, that it took considerable time for these effects to be realized and that the early transition to agriculture produced some puzzling health outcomes including the fact that "humans initially were more disease prone, smaller, less nourished, and shorter-lived". See Arthur J. Robson, "A Bioeconomic View of the Neolithic Transition to Agriculture", *Canadian Journal of Economics*, 43, 1 (February 2010): pp. 280-300. For a different perspective, see T. J. Wilkinson et. al., "Contextualizing Early Urbanization: Settlement Cores, Early States and Agro-Pastoral Strategies in the Fertile Crescent During the Fourth and Third Millennia BC", *Journal of World Prehistory*, 27, 1 (March 2014), pp. 43-109.

21. Approximate dates for the beginning of these first civilizations are Mesopotamia: 3000 BCE, Egypt: 3100 BCE, India: 2500 CE, and China: 1500 BCE. In Mesoamerica, this change occurs much later, although agriculture evolves there without any stimulus from elsewhere in the world as early as 5000 BCE.

22. Of course, precise boundaries of these three so named geographic locations have varied. This should be especially evident in that the modern demarcation of Iraq was made by the League of Nations in 1920 as part of its formal disintegration of the Ottoman Empire.

23. A 1400 BCE version is credited to an author named Shin-leqi-unninni. See Maureen Gallery Kovacs, *The Epic of Gilgamesh, (*Stanford, California: Stanford University Press, 1989). On parallels between Sumerian literature and the Bible, see Robert M. Best, *Noah's Ark and the Zuisudra Epic: Sumerian Origins of the Flood Myth,* (Fort Myers, FL: Enlil Press, 1999); Stephanie Dalley, *Myths from Mesopotamia. Creation, the Flood, and Others: A New Translation,* (Oxford: Oxford University Press, 1989); and Alexander Heidel, *The Gilgamesh Epic and Old Testament Parallels,* (Chicago: University of Chicago Press, 1963).

Chapter Three

Ancient Cultures and Economies

It was not wisdom that enabled poets to write their poetry, but a kind of instinct or inspiration.

Socrates

The most perfect political community is one in which the middle class is in control and outnumbers both of the other classes.

Aristotle

The world cares very little about what a man or woman knows; it is what a man or woman is able to do that counts.

Virgil

Don't think, just do.

Horace

Modern ideas have come from a number of civilizations that emerged during a period generally known as Classical Antiquity. These early cultures include Persia, Arabia, Babylon, Israel, Egypt, Greece, Rome, China, India, and several others. All tell us much about human progress at the dawn of recorded history and the struggles of everyday life during an era of limited, yet advancing, technology.

Seven centuries before the birth of Christianity, inventors in Persia developed the qanat, an irrigation system still used in parts of Iran today. The early Egyptians gave the world the ramp, the lever, papyrus (a form of paper), and the decimal system as well as, of course, the pyramids (whose precise origin is still a mystery). Ancient China is responsible for paper making, the compass, gunpowder, printing, bells made of pottery, lacquer, acupuncture, and nail polish. Plastic surgery began in India (20th century BCE) where the first cataract surgery was also performed (6th century BCE).

Early inventions in Greece included the catapult, cartography (mapmaking), cranes with winches, plumbing systems for baths and fountains, canal locks, alarm clocks, primitive cannons, and surveying tools. Soon afterward, Roman engineering produced aqueducts, dams, bridges, roads, and amphitheaters as well as advances in mining technology.

The focus in this chapter will be upon Greece and Rome, both of which rose to initial prominence during the eighth century BCE. Despite the prevalence of tradition and superstition in both cases, each made significant strides in advancing human knowledge.

Ancient Greece

The Greeks of antiquity profoundly influenced Western civilization, especially in the areas of politics, architecture, literature, science, philosophy, and art. Athens is where the ideals of democracy first developed in the late sixth century BCE. Portions of its Parthenon, the magnificent temple completed in 432 BCE, and remnants of other architectural wonders still stand today. Early Greek contributions to literature range from the eighth century(?) BCE epic poems of Homer to the second century CE biographies of Plutarch. Classic works throughout this period frequently offer insightful economic perspectives.

Homer and Plutarch

In the *Odyssey,* for example, Homer describes the self-sufficient household economy, efficiently cultivated orchards and gardens, and the trades of the blacksmith and potter in early Greek history.[1] He also provides vivid accounts of the shipping industry, the sailing profession, and at least one port city whose harbors made trade with neighboring ports possible. A recurring theme in the *Odyssey* is the waste of household resources by guests who overextend their welcome. Much of the *Iliad,* the other major work attributed to Homer, is about the distribution of income and wealth.[2] All of these topics would capture the attention of economists for centuries to come.

Plutarch (47–120 CE), who would later inspire Shakespeare among others, is well known for his biographies of famous Greeks and Romans. Ethical and religious in tone, his work in the area of philosophy is supportive of Plato[3] (discussed below) and highly critical of thought Plutarch dismissed as overly secular (the Stoics and Epicureans). Often considered puritanical, he was not without satire and humor.

One of his more than 200 titles, "Of the Love of Wealth" compares man's insatiable quest for gold and silver to eating disorders that cause obesity, to the forbidden pleasures of a mistress, and to a "covetousness which makes a man live the life of an ass or ant."[4] In another essay entitled "Against Borrowing Money," Plutarch criticizes not only people who lend at interest but also those who, because of their "love of lavish expenditure", borrow to emulate the lifestyles of the wealthy.

Although born into wealth himself, Plutarch tends to be critical of those who aspire to financial gain for its own sake. Eighteen centuries later, the American economist and social critic Thorstein Veblen would coin the term *conspicuous consumption.* Destined to become part of the vocabulary of twentieth-century America, this phrase means buying things to impress others. Veblen used it to describe the habits of the wealthy class in 1890s America.

Plutarch observed similar tendencies in ancient Greece and Rome when he wrote: "The happiness riches pretend to is such that it depends upon spectators and witnesses; else it would signify nothing at all."[5] His message is that many people desire possessions that are "useless and superfluous" simply for the sake of drawing attention to themselves. Ostentatious displays of wealth were hardly invented by Americans.

Plutarch does not describe the performance of the Greek economy per se. His experiences as a civic leader (mayor, diplomat, and other roles) no doubt inspired his several works on the management of city government. Centuries later, economists would finally be drawn to this topic. A renowned author in many fields but perhaps most distinguished for his biographies, Plutarch has fallen victim to a supreme irony. No one has yet to write a *detailed* biography of his life.[6]

Aesop and Xenophon

Other significant Greek literary works include *Aesop's Fables,* written in the early sixth century BCE, and the essays of Xenophon, written two centuries later. Aesop (620–560 BCE), a slave from Thrace, often uses animal characters to show both human virtue and frailty. The storyline in his classic "The Hare and the Tortoise" involves a race between an easily distracted hare with blinding speed and a slow but meticulously focused tortoise.[7] The moral is that steady, determined effort wins out over misused talent. Much of economics today is about doing the best with what we have. Aesop's turtle certainly applies that principle more efficiently than his rabbit.

Many of Aesop's other fables, while humorous and entertaining, also illustrate familiar economic principles. In "The Ant and the Grasshopper," an industrious ant who saved wheat all summer has something to eat during the winter, while a carefree, not so forward looking grasshopper goes hungry. "The Vain Crow" warns against borrowing for the sake of enhancing outward appearance. Anticipating the

Protestant ethic, “Hercules and the Wagoner” is the story of a lazy farm hand who, after his wagon becomes stuck in mud, prays for help to Hercules, the god of strength. Annoyed by the lack of physical effort, Hercules scolds the lazy man and prompts the moral: the gods help those who help themselves, a phrase that would gain popularity during the 16th century CE Protestant Reformation.

Aesop’s “The Farmer and His Sons” concludes with a similar moral: hard work can pay unexpected dividends. On his deathbed, a farmer tells his two sons that their only inheritance is in the vineyard. Expecting a buried treasure, the sons dig up the ground several times. While they find no gold, their tilling of the soil produces stronger vines and better wine than ever before. In another fable, “The Miser” converts all of his property into a large lump of gold, buries it, and has it stolen by a thief. The moral this time: the true value of money is in its use, not in its mere possession. In “The Goose with the Golden Eggs,” a farmer, whose goose lays one egg of pure gold each day, kills the goose and cuts her open in search of her entire treasure all at once. Finding nothing, he is left with the lesson that the greedy who want more may well lose it all.

The works of the versatile Xenophon (430?–354? BCE), a student of Socrates, address several economic concepts often credited to other writers.[8] In a story of the early Persian empire, he argues that the artisan can work in a single trade, if employed in a large city. In a small town, however, this worker must perform many different tasks just to earn a living. This idea is similar to the modern *division of labor* concept, which states that more can be produced if workers specialize. Mass production on the factory assembly line is perhaps the most vivid contemporary example. Most economists credit Adam Smith with explaining the significance of the division of labor principle. While the later statement is clearly more sophisticated and accurate, Xenophon gives us a preview some twenty-two centuries earlier!

In another work on household management, Xenophon offers a very modern view of property and wealth. In yet a third publication, he illustrates the superior economic growth potential of a nation at peace compared to one at war. Unfortunately, economists and world leaders have too infrequently heeded this advice.

In all three of Xenophon's major works, his discussion of leadership skills, administrative effectiveness, agricultural techniques, and military strategies[9] indicate his awareness of what is today perhaps *the* fundamental economic concept. *Opportunity cost* is what you have to give up in order to get something else. It measures opportunities forgone. To an economist, the cost of a high-tech weapon system, for example, is not just $2 billion; it is the number of schools that could not be built because the money was spent elsewhere. Xenophon's analyses of alternative goals and resource requirements of leaders, administrators, farmers, and defense planners consistently use this principle.[10]

Science

There are numerous outstanding figures in the scientific community of ancient Greece.[11] These include Pythagoras, a pioneer in mathematics; Euclid, widely known for his textbooks on geometry; Archimedes, the mathematician, physicist, and inventor who was arguably the foremost scientist in the world until Isaac Newton; and Ptolemy, the renowned astronomer. All have made lasting contributions to modern science. All have also indirectly influenced economists who would later use geometry and algebra in their formal economic models. Later advances in calculus, astronomy, and physics would similarly inspire an emerging economics profession intent on scientific precision.

Plato and Aristotle also contributed to the study of science and political economy. Their works in the latter area, however, were sufficiently path-breaking that they will merit separate attention momentarily. Finally, Hippocrates, considered the father of medicine, is credited (erroneously, according to most Greek scholars) with establishing the Hippocratic Oath, a standard of professional conduct and ethics for physicians. A similar oath for economists, by the way, has yet to be devised. Had one existed, some of the personalities to be surveyed later in this book would probably have been barred from the profession.

The Greek Economy[12]

The nomadic, pastoral tribes of early Greek culture eventually pursued subsistence agriculture in small, self-sufficient farms. As early as the eighth century BCE, iron replaced bronze in tools and in weapons (swords, spears, armor, and helmets). These changes allowed Greece to prosper economically and made it more aggressive militarily. While the traditional agricultural economy, now armed with iron tools, continued to flourish, craftsmen became increasingly prominent.

Bronze had always been expensive to produce because the copper and tin required to make it were scarce and rarely found in close proximity. Iron products could be made far more cheaply, since iron was more widely available. Industry, agriculture, and armament production, therefore, all became highly decentralized operations. Not coincidentally, a system of private property, which would both encourage productive activity and lead to income inequality, developed at about the same time.

Decentralization prompted the rise of dozens of city-states, the most important of which was Athens. Mountainous geography encouraged each urban area to seek economic independence, but trade between city-states (especially Athens, Sparta, and Corinth) eventually became significant. Overland routes ultimately complemented ventures by sea. Wealth acquired through trade helped to finance some of the major buildings of Athens.

Barter was used as recently as the sixth century BCE but merchants armed with money soon traded their wares with Egyptians, Phoenicians, and people of the Middle East. Objects traded included hides, wool, timber, wine, oil, fish, wheat, corn, and ceramics. The discovery of silver in Attica alleviated a precious metal shortage and enabled currency (the *drachma*) to assist the process of exchange. It was not until the fourth century BCE that gold currency (the *philip,* named after a succession of kings in Macedonia) was widely used. Small banks and even small stock exchanges (both largely unregulated) were also established during this period.

As population grew and as tensions between aristocratic rulers and their subjects rose, colonization of Mediterranean lands (Sicily, southern Italy, France, and Libya) and shores of the Black Sea expanded. Colonies provided new markets, especially for metal utensils, textiles, and pottery. The growth of commerce created increasing opportunities for small manufacturers, merchants, and ship owners. As a result, a capitalist class and a working class were soon very much in evidence.

Confrontation between classes became inevitable as capitalists prospered while the masses grew increasingly impoverished.[13] The ensuing class warfare prevented a more harmonious economic progress, as social pressures arose for redistribution of property. These pressures eventually brought on violent revolution.

Armed conflict among city-states was common, especially during the fifth and fourth centuries BCE. The Peloponnesian War between Athens and Sparta was fought intermittently for 27 years until the Spartan victory in 404 BCE. Sparta was a military state with virtually no inclination toward democracy. Its male citizens were highly disciplined and perpetually mobilized for war from the age of seven onward. Spartan authoritarianism did not last long after the conquest of Athens, however, and democracy was soon restored. Nevertheless, war continued until 338 BCE, when Macedonia, under the military leadership of Alexander the Great, conquered Athens and other urban centers, effectively ending the independent city-state system.

Some Negative Features

Even at its best, Athens had only a limited democracy. Although the political and economic system was based on individual rights, it also depended on slavery. Slaves were generally those non-Greeks captured in war or kidnapped from outlying regions. Their labor was utilized in industry, in construction of buildings and other public works projects, and in agriculture. The working conditions for slaves in the mines were especially harsh.

The ancient Greeks invented water clocks, cog-wheels, gearing systems, slot machines, and steam power. None of these devices were widely used or developed further by the Greeks, most likely because the large number of slaves reduced the need for labor-saving devices.

Women enjoyed no political rights whatsoever. Confined to domestic chores, they were virtually excluded from public affairs. They could not vote, hold office, own property, or conduct business legally. Educational opportunities for women were essentially nonexistent, marriages were arranged by the young girls' parents, and many women were routinely treated with indifference and even contempt by their husbands.[14] The good life of the few in ancient Greece was provided to a considerable degree by the labor of two groups of slaves, one based on ethnic origin, the other on gender.

Socrates

If he were alive today, Socrates (469–399 BCE) would probably be denied tenure at most American universities because, even though he was a brilliant teacher, he never published anything. It has also been argued that God himself might have problems achieving tenure today. After all, He wrote only one book (and it was not even in English), did not footnote his sources, conducted lab experiments (miracles) that succeeding generations of scholars have been unable to replicate, expelled his first two students for learning, rarely came to class and just told his students to read the book, had his son teach the class, and held office hours infrequently on an inconvenient mountaintop. When one experiment went awry, he tried to cover it up by drowning the subjects. Although there were only ten requirements, most students failed his tests. And finally, he may have created the world but what has he done recently? By comparison, the accomplishments of Socrates were far more modest but certainly noteworthy.

Like many great teachers, Socrates was quite a colorful character. He was eccentric, unorthodox, and, in the eyes of many, uncouth. His personal appearance was slovenly and often in disarray. He loved to say things in jest and, in many ways, must have appeared to be the ultimate nonconformist. He enjoyed confronting pretentious people and engaging them in dialogue. He spent considerable time in the marketplace of Athens challenging the conventional wisdom of the era. This frequently angered his wife who, given the limited economic opportunities available to women, understandably felt he should spend less time being combative and more time earning a living.

The latter seemed unimportant to a man who believed that having few wants was godlike and who allowed Crito, one of his more practical students, to invest what modest savings he had accumulated. (Before embarking on a career in teaching, Socrates served in the army of his native Athens and later held fairly minor administrative positions in the Athenian government.) As a result, he was able to teach without pay, which, come to think of it, would probably endear him to many frugal, present-day university administrators and improve his chances for tenure after all.

In ancient Greece, however, such a practice only made him the target of suspicion. Several fellow academics and even more influential citizens viewed him with disdain. His many enemies eventually accused him of irreligious behavior, not acknowledging the gods recognized by the state, and corrupting youth. For these crimes, he was officially charged, convicted, and sentenced to death. While the case against him was "merely a mask for a general animosity," his unwillingness to repent for a crime he did not commit "in effect, forced his judges to martyr a man whom they wished merely to intimidate into silence."[15]

The most significant contribution of Socrates was his *Socratic method* of inquiry, the investigation of concepts by question and answer. This approach, which encourages student/teacher interaction and response to those issues that interest students, served as a model to universities worldwide for centuries. It allowed openness to different points of view and encouraged creativity in learning. Given the current move toward diverse teaching methods in American universities, Socratic inquiry is making a comeback, especially in small seminars. With its many controversial issues, economics, both in ancient times and today, is easily suited to this teaching technique.

Many recent scholars hold the view that Socrates influenced the future of political economy by structuring many of his arguments from the perspective of individualism. At one point in his career, he even discussed the "economics" of the entertainment field by outlining the most efficient way of reaching a business goal.[16] Such fragments of ideas were the seeds that, when crossbred with others, later grew into an entire discipline.

During his lifetime, Socrates devoted considerable time to those who loved and respected him the most, his students, some of whom became accomplished philosophers in their own right. One, in particular, was destined to exert considerable influence on Western thought, including that of future economists.

Plato

With all due respect to Xenophon, many scholars of the classics believe that the greatest student of Socrates was Plato (427?–347 BCE). Born into aristocracy, this former wrestling champion lived during some of the most violent years in the history of Greece. The trial and death of Socrates affected him greatly. Plato's classic work, the *Republic,* utilized the Socratic method and was written as a dialogue between students and their teacher, none other than Socrates himself, who was always portrayed as the ultimate source of wisdom. Plato "never forgot the lesson of Socrates, that wisdom begins when a man finds out that he does not know what he thinks he knows."[17]

In Athens, Plato founded the Academy, a place of research, training center for future political leaders, and the first university in the Western world. The institution remained in existence until 529 CE, when it was closed by the Roman Emperor Justinian.

In the *Republic,*[18] Plato formulated his ideal state which was designed to achieve his concept of justice. In this quest, he explicitly argued the roles to be played by each class. The working class was best suited to producing goods. The warrior class possessed the necessary courage to provide defense. The philosopher or ruling class, filled with wisdom and insight, was fit to lead. Justice was attained, in Plato's view, when each class performed its functions well.

This concept of the division of labor was similar to that of Xenophon. Plato believed[19] that specialization was the natural result of the fact that different people have different talents and skills. Each person doing what he/she (in Plato's day, only he) did best was most likely to contribute optimally to the ideal, just state. As new occupations were required, Plato argued that people best suited to fill these roles would be drawn to them. Merchants, in Plato's view, probably lacked both the physical strength to be manual laborers and the mental capacities to be rulers, hardly a complimentary view of this group.

Such a division of labor concept recognized the potential for added production but primarily emphasized the ideal use of physical and mental abilities. That such labor specialization enforced long-existing income and class inequalities apparently did not bother Plato. Since class divisions were logical, long-term consequences had to be positive.

Plato accepted slavery as a long-standing tradition of Greek society. That he chose to ignore the economic contribution of one-third of the population in his ideal state indicated a certain naivete on his part. He did not argue that slaves were only fit for the type of work they did. Rather, he apparently believed that slaves were the unfortunate victims of being on the losing side during wars. In the *Laws,* a work written in his later years, his inability (or unwillingness) to address the economic advantages that slavery gave the wealthy class (of which he was a member) render his stature as a potential economist highly suspect.

On the questions of wealth and poverty, Plato held a fairly unique perspective. Since wealth produced an unwillingness to work and poverty led to crime and poor work habits, the ruling class must closely monitor both extremes. Both the warrior and ruling classes, however, should be free of the concerns that private property and family inevitably bring. In this way, both classes can concentrate on what they do best: soldiering and ruling. Plato proposed, therefore, that both classes share communal property.

Common housing, shared meals, and even shared women were part of Plato's prescription. His disdain for democracy and private property, his suspicion of commerce, and his bold proposals for restructuring of family life often discredit an otherwise brilliant mind. Fortunately for all, his "ideal" state was never achieved, either in Greece or anywhere else.

Plato's alleged communism has troubled generations of scholars, both sympathetic to and critical of the Greek philosopher.[20] His communal tendencies were, of course, only partial. The working class was free to enjoy both the benefits and curses of private property. Since they were the ones who physically produced material goods, they presumably appreciated them most. The other classes, meanwhile, desired goals on a supposedly higher plateau. Rather than displaying revolutionary propensities, Plato's proposal emphasized class distinctions which, of course, are the antithesis of modern communism.

Aristotle

Sometimes ideas are learned quickly and many people enjoy immediate benefits. At other times, it takes generations for ideas to reach their full fruition. Socrates, as we have seen, wrote nothing but communicated orally perhaps better than anyone before or since. His best student, as we have also seen, was Plato, who wrote a great deal, some of it profound, some hopelessly idealistic and misguided. Plato's best student was Aristotle (384–322 BCE), arguably the greatest mind and most insightful writer of antiquity. The philosophical "grandson" of Socrates, Aristotle tells us much about the transmission of innovative ideas from one great mind to another. He also tells us much about generation gaps.

Born in the Macedonian town of Stagira, Aristotle moved to Athens at the age of seventeen and remained there for twenty years as a student and colleague of Plato. After Plato's death, Aristotle traveled to Asia Minor, where he married the niece of a despotic ruler. He then returned to Macedonia, where he tutored its leader's son, a young man who would soon be known as Alexander the Great.

When Alexander ascended to the throne of Macedonia, Aristotle returned to Athens, where he established his own center of learning, the Lyceum.[21] There he taught art, politics, physics, natural science, and philosophy (quite a teaching load!) and revealed his encyclopedic abilities to amazed students for just over a decade. After Alexander's death in 323 BCE, his enemies charged Aristotle with false crimes, much like the character assassination of Socrates. Fearing a similar fate, Aristotle fled to Chalcis, where he died the following year.

While his early works were in the Socratic tradition of Plato, Aristotle's later writings, especially the *Politics* and *Nicomachaean Ethics* indicated a sharp break with his former teacher. Aristotle was clearly more practical, more analytical, more accepting of private property, more critical of communal life, more inclined toward democracy, less egalitarian, less enamored of the concept of an ideal state, more suspicious of state power, and more concerned about, although still accepting of, slavery.

In his *Politics,* Aristotle argued that the state originates with the household. Several families combined to make a village. As long as they were large enough to be self sufficient, several villages formed a state. This view was obviously more conservative than that of Plato and implicitly more interested in limiting state power. While Aristotle considered the formation of the state to be natural, he viewed the state as existing to assist in the preservation of the "good life."

Aristotle is more explicit about economics than any other writer of antiquity.[22] His formal writing on the subject begins with the following distinction: Economics *(oikonomik)* is the study of household management. It deals with the practice of producing and consuming goods to satisfy wants. *Chrematistics (chrematistik)* is the study of wealth acquisition,[23] including the art of making money and exchange.

Aristotle viewed economics as natural and proper since the household was the fundamental unit in the state. He viewed chrematistics as unnatural, improper, and artificial since exchange by merchants does not add to the wealth of the state.[24] Managing the household and the land around it efficiently was the natural way to satisfy family wants. Gaining wealth by retail trade was unnatural because nothing new was produced; hence, no additional wants could be satisfied.

The very word *economics,* therefore, is of Greek origin. Using Aristotle's terminology, there are many people today who claim to be interested in economics when they are really interested in chrematistics. The profession has generally lumped the activities of both under the general heading of economics. It is not difficult to see why. With apologies to Aristotle, how many students today would want to take a course in something called chrematistics?

Aristotle argued further that the most unnatural way to acquire wealth was usury. It is little wonder that he would be so respected by Church leaders such as Thomas Aquinas during the Middle Ages. Before dismissing this view as uninformed and hopelessly out of date, it may be useful to see the logic Aristotle used.

Most loans today are made either for productive investment, such as when a business builds a new factory, or for major consumption, such as when an individual buys a new car. Loans in ancient Greece were virtually never made for productive purposes. Instead, thcy were made to relieve distress, such as hardship when a crop was destroyed or a home was lost to fire. If loans were made today primarily to embarrassed friends or neighbors who were the victims of arbitrary misfortune, we would probably view interest more like the ancients did. Would you favor charging interest on food and shelter assistance to people today who lost everything due to flood, earthquake, or tornado? (Of course, no insurance industry existed in ancient Greece.) Aristotle may not have understood modern financial markets very well for the simple reason that they were fairly rare in his time.

What Aristotle grasped quite clearly was the role of money in the economy. As the number of products available multiplied, trade by barter became increasingly difficult. Money, therefore, functioned as a *medium of exchange* (it made trade go more smoothly as people worked for money and used it to buy what they wanted) and *standard of value* (it enabled people to value goods and services in terms of money). Money by itself was not wealth. Both the legendary King Midas and the actual seventeenth century mercantilists would learn this lesson the hard way.[25] On the issue of money, Aristotle was nearly twenty centuries ahead of his time.

From Homer and Aesop to Plato and Aristotle, therefore, the ancient Greeks set the stage for a modern discipline of economics, albeit at times indirectly. Early Greek writings addressed such issues as the search for wealth, the distribution of income between rich and poor, class conflict, efficiency, the division of labor, trade, and controversies over the role of government. These are precisely the issues that occupy the minds of economists today. Perhaps it is significant that, when formal discipline founder Adam Smith delivered his inaugural lecture at the University of Glasgow, much of it was devoted to a discussion of Plato.

Ancient Rome

To many people today, the Romans of antiquity convey an image of decadent excess, warlike behavior, raping and pillaging, some economic progress, and few scholarly accomplishments. There is much truth in this image, even though it may be slightly exaggerated. The well-to-do lived quite well. Roman leaders were aggressive. Economically speaking, they produced a fairly advanced civilization. Their soldiers, as well as those of foreign invaders, often engaged in ungentlemanly conduct. Wars and all that tend to go with them were all too common. And compared to Greece, contributions to Western thought were relatively few. The famous historian, Arnold Toynbee, has somewhat harshly written: "If (Rome) did give a thought to the world, it would be to plunder and exploit it."[26]

Roman engineering did produce bridges and roads, buildings made of concrete, large open-air theatres, a rudimentary form of central heating, and Hadrian's Wall (a 75-mile defensive barrier across northern Britain, which marked the northernmost boundary of the Empire and which still stands today). More importantly, the Romans built aqueducts, a system of channels and pipes, many of which were underground, to carry fresh water from springs and lakes to Roman towns and cities. Water was piped to fountains, to public baths, and to the homes of the wealthy.

Rome possessed its share of literary titans, including Pliny, Cato, Seneca, Cicero, Virgil, Horace, and Ovid, some of whom address issues of economic importance. In his thirty seven-volume *Natural History* (77 CE), for example, Pliny writes at length about trees and their products including pepper, ginger, sugarcane, cotton, resins, and papyrus. He also discusses the production of wine, olive oil, and various fruits and vegetables; managing an agricultural establishment; farming techniques; uses of metals; and exploitation of natural resources. Roman art has become increasingly appreciated with the passage of time. Roman contributions to science and philosophy, however, were negligible. Rome certainly produced no inspirational thinker comparable to Aristotle.

Roman Law

There is one area, however, where Rome would permanently influence economic thought. For economic prosperity to occur, a well defined legal system, which sets forth property rights and defines the boundaries within which commerce can operate, must exist. The greatest gift the Roman Empire left to the discipline of economics and to future systems of capitalism was Roman law.

Today, many nations of Western Europe, Asia, Latin America, and Africa as well as the United States use legal systems based to some degree on Roman legal principles. Frequently praised for their logic, practicality, and wide adaptability, these principles have survived for centuries.

To understand how Roman legal principles contributed to economic progress, consider the following three illustrations.[27] Roman law vigorously protected *property rights*, the rights to use property as the owner wished. It also upheld the principle of *freedom of contract.* One could enter into a business relationship with whomever one pleased. In addition, Roman law inspired the modern *doctrine of the corporation,* under which corporate assets were separated from the assets of stockholders. As a result, owners of corporations had *limited liability.* They could lose only the amount invested in the firm, not privately held assets such as their personal property. Without such legal principles, incentives for potential entrepreneurs would have been severely restricted and modern capitalism would not have been able to function.

Over time, the Romans succeeded in making their concept of the law more rational, more scientific, and based less on religion. Their law was consistent with their spirit of individualism, although later imperial edicts did attempt to regulate prices in the marketplace. Although the legal system of Rome eventually became fairly sophisticated, the country's political and social struggles were legendary. These can be understood, at least partially, by a selective look at early Roman developments.

Some Roman History

Official account credits Romulus and Remus with the

founding of Rome in 753 BCE. During most of the five centuries prior to the birth of Christianity, the Roman Republic was nominally a democracy. Much class conflict, however, between the *patricians* (wealthy aristocrats) and the *plebeians* (the ordinary people) existed throughout this period. Over time, plebeians gained the legal right to marry into the patrician class and the right to have government representatives, called *tribunes.*

The economic and political problems of ordinary Romans, however, continued.[28] Executive decision-making power remained with two consuls who were elected by an assembly dominated by the patrician class. Eventually, a middle class of sorts emerged. Its wealth derived from ventures such as banking and was often substantial.

Like its Greek counterpart, the Roman economy was based on slavery. Even though they numbered as much as half the total population, slaves had no legal rights, could not marry, and were often treated abominably. Eventually, many slaves became freedmen, some of whom even amassed wealth as part of the emerging class of merchants and craftsmen.

Despite the fact that few Roman citizens were either wealthy or influential, most considered themselves above manual labor. Many men pursued careers as small manufacturers, shopkeepers, and bankers (all with the assistance of slaves). Others aspired to be members of the military. Sons of aristocrats often became lawyers, the most respected profession of the era.

After a long and bloody struggle during the first century BCE, the Roman Empire replaced the collapsing Republic. The major figure in this clash of force was Julius Caesar (100–44 BCE), who, after a series of military ventures, became virtual dictator of Rome. His formal rule, however, was relatively short due to his assassination at the hands of Brutus and Cassius on the Ides of March. In the ensuing struggle for power, Octavian (63 BCE–14 CE) emerged victorious and later became the first emperor of the Roman

Empire in 27 BCE. The Roman Senate eventually gave Octavian the title of Augustus (meaning first among equals), by which he was known until his death.

The Roman Economy[29]

At its apex in the second century CE, the Roman Empire included all of what is now Italy, France, and Spain, as well as the southern half of Britain up to the boundary of Scotland. It extended eastward in central Europe to the Elbe and Danube rivers, eastward to the Nile River in Egypt, and southward to encompass areas of northern Africa that had easy access to the Mediterranean Sea. During this period, an effective system of safe seaways (piracy was minimal) and roads enabled trade and travel to flourish as never before. Water routes were the major source of commerce because the legendary roads were still fairly crude by later standards.

Archaeological evidence documents many small shops, bakeries, and other establishments, as well as the existence of nearly 100 different occupations in selected Roman towns.[30] Among the most common occupations were weavers, shoemakers, dyers, masons, smiths, carpenters, and jewelers. Some division of labor existed in industries that produced bronze, silver, glass, and pottery. This specialization, however, was fairly rare. It was far more common for a manufactured item to be produced from start to finish by the same worker.[31]

Aristocrats and emperors often owned pottery works, brickyards, shipping lines, and warehouses.[32] These ventures were characterized more by large scale rather than small enterprise. Other industries produced such items as lamps, bricks, tile, glass, and metalwork (both bronze and iron).

Large merchant fleets traded with places as far away as India and China, importing such items as silk, linen, ivory, precious stones, and spices. Roman ships ventured through the Bay of Bengal, past the Malay Peninsula, and up the

South China Sea to the ports of China. This was a rather substantial distance, considering the relatively crude ships in which goods (and merchants!) traveled. Using ports on the Black Sea, merchants also traded with their counterparts from the interior of Russia. Roman exports included pottery, textiles, furniture, silverware, wine, clothing, musical instruments, and slaves. The value of imports consistently exceeded that of exports. As a result, the Empire experienced what is known as an *unfavorable balance of trade.* To make up for the difference, coinage flowed out, causing a serious drain on the supply of precious metals.

The Roman position on usury changed with the passing of time. The laws of the Twelve Tables, codified in 450 BCE, originally condemned usury. Seneca and Cato both denounced it, with the latter even comparing usury to murder. As governor of Sardinia, Cato actively rounded up the usurers for public reprimand. Later in life, however, when the practice had evidently become more acceptable, Cato himself loaned money at interest.

In the later years of the Roman Empire, a number of aristocrats invested heavily in agriculture. Small land holdings were thus converted to large holdings called *latifundia.* In many cases, bigger is better, especially if larger firms can produce goods at lower unit costs. The latifundia did not do this. Instead, they came to be regarded as models of inefficiency. Small farms had produced basic foods, which fed much of the Roman population.[33] In the interest of earning more money, owners of the latifundia produced far less grain for food. Fields were converted to olive orchards and vineyards for wine. Not surprisingly, these changes caused food shortages, hunger, and much domestic unrest.

Women

Compared to their counterparts in Greece, Roman women enjoyed better, although hardly glamorous, lifestyles.

Rome was a male-dominated society. In the early years of the Republic, women were legal wards of their fathers or husbands. Their treatment varied according to individual circumstance.

By the second century BCE, upper class women were enjoying the benefits of education, inheritance, and greater freedom generally. Instances existed where women managed households without male supervision, where women became published authors, and even where women presided over literary salons. These were gatherings where poets and artists were encouraged in their work. When the Roman Empire was formed, divorce was not only more common but could be initiated by a woman. Although Roman women were never allowed to vote, their influence on men responsible for public policy is well documented.[34]

Decline of the Roman Empire

Despite some economic success, the Empire was plagued because no viable system of succession to the throne existed. When an emperor died, chaos usually prevailed. After lengthy civil unrest and frequent foreign invasion, the emperor Diocletian in 285 CE divided the Empire into eastern and western sections. Each was to be ruled by an *augustus* with a *caesar* as his second in command and heir after a period of twenty years. The Empire was reunited in 324 by Constantine (285–337), who made its capital the city of Byzantium, which he modestly renamed Constantinople. (And why not? His sons had names like Constantine, Constantius, and Constans!) Under Constantine, Christianity, which only decades earlier had experienced horrible persecution because Christians refused to worship the emperor, became the official religion of the Roman Empire.

The succession problem, however, was not solved. After the death of Constantine, efforts to divide and reunite the empire occurred so often that effective government became impossible. Barbarian invasion soon was the rule rather than the exception. (Roman leaders used the term *barbarian* to describe any nomadic tribe that originated outside the borders of the Empire. In addition to the infamous Attila the Hun, these groups included many of the ancestors of present-day England, Germany, and France. From the barbarians, therefore, came some of the most influential cultures of Western civilization.) One attack by the Visigoths at Adrianople resulted in the assassination of the emperor Valens (328–378), during whose reign many aqueducts had been built. Soon afterward, an increasing number of non-Romans migrated freely to lands of the Western Empire.

Unable to secure its borders, Rome watched its domestic influence decline further while internal strife rose. The fall of Rome was complete in 476, when German troops in Italy elected as their king an Ostrogoth named Flavius Odovacer. He deposed the last Roman emperor, Romulus Augustulus, and declared boldly, but with widespread support that Roman emperors were no longer needed.

Four centuries before the fall of the Roman Empire, Pliny the Elder (23–79) wrote prophetically: "The latifundia destroyed Italy."[35] Large land holdings simply did not produce enough to feed the Roman people. Why? Wealthy absentee owners lacked both the skill and the desire to manage the latifundia efficiently. They also cared little about the workers who actually produced the food. Owners paid their workers such low wages that there was no incentive for them to be productive. As a result, the agricultural system deteriorated.

Throughout history, when technological advance occurs, unit costs normally fall as output increases. Large farms capable of using more acreage, therefore, are generally more efficient than smaller ones. The startling fact is that virtually no new machinery was invented during the 500-year life of the Roman Empire. Apparently, the Roman imagination was never captivated by the possibility of scientific discovery and the practical application of new knowledge in the area of agriculture.

Since farm output was a major source of tax revenue, government funds fell rapidly as agriculture declined. With smaller incomes, farm workers were less able to buy manufactured goods from the cities. As owners of urban small businesses lost confidence in the economy, their output fell, causing yet a further drop in government revenue. Facing rising unemployment, government provided increasingly expensive "bread and circuses" to create the illusion that all was well. As the external threat of invasion and the internal threat of disorder intensified, the emperor simply lacked the money to pay his soldiers. Eventually, fewer and fewer soldiers were willing to risk their lives for nothing in return. Sensing a powerless government,[36] invaders from without and from within felt encouraged about the chances for revolution. The inevitable finally happened.

The aggressive drive of government leaders and entrepreneurs (both with the help of slaves) created, for a time, an economy of abundance, at least for the privileged classes. The live-for-today mentality, however, meant that little was available for tomorrow. No provision was made for the maintenance of a stock of *capital goods* (goods like machines used to produce other goods, especially in agriculture) and few incentives were provided for workers to be productive. In addition, armed conflict was both frequent and costly. In retrospect, it is surprising that such a system survived as long as it did.

The Rise of Christianity

In a manner of speaking, the fall of Rome and the rise of Christianity occurred simultaneously. One gradually filled the power vacuum left by the other. During the long decline of the empire, Church leaders were often critical of economic and social conditions within its borders. They were also sympathetic to the plight of non-Romans, who were regarded more as potential converts than enemies. Such philosophical stances endeared larger numbers of the masses to the Church than to the Roman government.

That government also fueled the erosion of its own power. Emperors after Constantine began persecuting pagans and promoting Christians to positions of influence. Decades before the official fall of Rome, its Senate was almost entirely Christian. The Romans themselves, therefore, grew increasingly wary of their ancient pagan gods and developed interest in religions, many of them monotheistic, which they had observed in their commercial travels. Christian leaders responded to this interest quite effectively.

The hierarchy of the Church also attracted talented young men who might otherwise have entered government service. As the popularity of the Church grew, it also diverted money in the same direction. This shift of resources, both human and financial, contributed to a changing power balance between Church and state.

For many years, the emperor and Church leaders cooperated in defining issues of Church dogma and in settling religious disputes. Councils or *synods* were frequently called by the emperor for such purposes. Decisions at these gatherings were made by bishops, although powerful emperors often influenced the outcome. During the fifth century, however, the authority of the papacy eventually ascended as that of the emperor declined. Even though an Eastern Church, led by the rival patriarch of Constantinople, often questioned papal authority, a succession of assertive popes successfully challenged imperial views on religious matters.

Roman strengths and weaknesses played a major role in sealing the fate of the Empire. Rome's major achievement, as we have seen, was legal. So long as a measure of lawfulness remained throughout much of its territory, the Empire possessed the means to deal with the occasional aberration from upstanding behavior. Its major weakness was philosophical and cultural. This restricted its ability to influence non-Roman people who lurked just outside the Empire. What Romans apparently offered was the following: Accept our ways and uphold our laws or face the wrath of our military might. This was not the most neighborly of approaches.

Given this limited interest in peacefully exporting Roman ideas and culture, it is not surprising that nomadic people remained *uncivilized,* at least in the sense in which the Romans understood that term. Christianity, by contrast, reached out to all, Roman and non-Roman alike. Predictably, more people became attracted to the value system of the Church than of the Romans. Those seeking human progress, both economic and cultural, thus responded with enthusiasm, to the civilization offered by Christianity.

Perhaps most importantly, Christianity presented an alternative lifestyle to that of traditional, decadent Rome. Corruption and greed of those in power took its toll on the loyalty of those who supposedly were being served. Government political institutions, in other words, had long since demonstrated their ineffectiveness. They therefore were viewed either with growing suspicion or indifference. As papal authority and Church membership rose, one fact became increasingly obvious: Christianity would exert an important influence over secular issues, including economic affairs, for many years to come.

Technology vs. Institutions in Antiquity

The Veblen-Ayres dichotomy is especially appropriate in analyzing the world of ancient Greece and Rome. The contributions of the Greeks to numerous areas of knowledge were considerable. Their impressive achievements in architecture, science, and mathematics all reached heights never before attained. Many of the subjects we study today including philosophy, rhetoric, politics, and economics can be traced to their Greek origins. The scholarly work of Greek historians and literary figures still commands respect. The Greeks even invented steam power although they did not fully utilize its potential.

The ancient Romans gave the world a complex legal system that later allowed capitalism to flourish. They also built impressive structures including buildings, aqueducts, and roads. Although their literary achievements were less impressive than those of the Greeks, the Romans did produce great work in this area and in art as well.

Both societies, however, still operated within established customs and traditions that limited the full potential of their discoveries. The acceptance of slavery not only reduced human potential but also may have been a factor in discouraging the development of labor saving technology, especially in Rome. The second class citizenship to which women were relegated prevented roughly half of their populations from contributing to human knowledge. This practice also limited the effectiveness of the Greek experiment in democracy.

Deities of questionable merit were still worshipped in both cultures and have provided the world with fascinating mythology and art. Gods and goddesses from ancient Greece included such time-honored names as Apollo, Poseidon, Zeus, Eros, Atlas, Athena, Helios, Phoebe, and Prometheus. The Romans have given us Venus, Neptune, Mars, Vulcan, Juno, Cupid, Diana, Minerva, and Saturn. The complete list of these fictitious beings is huge and is living testament to the creativity and paranoia of the ancient mind.

Some of the more interesting Greek deities included: Acratopotes, god of unmixed wine and incontinence; Agdistis, the hermaphroditic deity; Bootes, agricultural demi-god who was credited with being the inventor of the wagon and the plough; Dionysus, god of wine, drunken orgies and wild vegetation; Aura, goddess of the breeze and the fresh, cool air of early morning; Koalemos, god of stupidity and foolishness;

and Hybris, spirit of outrageous behavior and arrogance.

The Romans had their own unusual deities including: Bacchus, the god of wine and partying: Carnea, goddess of the heart, other organs, and door handles; Cloacina, goddess of the sewer system in Rome; Devera, goddess of brooms used for purification; Febris, goddess who protected people from fevers; Furina, goddess of thieves; Laverna, goddess of unlawful gain and trickery; Mefitas, goddess of poisonous vapors from the earth; Mena, goddess of menstruation; Saritor, god of weeding and hoeing; Volutina, goddess of the envelopes of the follicles of crops; Stimula, goddess who incites passion in women; and Viriplacaa, goddess of marital strife. (Perhaps the last two could have worked together closely to minimize marital difficulties.)

Temples erected to honor gods *that obviously did not exist* represented a substantial waste of money and human effort. The great care taken to avoid offending these humanly invented supernatural entities no doubt limited progress in explaining scientific principles and set artificial boundaries as to where human inquiry might otherwise go. Zeus, for example, was considered to be responsible for clouds, rain, thunder, and lightning while Poseidon, who oversaw an array of sea gods, was credited with causing floods and earthquakes. Scientific advance in explaining these phenomena would have to wait until investigators could proceed without fear of tampering in the domain of these powerful divinities. Socrates himself was ridiculed by the Greek writer Aristophanes for questioning the gods' responsibility for rain and thunder.[37]

Such restrictive behavior was clearly dictated by a strong path dependency several centuries in duration. Imagine what the great minds of ancient Greece might have discovered had they not been restrained by such ridiculous and blatant superstition.

Summary and Conclusions

The popular literature of ancient Greece contained a wealth of economic ideas. The writings of such diverse authors as Homer, Plutarch, and Aesop touched upon economic life in the early development of the Greek people. The work of Xenophon indicated a keen awareness of such important economic concepts as the division of labor and opportunity cost. Influenced by the oral tradition of Socrates as well as both the teaching and writing of Plato, Aristotle developed a fairly sophisticated theory of the role of money. The very word "economics" first appears in the writing of Xenophon and Aristotle.[38]

Early Greek history tells us of scientific advance, decentralized industry that enabled the city-state to flourish, and trade which was fueled by the development of coinage. Class conflict, however, eventually led to the collapse of the city-state system. The limited democracy of Athens created an economy based on slavery and blatant denial of rights for women.

Ancient Rome produced a society of builders, warriors, and plunderers. While not directly contributing to economic philosophy, the Romans developed a legal system that allowed the smooth functioning of capitalism. Especially important was the legal defense of private property and limited liability.

Roman history is replete with wars, internal class conflicts, and chaotic successions to the throne. For a time, however, the economy thrived as the empire expanded and trade with distant lands grew. Roman women enjoyed better lifestyles and economic opportunities than their Greek counterparts but never achieved political equality with men.

Among other reasons, the Roman Empire fell because of inefficient agriculture, limited technological innovation, a mismanaged and eventually bankrupt government, and both external invasion and internal strife. The fall of Rome enabled

Christianity to exert a growing influence in economic matters and in life generally.

Footnotes

1. H. D. F. Kitto, *The Greeks* (Middlesex, England: Penguin Books, Ltd., 1951), pp. 37–40, 68. Whether Homer was one person, two, a group, or never existed continues to be a matter of much speculation among scholars of antiquity. Since there is no definitive known information about his life, he remains an enigma.

2. S. Todd Lowry, *The Archaeology of Economic Ideas: The Classical Greek Tradition* (Durham, NC: Duke University Press, 1987), pp. 146–147. For more on the economics of Homer, see Walter Donlan, "Scale, Value, and Function in the Homeric Economy," *American Journal of Ancient History,* 6 (1981), pp. 101–117 and James M. Redfield, "The Economic Man," in Carl A. Rubino and Cynthia W. Shelmerdine, (eds.), *Approaches to Homer* (Austin: University of Texas Press, 1983), pp. 218–247.

3. For additional background on similarities and differences between Plutarch and Plato, see: James Warren, "Pleasure, Plutarch's *Non Posse* and Plato's *Republic*", *Classical Quarterly*, 61, 1 (May 2011), pp. 278–293.

4. *Plutarch's Morals,* Vol. II, (Boston: Little, Brown, and Company, 1878), p. 299.

5. *Plutarch's Morals,* p. 304.

6. This statement does require a qualification. As it stands, it is a frequent lament among scholars of ancient Greece. There are books that touch upon various aspects of the life of Plutarch but none of these can be considered thorough. See,

for example, Robert Lamberton, *Plutarch*, (New Haven, CN: Yale University Press), 2001; D. A. Russell, *Plutarch*, (London: Duckworth Publishing, 2001/1972); Christopher. P. Jones, *Plutarch and Rome, (*Oxford: Clarendon Press, 1971); and Reginald H. Barrow, *Plutarch and His Times, (*Bloomington: Indiana University Press, 1967).

7. Aesop, *Aesop's Fables,* (New York: Grosset and Dunlap, 1947) and Simon Stern (ed.), *The Life and Fables of Aesop,* (New York: Taplinger, 1970).

8. The three works of Xenophon referred to here are, respectively, *Cyropaedia, Oeconomicus,* and *On the Means of Improving the Revenues of the State of Athens.* Xenophon is also discussed in John Kenneth Galbraith, *Economics in Perspective: A Critical History, (*Boston: Houghton Mifflin, 1987).

9. Lowry, p. 11, and pp. 46–81.

10. Works on Xenophon include: James E. Alvey, "The Ethical Foundations of Economics in Ancient Greece, Focussing on Socrates and Xenophon", *International Journal of Social Economics*, 38, 8 (2011), pp. 714-733; James Tatum, *Xenophon's Imperial Fiction, (*Princeton: Princeton University Press, 1989); and Leo Strauss, *Xenophon's Socratic Discourse: An Interpretation of the Oeconomicus, (*Ithaca, NY: Cornell University Press, 1970).

11. Relevant dates for each: Pythagoras (580–500 BCE), Euclid (330?–275 BCE), Archimedes (287–212 BCE), Ptolemy (90–168 CE), and Hippocrates (460–377 BCE).

12. Recent discussions of the Greek economy may be found in Carl Hampus Lyttkens, *Economic Analysis of Institutional Change in Ancient Greece: Politics, Taxation and Rational*

Behavior, (London: Routledge, 2013); Zosia H. Archibald, John K. Davies, and Vincent Gabrielsen (eds.), *The Economies of Hellenistic Societies: Third to First Centuries BC*, (Oxford: Oxford University Press, 2011); Steven Johnstone, *A History of Trust in Ancient Greece,* (Chicago, IL: University of Chicago Press, 2011); and Panayotis Michaelides, Ourania Kardasi, and John Milios, "Democritus's Economic Ideas in the Context of Classical Political Economy", *European Journal of the History of Economic Thought,* 18, 1 (2011), pp. 1-18.

13. Michael Rostovtzeff, *The Social and Economic History of the Roman Empire,* 2nd ed., (Oxford: Clarendon Press, 1957), Vol. 1, p. 2.

14. Dotan Leshem, "The Ancient Art of Economics", *European Journal of the History of Economic Thought*, 21, 2 (June 2014), pp. 201-229. See also Kitto, especially pp. 131–133 and pp. 219–222.

15. J. D. Kaplan (ed.), *Dialogues of Plato,* (New York: Washington Square Press, 1951), pp. 2–3.

16. Lowry, pp. 172–176, p. 81 and William F. Campbell, "The Free Market for Goods and the Free Market for Ideas in the Platonic Dialogues," *History of Political Economy*, 17 (1985), pp. 187–197.

17. Francis M. Cornford, *The Republic of Plato,* (London: Oxford University Press, 1941), p. xxix.

18. James E. Alvey, "The Foundations of the Ethical Tradition of Economics: Plato's *Republic*", *International Journal of Social Economics,* 38, 10 (2011), pp. 824-846.

19. For additional treatment of this issue, see Vernard Foley,

"The Division of Labor in Plato and Smith," *History of Political Economy*, 6 (1974), pp. 220–242.

20. C. Bradford Welles, "The Economic Background of Plato's Communism," *Journal of Economic History,* 8 (1948), Supplement, pp. 101–114.

21. Recent work on Aristotle includes Ricardo F. Crispo, *A Re-Assessment of Aristotle's Economic Thought*, (London: Routledge, 2013) and Spencer J. Pack, *Aristotle, Adam Smith and Karl Marx: On Some Fundamental Issues in 21st Century Political Economy*, (Northampton, MA: Edward Elgar, 2010).

22. C. Tyler DesRoches, "On Aristotle's Natural Limit", *History of Political Economy*, 46, 3 (Fall 2014), pp. 387-407; Rodolphe Dos Santos Ferreira, "Aristotle's Analysis of Bilateral Exchange: An Early Formal Approach to the Bargaining Problem," *European Journal of the History of Economic Thought,* 9**,** 4 (December 2002), pp. 568–590; Scott Meikle, *Aristotle's Economic Thought* (Oxford: Oxford University Press, 1995); and Joseph J. Spengler, "Aristotle on Economic Imputation and Related Matters," *Southern Economic Journal* 21 (1955), pp. 371–389.

23. Aristotle, *Politics,* Book 1, Chapter 3. See also Dotan Leshem, "Oikonomia Redefined", *Journal of the History of Economic Thought*, 35, 1 (March 2013), pp. 43-61.

24. Lewis H. Haney, *History of Economic Thought* (New York: Macmillan, 1933), pp. 58–60.

25. A fictional character created by the Roman author Ovid, Midas was granted his wish that anything he touched would be turned into gold. He was quickly unable to eat or drink because, as soon as he made contact with his food, it was transformed into the precious metal. Mercantilism will be

discussed in Chapter 6.

26. Arnold J. Toynbee, *Hellenism* (London: Oxford University Press, 1959), pp. 176–177.

27. Henry William Spiegel, *The Growth of Economic Thought*, (Englewood Cliffs, NJ: Prentice Hall, 1971), p. 37.

28. Substantial poverty was prevalent in the slavery supported Roman Empire. See William V. Harris, *Rome's Imperial Economy: Twelve Essays*, (Oxford: Oxford University Press, 2011).

29. A thorough collection of essays on this topic may be found in Walter Scheidel, (ed.), *The Cambridge Companion to the Roman Economy*, (Cambridge: Cambridge University Press, 2012). See also Bernard S. Bacharach, "The Fortification of Gaul and the Economy of the Third and Fourth Centuries", *Journal of Late Antiquity*, 3,1 (Spring 2010), pp. 38-64.

30. Chester G. Starr, *The Roman Empire, 27 B.C.–A.D. 476: A Study in Survival,* (Oxford: Oxford University Press, 1982), p. 103. See also Claire Holleran, *Shopping in Ancient Rome: The Retail Trade in the Late Republic and the Principate*, (Oxford: Oxford University Press, 2012).

31. William Sinnigen and Arthur E. R. Boak, *A History of Rome to A.D. 565,* 6th ed. (New York: Macmillan, 1977), p. 363.

32. Peter Garnsey and Richard Saller, *The Roman Empire: Economy, Society, and Culture,* (Berkeley: University of California Press, 1987), p. 47.

33. Jason Linn, "The Roman Grain Supply, 442-455", *Journal of Late Antiquity*, 5, 2 (Fall 2012), pp. 298-321.

34. Sinnigen and Boak, pp. 85–86, 152–153, and 239–240.

35. Pliny, *Natural History.* His nephew and adopted son, Pliny the Younger, witnessed the eruption of Mt. Vesuvius and the destruction of the city of Herculaneum in 79 CE. The elder Pliny was a victim of that disaster.

36. For excellent, more-detailed accounts, see Peter Brown, *Through the Eye of a Needle: Wealth, the Fall of Rome, and the Making of Christianity in the West, 350–550 AD,* (Princeton, NJ: Princeton University Press, 2012); Donald Kagan (ed.), *The End of the Roman Empire: Decline or Transformation?* 3rd ed., (Lexington: D. C. Heath, 1992); and W. W. Rostow, *Politics and the Stages of Growth,* (Cambridge: Cambridge University Press, 1971), especially pp. 43–46.

37. Roger E. Backhouse, *The Ordinary Business of Life: A History of Economics From the Ancient World to the Twenty-First Century,* (London: Penguin Books, 2004), p. 15.

38. Since *Oeconomicus* ("The Economist") was written by Xenophon before Aristotle's works on the economy (especially his *Politics*), a case may be made to credit Xenophon with giving the discipline its name. Both men defined the subject as the study of household management. Because Xenophon in *Oeconomicus* claims to be quoting the views of Socrates, perhaps an even stronger argument can be made that Socrates gave the discipline of economics its name!

Chapter Four

The Influence of Religion on Economics

Choose a job you love and you will never have to work a day in your life.

Confucius

If there is any religion that could respond to the needs of modern science, it would be Buddhism.

Albert Einstein

You see a man skilled at his work? He will stand in the presence of kings.

Proverbs 22: 29

You household slaves, obey your masters with all deference, not only the good and reasonable ones but even those who are harsh.

1 Peter 2: 18

Societies appear to become considerably less productive whenever large numbers of people stop making widgets and begin killing their customers and creditors for heresy.

Sam Harris

Various religious influences existed in many parts of the world when polytheistic pagan gods were worshiped in ancient Greece and Rome. Because the historical accuracy and scientific awareness of their multiple authors are often challenged, the Judeo-Christian Bible along with other early religious texts may at first appear to be unlikely and unreliable sources of economic concepts. Selected passages, however, do address worldly matters and, if one is willing to infer verifiable economic principles from poetic verse, occasional surprising insight may be suggested.

Religious texts are probable written origins of early economic thought, especially since so many ancient civilizations were still so deeply rooted in pre-scientific superstition. Among the oldest surviving works of literature, these texts feature diverse perspectives and have influenced numerous cultures for more than two thousand years. Whether religion has stimulated human progress or has merely been another institutional resistance to change is one of the more engrossing issues evolutionary economists and others have addressed.

The Bible and prevailing religious ideas indirectly influenced the thinking and writing of some of the world's first European economists. How did this occur?

Thomas Malthus was an ordained minister. In his youth, Alfred Marshall was being groomed for ministry in the Anglican Church until he became more interested in mathematics. Some of his contemporaries believed his upbringing played a part in his later humanitarian concerns. David Ricardo, after being raised in a Jewish family, married a Quaker and converted to the ways of the Anglican Church. Their strong conflicting religious beliefs are said to have caused lifelong strife with their families. Some believe he eventually became an agnostic. Marshall eventually suffered a similar fate. John Stuart Mill, on the other hand, was an atheist from childhood but was careful not to reveal this fact in his published writing.

Adam Smith was a professor of moral philosophy in the late eighteenth century when that discipline was heavily rooted in faith-based thought. His two most prominent teachers were Francis Hutcheson, who was profoundly devout, and David Hume, who was an agnostic. Many scholars today challenge the view that Smith himself was religious despite the alleged Protestant influence of Hutcheson in some of his early work on justice and equity.[1]

Smith did not openly embrace religion and was more likely unimpressed by and even cynical about many of its claims.[2] To be sure, religion influenced him but *not* in the way many churchgoers have claimed it did. Rather than writing with a concern for humanity that was theologically inspired, a more likely scenario is that, in an effort to reach as wide an audience as possible, he was merely careful not to offend those who embraced existing doctrine.

In the early nineteenth century, economics textbooks in the U. S. were frequently written by Protestant ministers,[3] many of whom did have some formal training in economics. At this time, it was not only religion, but specifically Protestant fundamentalism, that constituted the major "spiritual" influence on economic ideas. These textbook writers often inferred religious positions from the work of early economists that those economists never intended. Economics was a newly emerging field that was drawing wide interest. If some of its principles could be advertised as godlike, church attendance just might increase as well. Institutions seek self preservation. A wealth of fragmentary economic ideas could be found by those willing to dig deeply enough and selectively enough.

General Observations

Among other economic stances, the Bible praises hard work,[4] justifies private property,[5] and endorses private markets.[6] Of course, it also claims that divine providence rewards human effort[7] and it extols the virtue of saving.[8] In addition, it condemns: "love of money as the root of all evil",[9] monopoly,[10] and, in several instances,[11] the rich, while it dignifies poverty.[12] It even states in two separate gospels that "it is easier for a camel to pass through the eye of a needle than for one who is rich to enter the Kingdom of God".[13]

Elsewhere, the Bible praises the rich and condemns the poor.[14] Apparently, the eye of the needle had gotten wider in these cases. In yet other places, the Bible appears to endorse socialism by commanding the wealthy to sell their property and distribute the proceeds to the poor.[15] Neither Karl Marx nor Mao Zedong could have articulated the principles of modern day socialism more effectively than a number of biblical verses do. Was the Bible even their inspiration?

It should not be surprising that the Bible contradicts itself since it is actually a collection of chapters written by numerous authors roughly between 500 BCE and 200 CE. Such contradictions, however, suggest that those who claim to believe in its every literal word are likely candidates for extreme schizophrenia.

In some of its more astute observations, the Bible alludes to racism negatively[16] and supports the dignity of labor[17] plus fair treatment of workers.[18] There are also those today who would applaud its recognition of the burden of heavy taxes and even its suggested criticism of progressive taxation.[19] A tax is progressive if the rich pay a higher percentage of their income than those of more modest means. Some economists believe that such taxes harm work incentives and discourage investment among those who are prone to seek business opportunities, some of which create new jobs. The limited government attitude, so prevalent at the end of the mercantilist era and the beginning of classical economic influence, likely drew some inspiration from biblical anti-tax statements.

The Bible also documents the use of barter or the exchange of goods for goods without the use of money.[20] Perhaps its most insightful explanation of an economic concept, however, is its illustration of the comparative advantage principle in the book of Ezekiel.[21]

A nation has a comparative advantage when, compared to nations with which it trades, it is relatively more efficient in producing *some* goods than others. The United States today, for example, exports manufactured goods to nations of the Middle East which export oil to us. Japan imports beef from Argentina while sending TVs and automobiles to countries throughout the Americas. Each country trades what it is relatively more efficient at producing.

The passage in Ezekiel describes a ship built from cypress (for decks), cedar (for the mast), oak (for oars), and linen (for sails). Each raw material came from a different country. Why? Because the forests of Jordan were known for their fine oaks and the weavers of Egypt produced excellent embroidered linen.[22] Jordan, therefore, had a comparative advantage in the production of wood products while Egypt had a comparative advantage in woven cloth.

This passage also revealed some of the major products traded by individual nations in ancient times. These included metals such as silver, iron, tin, lead, and bronze; fine delicacies such as cloth, linen, garments, "varicolored carpets," and rubies; and animals such as horses, steeds, mules, lambs, rams, and goats. The mutual benefit of trade resulting from comparative advantage may well have been in evidence as early as the sixth century BCE.

Some Suspect Biblical Advice

Despite biblical support for seemingly opposite positions, the Christian Church during the first three or four centuries of its existence did establish an early pattern. Religion would continue to exert considerable influence on economic thought for some time, as Church leaders would routinely comment on matters pertaining to the conduct of everyday life. Church councils, for example, eventually decided that passages about communal ownership were simply intended to encourage charitable giving and a lifestyle that valued something other than the blind pursuit of riches.

Literal interpretation of individual Bible passages would lead to much controversy and to endorsement of some highly questionable behavior.

For example, the Bible contains statements supporting such morally dubious practices as the legitimacy of slavery;[23] circumstances under which the murder of slaves is justified;[24] the submissiveness of wives to their husbands[25] and of women to men generally,[26] and death as punishment for homosexuality,[27] for cursing parents,[28] and for adultery.[29] The Bible also states that a woman who does not bleed on her wedding night should be stoned to death[30] and that women must remain silent during religious services.[31]

The fact that the Bible does not condemn slavery and even justifies the murder of slaves under any circumstance seriously reduces any moral credibility its readers may assign to it. (Stoning women to death for any reason also seems to fall far short of any reasonable moral standard.) Of course, its position on slavery and its praise for the dignity of labor provide yet another glaring contradiction. Further, there are specific biblical passages that call for those who are guilty of heresy to be put to death.[32] During the intellectually stagnant Middle Ages, Church leaders would condone unspeakable acts of torture and murder, presumably in the interest of enforcing these biblical directives.

Less ethically suspect but equally eye-opening are several fascinating biblical passages that describe possible UFO visits in ancient times.[33] Serious scholars of history and science are currently debating whether these accounts might be scientifically accurate or are merely the product of an author's excessively creative imagination. While all of these controversial(!) moral and scientific accounts have invited varying interpretations and feeble attempts at justification, the following discussion will be limited to questionable *economic* practices.

In this area, the Bible is filled with directives condemning the practice of usury (the lending of money at interest). The following passage is typical: "You are to lend him (your countryman) neither money at interest nor food at a profit".[34] Similar statements may also be found elsewhere.[35] One passage even instructs that debts be canceled in the seventh year.[36] Imagine the implications for the modern 30-year mortgage! Pronouncements on usury would trouble Church leaders until the Protestant Reformation in the sixteenth century.[37] A more tolerant view of lending would emerge just in time for the arrival of modern capitalism and for the Church itself to participate as a lender, while making a tidy profit in doing so.

In addition to the usury issue, a famous biblical parable concerns compensation of employees. Workers in a vineyard are paid the same wage no matter how long each worked: some toiled all day, others only an hour. When questioned about the fairness of such a policy, the landowner replied: "Am I not free to do as I wish with my own money?"[38] An employer who expressed such a view today would not only be subjected to much ridicule by workers (and unions) but would also have considerable difficulty in hiring workers tomorrow.

Several biblical passages encourage giving money to charity with the promise that such donations will be repaid tenfold. For those who believe such statements, the logical conclusion would be to give away as much as one has to secure an even greater return. (Ten times a large number is greater than ten times a smaller number.) While charitable contributions are indeed humane and no doubt reduce social tensions, this biblical directive is hardly a sound, and clearly an unproven, investment strategy.

Of course, the frequently stated charge to tithe ten percent of one's income proved to be far more beneficial to the Church hierarchy itself than to those in genuine need. The command to tithe implies that Church leaders are better able to redistribute funds to worthwhile recipients than the person doing the tithing. Lavish lifestyles of some of these leaders along with the considerable value of property owned by religious institutions have seriously questioned this claim and have obviously proven otherwise.

The principle of self-interest that would one day become the basis of Adam Smith's invisible hand metaphor as well as the motivating force in mainstream economics is also viewed from opposite perspectives in different biblical chapters. In some places, self-reliance and self-support are viewed favorably[39] while elsewhere they are treated with far less reverence.[40] Yet another biblical contradiction would be astutely and cleverly repackaged when Adam Smith would later attempt to argue that, by pursuing one's own self-interest, others would benefit.

Religions Other Than Christianity

Economic ideas may be found in the early texts of virtually all religions.[41] Material success, self-discipline, work, and the attainment of status are among the themes addressed in the *Talmud* of Judaism, the *Bhagavad Gita* of Hinduism, and the *Qur'an* of Islam. Both Christian and non-Christian treatises attempted to address, among other things, the practical conduct of daily life, which after all, was fundamentally the focus of an emerging discipline of economics several centuries later.

Judaism and Hinduism

Judaism is based on both the *Talmud* and the Hebrew Bible. The latter includes the Old Testament's first five books, called the *Torah*;[42] the *Nevi'im*, or words of the prophets; and the *Ketuvim*, or writings. A collection of works by ancient rabbis, the *Talmud* contains laws pertaining to agriculture, festivals, and ceremonies, as well as family, civil, and criminal laws. Passages from the *Torah,* in addition to supporting the notion that wealth is a sign of favor from above, are consistent with mainstream economic principles, especially the defense of private property, the efficiency of trade, and the buying and selling of land. The *Torah* also expresses concern for the working class and advocates distribution of food surpluses to the poor.

According to one view,[43] Jewish prophets denounced wealth inequality, not because material possessions are evil, but rather because "they are so good that more people should have more of them." That same author, however, also argues that, when collective action was the only way to promote constructive change, Judaism generated an atmosphere of social protest and reform.[44] Therefore, Jewish *prophets* did not oppose *profits* but favored social change so more people could make them. Given strong religious endorsement, it is little wonder that so many early Jewish entrepreneurs were economically successful.

Hinduism traces its origin to several primary sources, the oldest of which were written during the second millennium BCE. Four books called the *Vedas* and two epic poems, the *Mahabharata* (which includes the *Bhagavad Gita*) and the *Ramayana*, provide much of the basic religious philosophy. One of the explicit goals of Hinduism is material success *(artha).* The religion has exerted a long-standing influence on the economic policies of India, whose governments have stressed the principles of self-sufficiency, nationalism, and government programs of income distribution.

Another early influence (with religious overtones) on Indian economic thought was the writing of Vishnugupta Chanakya Kautilya, especially his *Arthashastra* ("Instructions on Material Prosperity"). Considered by some Indian economists[45] to be the first book on economics ever written, this 4th century BCE work advocates protection of private property rights. It also discusses the legal basis of loans, bank deposits, mortgages, labor contracts, partnerships, and the sale of property. Chanakya was even aware of problems involving the separation of ownership and control in large businesses, an issue that would not command attention in the United States until the late 19th and early 20th centuries! Chanakya was devoted to Vishnu, a central god in Hinduism, and a widely recognized scholar of the *Vedas.*

Islam

Islam was founded in seventh century Arabia by Muhammad (570–632), himself a wealthy merchant in Mecca. Its primary sources are the *Qur'an* and the *Hadiths*, the latter consisting of oral reports and comments on the words of Muhammad. From these two ancient texts, Muslims have accepted the Islamic law code, known as the *Shari'a,* an Arabic word that originally meant path or way.

According to Islamic economists, the *Qur'an* recognizes people as being rational, free, acquisitive, and ethical.[46] It encourages moderation[47] and a harmony of spiritual and material pursuits. It blesses consumption[48] but condemns wastefulness[49] and extravagance.[50] The right of private property is explicitly stated,[51] provisions of contract law are outlined,[52] fraud is prohibited,[53] and a system of standard weights and measures is encouraged.[54] The charging of interest, or *riba,* is banned[55] although assessment of banking fees has been the subject of much debate in the Islamic world.[56]

Islamic economists also emphasize the importance of working hard in honorable professions, dealing fairly with others, paying just wages, and avoiding speculation. One of the principal duties of Muslims is almsgiving, or *zakat.* Supposedly a voluntary contribution to the poor, almsgiving eventually became a religious tax used by many Islamic governments. This policy is consistent with the traditional Muslim view that wealth be widely distributed in the interest of maintaining a stable and healthy social fabric.

Since the seventh century, a number of internal

struggles within Islam have occurred. The first concerned selection of a successor to Muhammad that produced a split into the *Sunni* and *Shiite* branches. Another has involved a general reluctance to accept industrial modernization and a suspicion of Westernization. A more basic conflict has emerged between mainstream Islam and its more radical fundamentalist fringe. Islamic fundamentalism demands imposition and enforcement of a strict *Shari'a* law code. Several countries, including Saudi Arabia, Iran, Pakistan, and the Sudan have adopted selected portions of this code. So did Afghanistan under the Taliban before that government was removed from power, but not entirely defeated, in 2002.

Women have been oppressed by male dominated governments in the name of Islam for centuries. Neither the *Qur'an* nor the *Hadiths* requires wearing of the veil; yet fundamentalist influence has sometimes used extreme methods in enforcing this and even more restrictive attire. The *Qur'an*, however, does place women in an inferior economic status compared to men through unequal inheritance laws, the right of men but not women to have multiple spouses, and divorce laws that favor men.[57] One text passage apparently endorses beating wives who misbehave.[58] In Iran as well as in several other Islamic countries today, a woman needs her husband's permission to work or to travel abroad and a man's court testimony is twice as important as a woman's.

In Pakistan, a woman can prove she has been raped only if four adult men testify they witnessed the event. In several Middle Eastern countries, women who have claimed rape but who have been unable to produce four adult male witnesses are often imprisoned for admitting "illicit" sexual activity. A woman who was raped in Nigeria was sentenced to be stoned to death by a *Shari'a* court before the sentence was finally overturned in 2002. A similar incident with the same outcome occurred in Iran in 2010. In some Islamic countries, women are allowed to own property and enter highly skilled professions, although tradition often dictates that educational levels attained by women are considerably lower than those of men.

One of the most extreme forms of Islamic fundamentalism is called Wahhabism.[59] Based on the teachings of an eighteenth-century Arab cleric, it preaches holy war *(jihad)* targeting all nonbelievers including Westerners and Jews. Its message is taught in so-called religious schools or *madrassas*, especially in Saudi Arabia and Pakistan. There are numerous statements in both the *Qur'an* and the *Hadiths* that explicitly call for jihad against "infidels", those who are not Muslims. Many of these statements openly condone violence.[60] Of course, some Islamic religious leaders still profess that the penalty for converting from Islam to Christianity is death. A Wahhabi Saudi sheik decreed in 2010 that even those moderate Muslims who advocate easing gender segregation in public places like swimming pools should be put to death.

A major global concern is the extent to which Wahhabis and their sympathizers have been able to engage in acts of mass terrorism in the name of a supposedly peaceful religion. Whether the primary Islamic influence on future economic and social policy comes from mainstream[61] or fundamentalist Islam is one of the most serious issues facing the world today.

Confucianism, Buddhism, and Taoism

Because the teachings of Confucius (551–479 BCE) emphasize the responsibility of rulers to their subjects, Confucianism helped to maintain for centuries the economic status quo and privileged position of the Mandarin class in China. The original writings of Confucius, called the *Analects*, contain several statements that support free market principles, including hard work and thrift. Confucianism today contains a similar pro-market focus but also sanctions strong government interference, especially in the emerging industrial giants of East Asia.[62] Many scholars argue that the Confucian ethic has played a major role in the late twentieth century economic miracle of Japan, Taiwan, Singapore, and South Korea.

Founded in India by Siddhartha Gautama in 528 BCE, Buddhism seeks the extinction of craving, suffering, and selfishness. Buddhist economics questions the importance of economic growth and materialism generally, encourages conservation of resources, and stresses local self-sufficiency to reduce the need for international trade. It also seeks the path to long-run harmonious coexistence of humans and the natural environment by reducing both consumption and the negative effects of technology, such as pollution.[63] Historically, the economies of China and Japan, where Buddhist religious devotion has been strong, have been influenced little, if at all, by these principles. Buddhist economics has attracted a much larger following, however, in nations such as Thailand, Laos, Myanmar, and Sri Lanka.

Based on the sixth century BCE work of the Chinese scholar Lao-tzu, Taoism stresses conserving energy in the pursuit of life's goals.[64] This does not imply laziness or inactivity. In fact, the principle bears a striking resemblance to doing things in the most efficient manner possible, one of the most fundamental economic concepts. The Taoist, however, rejects competition and self-assertiveness. In direct contrast to Western dominance of the physical world, Taoism emphasizes harmony with nature, an important issue in the economics of the environment.

Non-Christian religions, therefore, have clearly exerted some influence on economic thinking in many parts of the world. Like the Bible, however, their ancient texts have remained open to numerous interpretations, some of which have nominally encouraged human progress while others have clearly hindered it.

Out of this hodgepodge of contradictions and morally

dubious collection of principles, how could anyone, let alone supposedly intelligent scholars of the economy, find anything upon which to influence human behavior and the conduct of economic affairs in daily life? The answer is that those who aspired to, and claimed the influence of, a higher authority selected those passages that suited their needs and ignored that which was morally repulsive. In times when literacy was limited, finding people to live their lives based on a handful of poetic verses was an easy sell. "Cherry picking" selected sacred text content became widespread among religious leaders and economists who followed their lead.

As noted above, some of the early economists were religious. It should not be surprising, therefore, that they advocated economic principles that drew upon their individual beliefs. Those who were agnostic or atheistic appreciated the difficulty of openly espousing these views during an era when religious beliefs were not routinely challenged.

Technology vs. Institutions in Ancient Religious Texts

On the surface, it would appear that religious encouragement of hard work, saving, respect for private property as well as private markets, and the efficiency of trade have contributed to economic growth and human progress. Such endorsements appear in the ancient texts of Christianity, Judaism, Islam, Hinduism, and Confucianism. The Islamic condemnation of wastefulness, extravagance, and fraud may also have produced practices consistent with advances in the state of knowledge. Even though Buddhism has questioned the need for economic growth and materialism generally, its encouragement of resource conservation and environmental quality may be loosely interpreted as exerting a positive influence on the human condition. If the sayings of Confucius did, in fact, inspire recent economic progress in East Asia, if

Jewish entrepreneurs have received additional motivation from the Torah and the Talmud, and if the sixteenth century Protestant work ethic played a significant role in "the rise of capitalism", these influences should be duly noted.

Of course, it is still unclear whether religiously instilled values like hard work have contributed to human progress or have merely kept the masses in a state of subservient fear so that those with power, in religious bureaucracies and elsewhere, could call the shots.

On the other hand, institutional resistance to change over several centuries as codified in the texts of numerous established religions clearly illustrates the power of habit, ritual, myth, custom, tradition, ceremony, and even superstition. Many of these teachings have severely slowed human progress and have even contributed to backwardness along with brutally savage behavior.

The explicit biblical endorsement of slavery, submissiveness of women to men, and death as punishment for homosexuality, for cursing parents, and for adultery are examples of genuinely barbaric practices rooted in ignorance, no matter how cleverly Christian and other religious spin doctors have attempted to reinterpret such statements. Arguing that the world is a better place because people have been tortured and/or killed for their religious beliefs is still a difficult case to prove.

Fundamentalist Islam's abuse of the *Shari'a* law code under which women may be stoned to death because they are unable to produce four male witnesses to a rape is a similarly unspeakable tragedy and detriment to human advancement. Even mainstream Islam's unequal inheritance laws, the right of men but not women to have multiple spouses, and divorce laws that favor men are rooted in dubious customs and traditions. In much of the Middle East, suspicion of Western ideas, denial of educational and career opportunities for women, and only gradual acceptance of industrial modernization have slowed progress. Of course, a call for the murder of those who possess different ideas about what is morally permissible has done little to promote economic progress either in medieval Europe or in present day Middle Eastern societies.

In Judaism, laws pertaining to festivals and ceremonies in the *Talmud* pay substantial attention to the regulation of ritualistic behavior. The long time Christian (Roman Catholic) prohibition of lending money at interest prevented many of its members from engaging in legitimate business practices. Under Confucianism, emphasis on the responsibility of rulers to their subjects helped to maintain for centuries the economic status quo and privileged position of the Mandarin class in China. Buddhist rejection of both material values and reliance on international trade has reduced economic growth possibilities for those who strictly adhere to its principles. The disapproval of competition and self-assertiveness under Taoism is hardly a formula for economic advance.

All of these examples barely scratch the surface of religious opposition to human progress. More importantly, this resistant force has hardly been limited to ancient times. During the past fifteen years alone, religiously inspired wars have been responsible for *millions* of deaths in the following places:[65] Palestine (Jews vs. Muslims); the Balkans (Orthodox Serbians vs. Catholic Croatians), (Orthodox Serbians vs. Bosnian and Albanian Muslims); Northern Ireland (Protestants vs. Catholics); Kashmir (Muslims vs. Hindus); Sudan (Muslims vs. Christians); Nigeria (Muslims vs. Christians); Ethiopia and Eritrea (Muslims vs. Christians); Sri Lanka (Sinhalese Buddhists vs. Tamil Hindus); Indonesia (Muslims vs. Timorese Christians); and the Caucasus (Orthodox Russians vs. Chechen Muslims), (Muslim Azerbaijanis vs. Catholic and Orthodox Armenians). Over one million people have died in the long running religious border conflict between India and Pakistan that threatens to escalate into full-fledged nuclear confrontation.

The issue has perhaps most cogently been summarized as follows: "No doubt an obscure truth of economics is at work here: societies appear to become considerably less productive whenever large numbers of people stop making widgets and begin killing their customers and creditors for heresy."[66]

Except for occasional, generic, and vaguely defined support to "acquire wisdom…(and) understanding",[67] statements encouraging advances in human know how and the development of better ways of doing things are seldom, if ever, found in ancient religious texts.

The influence that religion has exerted on human behavior, concerning economic matters and everything else, is a classic example of a rigidly locked-in path dependency. Reluctance to challenge authority that has claimed a divine mandate has clearly limited human progress throughout history. Even the thoughtful polytheistic Greeks only allowed their inquiry to go so far. The vague and sometimes contradictory guidance provided by monotheistic religions has cast a shadow of fearful caution that limited many forms of inquiry, from scientific to philosophical. In Europe, a liberating Renaissance would eventually occur in the middle of the second millennium CE. Before that reawakening, the human race would have to endure more than a thousand years of harsh religious oppression after the fall of the Roman Empire. The consequences of those restrictions on creative thought would be overwhelming and would diminish only gradually yet incompletely even to the present day.

Footnotes:

1. Jeffrey T. Young, "Law and Economics in the Protestant Natural Law Tradition: Samuel Pufendorf, Francis Hutcheson, and Adam Smith", *Journal of the History of Economic Thought*, 30, 3 (September 2008), pp. 283-296.

2. Terry Peach, "Adam Smith's 'Optimistic Deism', the Invisible Hand of Providence, and the Unhappiness of Nations", *History of Political Economy*, 46, 1 (Spring 2014), pp. 55-83 and Gavin Kennedy, "The Hidden Adam Smith in His Alleged Theology", *Journal of the History of Economic Thought*, 33, 3 (September 2011), pp. 385-402. See also Paul Oslington, (ed.), *Adam Smith as Theologian*, (New York: Routledge, 2011) where several opposing points of view are voiced.

3. Bradley W. Bateman, "Reflections on the Secularization of American Economics", *Journal of the History of Economic Thought*, 30, 1 (March 2008), p. 3. For early religious influence on the conduct of American business, see: Mark Valeri, *Heavenly Merchandize: How Religion Shaped Commerce in Puritan America*, (Princeton, NJ: Princeton University Press, 2010). On the specific link between evangelical Protestantism and laissez faire-based neoclassical economics plus how this link has produced even more extreme positions in the 21st century, see: Donald E. Frey, *America's Economic Moralists: A History of Rival Ethics and Economics,* (New York: SUNY Press, 2009). A more reasonable Christian approach which argues for complete separation of church and state is given by Dennis C. Mueller, "The State and Religion", *Review of Social Economy*, 71, 1, (2013), pp. 1-19.

4. 2 Thessalonians 3:10; Proverbs 10: 4-5

5. Exodus 21: 33-37; Exodus 22: 6-13; Exodus 20: 15, 17

6. 1 Corinthians 10: 25; Amos 8: 4-6; Leviticus 25: 14

7. Genesis 26: 12-14; Proverbs 10: 22; Psalms 127:1

8. Proverbs 21: 20

9. 1 Timothy 6: 8-10

10. Proverbs 11:26

11. Luke 6:24; Sirach 27: 1-2; Luke 16: 19-31; Matthew 6: 24; Proverbs 16: 16; Sirach 13: 4; Proverbs 28: 3; James 5: 1-5

12. Proverbs 19: 1

13. Mark 10: 25; Matthew 19: 24

14. Proverbs 13: 18; Proverbs 14: 20; 1 Timothy 6: 17-19

15. Acts 2: 44-45; Acts 4: 32, 34-35; Matthew 19: 21; Mark 10:21; Luke 18: 22

16. Colossians 3:11

17. Proverbs 22: 29

18. Leviticus 19:13

19. Exodus 30: 15; Proverbs 29: 4

20. Genesis 47: 15

21. Ezekiel 27: 1-25

22. Comparative advantage will be contrasted with absolute advantage in Chapter 7. Since absolute advantage was not formally developed until the late eighteenth century and comparative advantage not until the early nineteenth century, a biblical illustration of either is somewhat surprising.

23. Leviticus 25:44–46; Ephesians 6:6; 1 Timothy 6:1;

Colossians 3:22; 1 Peter 2:18

24. Exodus 21:20–21

25. Titus 2:5; Colossians 3:18; 1 Peter 3:1, 7

26. 1 Corinthians 14:34–35; 1 Timothy 2:9–15; Ephesians 5:21–24

27. Leviticus 20:13

28. Leviticus 20:9

29. Leviticus 20:10

30. Deuteronomy 22: 21

31. 1 Corinthians 14: 34-36 and 1 Timothy 2: 9-15

32. Deuteronomy 17: 12-13; 13: Deuteronomy 12-16; and John 15: 6. Elsewhere in the New Testament, heresy is also dealt with harshly. See, for example, 1 Corinthians 11: 19; Galatians 5: 20; 2 Peter 2: 1; Romans 16: 17; 1 Corinthians 1: 10; 3: 3; and 14: 33; and Jude 19.

33. See, for example, Ezekiel 1:4–28 and Joseph F. Blumrich, *The Spaceships of Ezekiel,* (New York: Bantam Books, 1974).

34. Leviticus 25:37

35. Nehemiah 5:10–12; Deuteronomy 23:20–21; Luke 6:35

36. Deuteronomy 15:2

37. Carl F. Taeusch, "History of the Concept of Usury," *Journal of the History of Ideas*, 3 (1942), pp. 291–318. The

forbidding of interest in the Qur'an (2:275) has been the subject of similar controversy in the Muslim world.

38. Matthew 20:15

39. Proverbs 11: 25; 1 Thessalonians 4: 10-12; 2 Thessalonians 3: 10

40. Philippians 2: 3–4; Proverbs 19: 22

41. For an excellent survey of economic principles in the religions of the world, see J. Barkeley Rosser Jr. and Marina V. Rosser, *Comparative Economics in a Transforming World Economy,* (Chicago: Richard D. Irwin, Inc., 1996), especially Chapter 5.

42. The first five books of the Bible are Genesis, Exodus, Leviticus, Numbers, and Deuteronomy. A call for a "new moral capitalism" based on the Hebrew Bible may be found in Hershey H. Friedman and William D. Adler, "Moral Capitalism: A Biblical Perspective", *American Journal of Economics and Sociology*, 70, 4 (October 2011), pp. 1014-1028. For interpretations of the economic content of early Jewish religious writings, see Jacob Neusner, *The Economics of the Mishnah,* (Chicago: University of Chicago Press, 1990) and Meir Tamari, *"With All Your Possessions": Jewish Ethics and Economic Life,* (New York: Free Press, 1987).

43. Huston Smith, *The World's Religions: Our Great Wisdom Traditions,* (San Francisco: Harper Collins Publishers, 1991), p. 278.

44. Smith, pp. 283–286.

45. Balbir S. Sihag, "Kautilya on Administration of Justice

During the Fourth Century B.C.", *Journal of the History of Economic Thought*, 29, 3 (September 2007), pp. 359-377.

46. The following citations from the Qur'an are taken from Imad A. Ahmad, "An Islamic Perspective on the Wealth of Nations," paper presented at the International Conference on Comprehensive Development of Muslim Countries, Subang Jaya, Malaysia, August 1–3, 1994. See also Imad A. Ahmad, "Islamic Social Thought," in W. Block and I. Hexham, (eds.), *Religion, Economics, and Social Thought,* (Vancouver, British Columbia: Fraser Institute, 1986), p. 465.

47. *Qur'an* 7: 31–32, 18: 26 and 17: 29

48. *Qur'an* 2: 168

49. *Qur'an* 6: 141

50. *Qur'an* 17: 27

51. *Qur'an* 2:188

52. *Qur'an* 2: 282–283

53. *Qur'an* 26:181

54. *Qur'an* 55: 9

55. *Qur'an* 3: 130, 2: 275–279

56. For a thorough study of recent performance of Islamic banks, see Mehdi Mili, Jean-Michel Sahut, and Eryj Trimeche, "The Role of Islamic Banks in the Transmission of Liquidity Shocks Across Countries", *Journal of Economic Issues*, 49, 1 (March 2015), pp. 197-225. For a critical view of Islamic economics, especially its handling of the controversy

over the charging of interest, see Timur Kuran, *Islam and Mammon: The Economic Predicament of Islamism,* (Princeton: Princeton University Press, 2004).

57. Rosser and Rosser, p. 112.

58. *Qur'an* 4: 34

59. For a history of the early years of Wahhabism and its role in helping bring the current Saudi leadership to power, see Madawi Al-Rasheed, *A History of Saudi Arabia,* (Cambridge, England: Cambridge University Press, 2002), especially pp. 16–23. For a description of the rigidity of Wahhabi restrictions, see Sandra Mackey, *The Saudis: Inside the Desert Kingdom,* (New York: W. W. Norton, 2002), especially pp. 83–97.

60. For an exhaustive list of such statements, see Sam Harris, *The End of Faith: Religion, Terror, and the Future of Reason,* (New York: W. W. Norton, 2005), chapter 4, especially pp. 117-123.

61. For recent discussions of the relationship between the Islamic faith and economic progress, see: David L. Johnston, "Islam and Human Rights: A Growing Rapprochement?" *American Journal of Economics and Sociology*, 74, 1 (January 2015), pp.113-148; Ayman Reda, "Weber and Baqir as-Sadr: The Paradox of Economic Development in Islamic Societies", *American Journal of Economics and Sociology,* 73, 1 (January 2014), pp. 151-177; Ayman Reda, "Islam and Markets", *Review of Social Economy*, 71, 1 (2013), pp. 20-43; Abdulkader Cassim Mahomedy, "Islamic Economics: Still in Search of an Identity", *International Journal of Social Economics*, 40, 6 (2013), pp. 556-578; and Timur Kuran, *The Long Divergence: How Islamic Law Held Back the Middle East*, (Princeton, NJ: Princeton University Press, 2010).

62. An interesting recent view of Confucianism is given by Sungmoon Kim, "Confucianism, Moral Equality, and Human Rights: A Mencian Perspective", *American Journal of Economics and Sociology*, 74, 1 (January 2015), pp.149-185.

63. Peter L. Daniels, "Buddhist Economics and the Environment: Material Flow Analysis and the Moderation of Society's Metabolism," *International Journal of Social Economics,* 30 (1, 2) (2003), pp. 8–33. The classic book on Buddhist economics is E. F. Schumacher, *Small Is Beautiful: Economics as if People Mattered,* (New York: Harper and Row, 1973). A more recent work is Sulak Sivaraksa, *The Wisdom of Sustainability: Buddhist Economics for the 21st Century,* (Kihei, Hawaii: Koa Books, 2009).

64. The overall philosophy is presented in Max Kaltenmark, *Lao Tzu and Taoism,* (Stanford, CA: Stanford University Press, 1969).

65. Harris, p. 26 which also contains the listing of recent wars cited in this paragraph.

66. Harris, p. 17.

67. Proverbs 16: 16

Chapter Five

Feudalism and the Momentary Triumph of Institutions

Medieval cottages were dismal, depressing, unhealthy, foul-smelling.....and serving as common, one-room homes for man and wife, children and animals.

John Joseph Bagley

Medieval villages were conservative and inefficient, but they produced enough food to keep Europe alive, and that was all that they were trying to do.

Joseph R. Strayer and Dana C. Munro

The purpose of separation of church and state is to keep forever from these shores the ceaseless strife that has soaked the soil of Europe with blood for centuries.

James Madison

There is no general consensus among historians on the boundaries of the Middle Ages.[1] Many suggest the period began as the result of either military triumphs or the rise of Christianity. In both cases, specific dates vary, sometimes widely. Examples of the former include the fall of Rome in 476, the first Germanic invasions in 256, the assault on Rome by Alaric in 410,[2] and the Muslim invasions during the seventh and eighth centuries. Claims for the latter include the reign of the emperor Diocletian (284-305, during which the empire was formally divided into east and west), the founding of Constantinople in 330, the accession of Theodosius to the throne in 392, or the coronation of Charlemagne in 800. Heavily influenced by Christian orthodoxy, the last three of these emperors all helped establish Christianity as the official religion of the Roman Empire.[3]

There is somewhat greater consensus that the end of medieval Europe coincides with the early years of the *Renaissance,* although its specific timing is uncertain. This great cultural reawakening commences in Italy with the late 12th- and early 13th-century writings of authors like Dante, in England with the 14th-century work of Chaucer, and in Germany with the printing of the Gutenberg Bible in the middle of the 15th century. Others, apparently less impressed with the Renaissance, argue the Middle Ages ended either with the Turkish assault on Constantinople (which effectively ended the eastern or Byzantine Roman Empire[4]) in 1453, the appearance of the first Czar in Moscow in 1493, or even the Russian Revolution of 1917.

Between the ancient and modern worlds, therefore, an approximately thousand-plus-year (476-1500?) span of time had passed. It had to be called something. During the Renaissance, humanist philosophers[5] somewhat derogatorily christened it the *Middle Ages*. The name originally implied that, during this lengthy period, not much had happened in terms of the evolution of culture and growth of the economy. Even less flattering, the years from the end of antiquity until the tenth century were often called the *Dark Ages,* suggesting an even more serious stagnation, lack of accomplishment, and even retreat into ignorance. After the numerous accomplishments in Greece, Rome, and other societies of antiquity, the reemergence of superstition along with the near disappearance of vital human knowledge was arguably the most tragic episode in human history. The story of how this happened, what it involved, and how it finally ended is the subject of this chapter.

The Search for Order

The collapse of the Roman Empire created a need for some type of order and political stability. Germanic tribes, now nominally in control, lacked the tradition of a strong central government and legal system that had existed under Roman rule.[6] For a time, subsistence agriculture in a semi-civilized setting enabled a meager existence, although certainly not a prosperous economy.[7] Especially during the seventh and ninth centuries, however, Europe was in a state of anarchy. These were periods of violence, lawlessness, and much uncertainty.

While the Christian Church continued to gain influence, even its authority was threatened by Muslim invasions, which began in 622. The territories eventually captured included some of the wealthiest provinces of the former Roman Empire. By mid-century, Arab soldiers had conquered most of Spain, Egypt, Syria, Persia, and Palestine. Within the next two hundred years, Arabs also controlled southern Italy, Sicily, Corsica, Sardinia, and other Mediterranean islands. As a result, trade via shipping slowed considerably, warfare[8] severely hindered economic performance, and European culture and religion faced a formidable eastern rival.

Scandinavian invasions during the eighth and ninth centuries further upset the prospects for order on this troubled continent. The Vikings initially looted wealthy monasteries and churches. Eventually, they captured what is now northern England, northern France, and selected portions of Spain and Italy. A hearty group of Norwegians, known as Norsemen, journeyed to Ireland, Iceland, Greenland, and, at the close of the tenth century, even America, preceding one Christopher Columbus by nearly five centuries. The Magyars[9] from Hungary advanced upon western European territory from the east. Civil wars also raged as ruling groups competed for power, influence, and land.

Threatened from both external and internal sources, people of all economic classes sought security and protection through any institutional apparatus that appeared capable of delivering them. Not surprisingly, those with few economic resources desired the protection of the rich and powerful. The latter, however, needed help from those of lesser means, especially men with fighting potential, to protect their property and assure their safety. A natural local alliance was about to take shape.

The arrangement that resulted from this mutual insecurity in a troubled environment would later become known as feudalism. *Feudalism* was a decentralized system of government designed for mutual protection of different social classes. It began in seventh-century France as a very personal bond of loyalty and obligation. During the eighth and ninth centuries, it spread to much of Western Europe but did not develop in England until the Norman Conquest of 1066. Soon afterward, it spread to southern Italy, to Constantinople, and to the Slavic and Scandinavian states. Although forms of feudalism also existed in Japan, India, China, and the Middle East, the more familiar Western European version will be examined first. The basic institutions of European feudalism were vassalage and the fief.[10]

Vassalage was a binding contractual agreement between the lord (a king or holder of land) and a vassal. A *vassal* was a nobleman who pledged loyalty and various services (especially military) to the lord in return for protection and a means of livelihood called a fief. Although occasionally some other source of income such as the right to charge tolls, the *fief* was generally a parcel of land that the vassal was allowed to use while the lord maintained rights of control, if not outright ownership.

If kings had possessed sufficient sums of money to pay armed soldiers, the system of feudalism would not have been necessary. Lacking adequate funding but holding more land than they could possibly cultivate, kings instead carved up royal properties and endowed them to those who could provide the needed services. The lord–vassal relationship was part of a very rigid feudal hierarchy.

At the top of the pyramid was the *king,* who, in search of support against aggressors, granted fiefs and secured oaths of loyalty and homage from his *vassals*. Various *princes, dukes,* and *counts* might be vassals to the king but lords to the vassals below them. It was common practice for many lords to re-grant portions of their fief to men who then became their vassals. Some of the wealthier lords who had castles,[11] who held their own courts, and who functioned much like kings in their own realm were called *barons.* The baron was a lord to a lower level of vassal called *knights,* who actually did the fighting when called into battle. A distinct chain of landed dependency, therefore, developed. In the (slightly inaccurate) words of one observer, "All land was someone's fief and every landholder except the king was someone's vassal."[12]

All of these groups were considered nobility. At the very bottom of the feudal structure were the *peasants* or *serfs,* who worked the land and performed other manual tasks as required. Some serfs possessed fairly specialized skills and worked part of the time as blacksmiths, masons, carpenters, millers, and herdsmen. Because they enjoyed certain rights and freedoms, serfs were not slaves. Much freedom was voluntarily surrendered by both serfs and nobles in the interest of security. The alternative was viewed as a freedom to be attacked while defenseless, enslaved or killed by perpetrators of aggression, or forced into starvation.

Feudal society was hierarchical in the sense that virtually no upward mobility was possible. Generation after generation was born into serfdom and remained in that state of life until death. Hard-working, productive serfs did not become lords, and ineffective lords did not one day find themselves demoted to serfs.[13]

The pyramid, however, is more precise than the reality of feudal life. Feudalism was not constructed according to some definitive plan. Customs varied over time and from place to place. Services required of vassals were often vaguely stated and even more selectively enforced. Exceptions, exemptions, and special arrangements were common.

As a result, a maze of fragmented rights and obligations developed. One vassal might be given legal authority in matters involving theft but not murder. Another vassal might be charged with control over a piece of land but not the road that ran through it. The king levied taxes but granted immunity to some vassals, usually churchmen. The boundaries where one lord's influence stopped and another's began were often poorly defined. Some vassals might have sworn allegiance to more than one lord. This situation could produce some interesting divided loyalties when conflicts arose between lords.[14]

The lord–vassal–serf pyramid, therefore, is more of a caricature or model of how feudal society was supposed to work. In some cases, it was generally accurate. In others, however, confusion, special privileges, disputes, and questionably stated rights and obligations all made medieval life less symmetric than this model implies. A rigid, vertical set of relationships existed to be sure but they were not uniform in all times and places.

The Rise of the Manor

The center of economic activity under feudalism was the *manor,* a portion of a fief under the control of an individual lord. Not intended to make a profit, manors instead sought to be a wholly self-sufficient economic unit, a goal that few, if any, actually achieved. Items such as salt, pottery, armor, and various tools often had to be acquired via trade with other manors or purchased in nearby towns.

The land area of the typical manor was composed of three divisions: the demesne, open fields, and the commons.

The *demesne* was that portion of arable land reserved for the lord. Serfs tilled the soil, harvested crops, built fences, cared for cattle, and did whatever other work the lord requested. All agricultural output from this land went directly to the lord who often appointed a bailiff to manage the demesne. The *open fields* were reserved for use by the serfs who grew their own food on specifically designated strips of this land.

The *commons* was land not used for growing crops and was open to all. The peasant's animals could graze there. The commons might also have included wooded areas where peasants hunted, fished, and gathered wood for warmth.

The *village* of the manor typically consisted of the residence of the lord, peasant cottages, a blacksmith shop, grain mill, weaving facility, brewery, barns, storage sheds, and a centrally located church. Buildings were often clustered near a well or stream in fairly close proximity to the demesne. Animals roamed freely along village streets or paths.

Several village and manor patterns were possible. The village might be circular or rectangular with its buildings surrounding a green or it might be located along a single, lengthy street. Large manors might have more than one village while several smaller manors might be located adjacent to a single village. The following description of living conditions should dispel any nostalgic notion that medieval life was cozy and quaint:[15]

> Medieval cottages were dismal, depressing,…. unhealthy, foul-smelling, ….and short of head room. Many were built of clay and stone, and serving as common, one-room homes for man and wife, children and animals……Walls were made by tightly packing a mixture of clay,….. dung, and straw. Roofs were thatched with rye or wheat straw.
>
> The lord of the manor and the priest . . . might

> live in a wooden house built on stone foundations but, apart from more room and surer protection from the weather, such a house offered no more amenities than the peasant's cottage. There was no better lighting in either than a wax candle. . . . Smoke from the fire, which burned in a clay-lined hole in the floor, had to find its curling and sooty way out of the narrow windows (and) doors. . . . sanitary arrangements were primitive earth closets or pits. The floors.....were the natural earth trodden or beaten hard, but in wet weather muddy and oozing water. . . . Dampness encouraged decay, and the lack of ventilation from the small . . . windows made the atmosphere none the sweeter.

Custom dictated that the serfs pay the lord certain dues, which might include grain, chickens, or pigs. The lord also charged fees for the use of mills and ovens and received revenue from fines (which could not be appealed) charged by his court. Peasants had to tithe 10 percent of their personal harvests to support the local church. They also could not marry without permission of the lord; when permission was granted, a marriage fee was paid.

Feudalism had both Roman and Germanic origins. Some manors rose from the remnants of Roman estates (latifundia) while others could trace their roots to old German villages. In both earlier cultures, fighting men had freely pledged loyalty to a patron or leader who in return provided food, shelter, and protection. The stronger influence on medieval vassalage was probably that of the ancient Germanic tribe known as *Teutons.* More than a century before the time of Christ, they developed a similar quid pro quo arrangement based on mutual respect. Medieval lords intended, at least in principle, the same type of dignified support for those who had paid them homage. The more exploitive feudal lords, however, regarded their vassals as distinctly inferior, much like the ancient Romans treated their clients. The medieval manor clearly drew on both Roman and German traditions.

As the feudal structure matured and as kings became weaker, manors grew increasingly independent. Vassals governed, administered justice, and even waged war while maintaining only the most superficial connection to the king. Peasants, in particular, understandably felt a greater sense of loyalty to the lord of their manor than to some distant ruler whose precise location was often unknown to them. Both government and economic activity, therefore, became increasingly decentralized. Although the concept of the sovereign ruler did not disappear, Europe eventually evolved into a continent of small principalities rather than vast, powerful kingdoms. Indeed, feudalism may well have been the only practical system in a land of local economies facing perpetual threats of violence.

Feudal Economics

The economic base of feudalism was agriculture. Perhaps as much as 90 to 95 percent of the population worked the land. During the Middle Ages, there were no stunning advances in mechanization or in knowledge of production techniques. For the most part, custom rather than experimentation dictated farming methods.

> The medieval village . . . could not afford experiments; there was too narrow a margin between survival and starvation. People could not be very enthusiastic about the process of trial and error when one error might mean that no one would be left to make further trials. Medieval villages were conservative and inefficient, but they produced enough food to keep Europe alive, and that was all

that they were trying to do.[16]

Three modest but important technological innovations, however, occurred in agriculture between the ninth and thirteenth centuries.[17] In Roman times, the old scratch plow worked fairly well in the dry, light soils of the Mediterranean but literally could not penetrate the rich and heavy soils in northwestern European lowlands. The invention of the heavy-wheeled plow brought this fertile acreage under cultivation. It also reduced plowing time, since fields now needed to be tilled only once instead of twice. Second, the introduction of the horse collar, harness, and nailed horseshoe made the agile team of horses more productive in plowing than the slower but stronger team of oxen.

Third, rotating crops and leaving some land idle during the growing season enhanced yields and slowed soil exhaustion. Grazing cattle would fertilize this idle land, thereby augmenting its productivity in the long run. In addition, iron increasingly replaced wood in the construction of agricultural tools, especially the toothed harrow (a cultivating implement that pulverized the soil, somewhat like the modern handheld rake) and the hinged flail (a handheld threshing implement that separated seeds from the plant). Such iron tools were stronger, more durable, and more efficient than their wooden predecessors.

There is some evidence of deforestation as more land was brought into cultivation. Despite steady cutting of the forests and erosion of soil due to primitive farming methods (not everyone practiced crop rotation, for example), the environment was not severely threatened. The Western European population of only about ten million people was not large enough to cause serious environmental damage.[18]

Outside of agriculture, technological advance was sparse. At the conclusion of the Middle Ages, sources of power were limited to wind, running water, and the muscles of humans and beasts. Windmills helped to grind corn while watermills[19] cut lumber and powered hammers. Iron manufacturing, tanning, and metal-working operations eventually used wind and water power. During the 12th and 13th centuries, the new spinning wheel enabled faster and less costly production of textiles, the wheelbarrow aided in construction, and the invention of eyeglasses helped the craftsmen and the few who were literate.

The major economic goal of the period was not accumulation but survival. The lord was motivated by the continued existence of the manor, not by the pursuit of profit. This was a subsistence, barter economy with virtually no savings whatsoever. Feudal relationships came about in a situation where money was scarce.[20] This severely limited the opportunities for trade, long-term investment, and production for profit. All three of these concepts, however, were not part of the medieval mindset.[21]

In addition to agriculture, the medieval economy was also based on theft. Royalty expanded its wealth, not only by taxes that were often poorly administered, but by stealing from the subjects of other royalty. The English epic *Beowulf* (probably composed during the eighth century by an unknown author) captures the barbarism of Germanic advances during the early Middle Ages. The violence of the period, therefore, was motivated by both the thrill of adventure and economic gain.

The rich and powerful overate and overdrank while many peasants suffered from hunger. The most widely available food consisted of grain (such as wheat or barley) made into bread or porridge, both of which were nutritious but hardly tasty. Adding honey or sour milk helped only slightly. Popular drinks included beer, milk, and cider. Given sanitation standards, water was often consumed at great risk. Hunting and fishing provided occasional protein, wild fruit and nuts infrequent diversity. Meat, butter, and cheese were staples only of the well-to-do who, like their less-well-off contemporaries, lacked sufficient vitamins and fat in their diets.[22] Lords sometimes kept cellars of imported wine,[23] an expensive luxury not shared with those who worked the land.

Productive manual labor was considered degrading and crude. It was performed by peasants who had neither the skills to be knights nor the knowledge to be clergy (and certainly not the social position to be lords). Aside from the Church, there were no professions that offered possibilities for advancement to anyone. Given their illiteracy, serfs were unlikely candidates for the clergy. Economic opportunities for peasant women outside of the home simply did not exist.

Even women who were not peasants had limited legal rights.[24] The right of inheritance existed only if there were no male heirs. An unmarried or widowed woman was placed under the guardianship of a lord, who could sell her in marriage to a man of his (the lord's!) choice. Single women paid for the right to choose their own spouse.

Serfs suffered constant hardship.[25] Although impossible to measure precisely, infant mortality rates were extremely high. Death of either mothers or infants during childbirth was common. Few serfs (and not that many nobles) lived beyond their twenties. Malnutrition, respiratory diseases, malaria, leprosy, plagues (especially during the 1340s and 1370s), and violence all limited life expectancy.

Under such frightful conditions, superstition was prevalent. Many people were prone to believe in signs from above and in supposed visions. *The Canterbury Tales,* a collection of narrative poems written over a twelve-year span by Geoffrey Chaucer (1340?–1400), records daily activities of medieval peasantry. Some of these accounts are humorous but most portray the harsh reality of the times in warm yet serious human terms.

Throughout the Middle Ages, royalty and nobility were locked in a perpetual power struggle. Kings sought centralization of their authority while lords became increasingly successful at achieving local independence. This decentralization reduced the power of the king and created potential for warfare among what were, in effect, many petty kingdoms. The economic loss caused by warfare during the Middle Ages[26] is incalculable but huge. Destruction of property and loss of human life was so commonplace that it was simply not possible to plan for long-term economic growth. Not until the late Middle Ages does Western Europe achieve a standard of living comparable to that of the Roman Empire.

Medieval Europeans had at best an inexact concept of time.[27] Sand clocks, sun dials, and the village rooster were the most sophisticated time pieces of the era. All were highly inaccurate. Mechanical clocks did not appear until the 1350s. Even the modern calendar was not devised until the late thirteenth century. Prior to that time, therefore, virtually no medieval resident knew the century or year in which he or she lived; few apparently cared. In today's world, such imprecision seems inconceivable. The medieval serf and lord, however, seldom needed more than a rough estimate of the number of remaining daylight hours. Furthermore, the uncertainty posed by disease and violence caused most people to live one day at a time.

In a similar vein, the use of numbers and measures was not widespread. When employed, units of measurement frequently varied from place to place. Because buildings were sometimes constructed haphazardly, they occasionally turned out far differently than originally designed. Architects of the era, however, did create many of the most magnificent castles and cathedrals ever built. Some of the more elaborate cathedrals, which still stand in European cities today, took more than a century to erect.

Between the fifth and tenth centuries, European cities actually lost population and declined in economic importance. Muslim invasions of the southern continent and Scandinavian attacks on northern ports crippled trade, which had been the lifeblood of an urban economy. There was little or no communication among people living in different areas.

During the more peaceful eleventh century, trade expanded, demand for manufactured products rose, transportation improved, and urban areas began a process of revival.

An important medieval institution, the *guild,* regulated economic activity as well as political and social life in cities.[28] Over time, the guild attained sufficient power to become a vital voice in city politics and administration. Different types of guilds frequently were rivals for local influence. Organized by merchants engaged in international commerce, the *merchant guild* regulated trade, encouraged production of goods for the market, and oversaw various aspects of commerce in the community. It also prevented competition from outsiders and established courts to handle commercial disputes.

Conflicts between merchants and artisans led the latter to form their own guilds. In some ways similar to a modern labor union, the *craft guild* was an organization of producers in the same occupation. The craft guild set quality standards for products, controlled prices and wages, and determined the total amount to be produced. There were guilds for blacksmiths, leatherworkers, bakers, butchers, weavers, dyers, metalworkers, and virtually every other occupation. In Paris and Toulouse, even prostitutes belonged to a guild.[29]

Much like the manor, the craft guild sought to maintain the existing order. It restricted both competition and profits, limited membership, and outlawed advertising. It even prohibited sneezing by merchants to attract the attention of shoppers to their wares.[30] The craft guild also set other standards of private conduct, including rigidly enforced directives on dress, church attendance, and gifts to charity.

Like other aspects of feudal society, the structure of the craft guild was hierarchical. At the bottom was the *apprentice,* generally a young boy learning the skills of a given craft and receiving room and board in return.[31] After a specified number of years, an apprentice could become a *journeyman* or hired day laborer. After proving he was proficient in his craft by completing a major project, the journeyman might attain the stature of a *mastercraftsman,* one who operated his own shop, hired journeymen, and trained apprentices. Unlike the king–lord–vassal–serf hierarchy, upward mobility in the guild was possible but not guaranteed. Most journeymen never became mastercraftsmen, simply because more laborers were needed than masters.

Although guilds successfully protected their members, they were inherently resistant to change. Neither new technology nor new ideas infiltrated the established production process until guild leaders incorporated them into existing regulations. Gaining official approval was so cumbersome that creative thinkers soon became hopelessly discouraged. Innovative manufacturing methods ultimately had to be developed in distant places not subject to guild restrictions. The guilds, in other words, achieved temporary economic security for some craftsmen but provided a barrier to long term economic progress.

Whether rural or urban, therefore, the medieval economy was governed more by tradition than the market. The absence of a strong central government meant that a command economy from that source was not possible. Authority played a role in medieval economics but central direction did not come from government. Rather, it came from the Church. Since religion was at least nominally designed to prepare people for life in the next world while economic motivations guided life in this world, religion and economics were potentially in conflict. The authority of the Church minimized such conflict by making sure that economic activity was kept in its proper place. During the Middle Ages, that place was consistently secondary to religion or, perhaps more discreetly stated, strongly guided by religious principles.

Influence of the Church

The most widely practiced religion in medieval

Europe was Roman Catholicism. Others present included Germanic and Slavic paganism, Islam (which dominated most of Spain for about 300 years until the 1490s), Judaism, Arian Christianity, Celtic Christianity, and Greek Orthodox Christianity.

Because of tithes from peasants and donations of land from lords, the Catholic Church prospered greatly during the Middle Ages. Eventually, the earthly branch of the institution achieved the status of a major landholder. Bishops often became vassals of the king who desired to benefit from these landholdings. Thrust into the role of nobles, some bishops succumbed to the temptations of wealth and power, the pursuit of which occasionally took precedence over spiritual concerns.

Religion in the Middle Ages was modeled after the feudal hierarchy. The faithful pledged loyalty to a sovereign deity much like a vassal swore allegiance to his lord. Satan was depicted as a vassal gone astray and as one destined to lose in battle. Just as there existed a political hierarchy with kings, dukes, counts, barons, earls, and knights, so too a religious hierarchy was constructed with popes, archbishops, bishops, priests, abbots, and monks. A classic work of literature during this period, the *Divine Comedy* (1321) written by Dante Alighieri (1265–1321), illustrates the medieval fascination with hierarchical structures as well as its commitment to spirituality.

The most influential medieval scholarship was *scholasticism,* which attempted to apply reason to religious principles. Drawing on Greek philosophy, its goal was to prove through logic what Christians accepted as true according to their faith.[32] Arabic and Jewish scholars had reintroduced Greek writings into western Europe during the twelfth century. Some conservative theologians resisted this approach on grounds that Greeks were pagans and beliefs such as miracles could never be explained. Subjecting miracles to rational analysis, they feared, would encourage disbelief. The scholastics (also called *schoolmen*), however, sought to enhance faith, not discredit it.

The leading scholastic thinker was Thomas Aquinas (1225?–1274). His classic *Summa Theologica* (1266–1273) was an attempt to reconcile Christian theology with the philosophy of Aristotle. What emerged from this work was a set of principles that Church leaders used as guidelines for economic policy. One principle was the *just price,* defined as the price that kept both buyer and seller in their existing social position. Although this may seem like an odd criterion of justice, it is wholly consistent with feudal thinking. Maintenance of the status quo, after all, was the goal. Ascending the ladder of success was not an accepted concept.

How was this just price to be determined? The process had little to do with the pursuit of profit since few in medieval society thought along those lines. Rather, sellers were not supposed to sell an item for more than it was worth. But how was this worth, or true value, decided? Over the years, various interpretations of what the scholastics actually intended have been given. Some have argued that the just price was based on the costs of production, most of which were labor costs. The more popular view equates the just price with the current market price.[33] Further, if price was regulated by government, that price was considered just. Three different possibilities, therefore, existed.

The plain truth is that the scholastics were rather vague and imprecise. Aquinas never specified how the just price was to be achieved but he clearly did not base just price on labor costs. Other scholastics (Albertus Magnus and San Bernardino of Siena) talked about a fair or customary price in the market, despite the fact that markets were not yet well developed. Aquinas does link the just price idea to Aristotle's notion of justice in exchange. Aquinas is explicit in saying that, if a seller charges more than the just price, he must pay restitution.

The preceding three statements suggest that

scholasticism was more concerned with the ethical aspects of exchange than with how prices were determined in practice. The schoolmen wanted to assure justice, fairness, and equity based on the customs and traditions of the time. Bluntly put, they were theologians, not economists, and they either did not understand how price might result from market forces or were unimpressed by the process. They were, however, medieval men who wanted the status quo upheld with a minimum of discomfort to those involved in exchange.

A second scholastic principle dealt with the familiar concept of *usury* or lending money at interest.[34] Both Aristotle and the Bible, you will recall, condemned it. Medieval churchmen initially reiterated classical Greek and biblical views. Violators were threatened with punishment, ranging from restitution to excommunication from the Church, although escaping these sanctions was fairly easy, especially for the 14th-century Italian banks. As in other feudal arrangements, exemptions were common, especially if risk was involved or the lender was not Christian. As one writer has stated tongue in cheek: "Jews and Lombards, being damned anyhow, were permitted to take usury."[35]

The practice of usury was fairly easy to condemn in an economy in which there was very little money. In one sense, medieval relationships involved a close personal touch. People in the manor all knew each other. The same may be said for residents of a village or even members of a guild. If hardship befell one person or family, lending at interest might well seem uncharitable. Most loans were not made for long-term investment, but rather, for meeting some immediate need like food or shelter. Eventually, as cities grew and markets expanded, lending became more impersonal and geared more toward investment needs. Charging interest appeared more logical under such circumstances. Ultimately, the Church itself became a lender at interest.

Scholastic writings also addressed questions of justice in wages, taxation, foreign trade, and other commercial activity. Selling defective merchandise was prohibited unless buyers were made fully aware of the product's condition. The practice of charity among Church members was encouraged as a means of attacking the problem of widespread poverty.

One reason for the pervasive influence of the Church in worldly matters was that few beyond the clergy were literate.[36] *Most medieval kings could neither read nor write.* Therefore, it should not be surprising that medieval society was static and unprogressive. Land and people were often used inefficiently, innovation was minimal, educational opportunity was limited, and maintenance of the existing order was the primary goal. Few people challenged existing patterns of thought because there were few incentives to do so. Creative thinking might get one charged with heresy, excommunicated, or burned at the stake.

The "Holy Inquisition" began in 1184 under the watchful eye of Pope Lucius III. In 1199, Pope Innocent III decreed that the property of convicted and executed heretics could be confiscated by the Church! In 1215, the Fourth Lateran Council officially sanctioned torture as a means to induce confessions of heresy. Specific tortures which clergymen, including bishops and priests, considered effective included, but were not limited to, stretching suspected heretics on a rack, scorching them with fire, cutting them with iron claws, and beating them with rods.[37] Once "convicted", burning was the preferred method of execution.[38] Sometimes the live bodies were not engulfed in flames but were only subjected, while chained, to controlled fire at close range so that roasting could induce a slower and more painful death. Incidents of such multiple forms of torture and murder were neither isolated nor rare. In fact, they were rampant for more than six centuries! The Spanish Inquisition did not officially cease such practices until 1834.

Lest the above statements be considered inappropriately biased against Catholicism, it should be noted that Protestants later subjected their heretics, renegade scholars, and fornicators to equally brutal treatment.[39] Public burnings and other forms of murder continued with a vengeance even after some other practices of the Church of Rome had been "reformed". The lengthy Inquisition in its various forms was clearly one of the most shameful periods in the history of organized religion, either Christian or otherwise "inspired".

Arab–Islamic Influence on Early Economic Thought

Recent scholarship documents that a number of economic ideas previously credited to Thomas Aquinas were put into print nearly two centuries earlier by an Arab-Islamic scholar named Abu Hamid Al-Ghazali (1058–1111).[40] His major work titled *Ihya Ulum al-Deen (The Revival of the Religious Sciences)* contains arguments, which closely parallel the *Summa Theologica.* Aquinas was educated at the University of Naples where the curriculum was based on works of Arabic Islamic philosophers and their translations of Greek classics.[41] While Aquinas acknowledged Islamic influence in the *Summa,* this source of his ideas has largely been ignored by Western authors.

In the Arab world, Al-Ghazali is widely regarded as the most influential thinker of medieval Islam. Like Aquinas, his writing in economics is only part of a larger concern with religion, ethics, and philosophy. Al-Ghazali sought to synthesize the works of Aristotle and Plato with the teachings of Islam and thereby create a balance between religion and reason. Aquinas attempted a similar synthesis of Greek thought and Christianity. An increasing number of Western authors are finally beginning to accept the degree to which Christian medieval scholasticism originated in the Middle East under the influence of a rival religious tradition.

A later Arab-Islamic scholar would have an even greater influence on western economic thought but would receive even less acknowledgement than Al-Ghazali. Historian and philosopher Abd Al-Rahman Ibn Khaldun (1332–1406) published a landmark book titled *Muqaddimah (Introduction to History)* which, among other things, contained insights into economics that Western writers would not "discover" until the 18th, 19th, and 20th centuries.[42] While Ibn Khaldun emphasized the importance of labor in determining the value of products and discussed regional differences in wages within the same occupation, he argued even more insightfully that the cost of production helped to determine supply and ultimately price. Other factors he believed determined price were the affluence of people, the concentration of wealth, and the amount of taxes that government levied on middlemen and traders.

Ibn Khaldun also maintained that profit is a reward for taking risk and even explicitly stated the rule that investors have used for centuries: "buy cheap and sell dear" (or buy low and sell high).[43] He discouraged government interference to alter market prices, such as through subsidies. He argued further that, when supply is restricted by a sales tax, prices rise. Because of these and other insights, a number of Arab and Arab-American economists today believe that Ibn Khaldun, rather than Adam Smith, deserves the title "Father of Economics."

In fact, even though Smith acknowledged neither Arab writer, it is the contention of some economists today that Smith was influenced by both Ibn Khaldun and Al-Ghazali. When Smith explained the division of labor in 1776, he used the now-famous example of a pin factory. Writing some seven centuries earlier, Al-Ghazali's strikingly similar division of labor concept is explained using the example of a needle factory![44] Aquinas also had a division of labor concept that more closely resembled the Al-Ghazali version than Plato's version.[45]

The somewhat surprising refusal of Western scholars to acknowledge the contribution of Middle Eastern thought to the history of economic ideas may well have been more intentional than accidental. However, Western influence in much of the Arab world has also been limited. The Christian-Islamic rivalry rooted in medieval times has apparently lived much longer than all other outdated medieval institutions.

Collapse of the European Feudal System

Change came slowly but inevitably. European feudalism reached its apex during the twelfth century. By that time, a series of forces that began the erosion of feudal institutions was already in motion. Each force was important in its own right but the cumulative effect ultimately spelled the death of the feudal system.

The *Crusades* were an attempt to recapture control of the Holy Land from "infidel" Muslims and to reduce the influence of Islam in Europe.[46] Called by Pope Urban II at the Council of Clermont in 1095, these *holy wars* continued intermittently for nearly two centuries! From military and religious standpoints, the Crusades were a dismal failure. The cost in terms of money and lost lives was staggering. Included among the casualties, however, were many feudal lords whose control over manors was consequently broken. Other lords met their premature demise either during the Hundred Years War (1337–1453) between England and France or the War of the Roses, a thirty-year English civil war during the late fifteenth century. Whenever and wherever the lords fought, they were not minding their manors.

Even more important, crusaders in the Middle East were introduced to a generally more advanced standard of living and more sophisticated tastes in consumer goods. Lords took along many serfs to carry baggage and perform other types of service. While there, the eyes of both classes were opened. Those who safely returned home sought change from the drab manorial or village way of life. Ultimately, the Church-led Crusades helped to create an economic transformation based on money-making principles that the Church opposed.

Traveling merchants operated on a modest scale as early as the late eighth century. Initially viewed with disdain partly because of religious opposition to trading practices, some of these sellers came from villages; others were serfs or sons of serfs who fled the manor. By the eleventh century, these merchants were participating in huge fairs along major trading routes between Italy and Flanders.[47] Products ranging from spices and fine silk to horses and armor were sold to local residents.[48]

In Champagne, France, the most famous of these fairs was held six times a year, with each session lasting as long as six weeks.[49] Three-week sessions held only once or twice per year were more common in other locations. At the close of the 13th century, fairs became scarce. Merchants, forced by kings to pay increasingly higher taxes, developed alternate trading routes and eventually established permanent shops in small communities.

The *spread of local food markets* and the *decline of the manor* went hand in hand. As manors became more productive during the 11th century, serfs were able to generate more food than their families needed. They brought this extra food to towns where they exchanged it for locally produced items or sold it for cash.[50] Serfs, therefore, began to participate in a market economy (albeit a small one) which involved transactions based on money, not barter or tradition. Lords, attracted by goods sold at fairs, began seeking money payments from serfs (rent for their huts and strips of land) instead of payment in crops or labor services. Lords also began renting demesne land to tenant farmers for cash payments. Since serfs paid rent in place of services to the lord, the lord no longer felt obligated to provide protection to the serf. As these arrangements became more established by the end of the 15th century, the old feudal relationships vanished.

A *rebirth of cities* resulted from the activity of merchants and artisans as well as from the growth in international trade.[51] Strategically located cities such as Venice benefited considerably from enhanced shipping activity. Cities near bodies of water or major overland routes throughout Europe found markets in the East for such products as furs, hides, wool cloth, and metals. Merchants in these cities imported such Eastern fare as rice, garlic, cotton, silk, muslin, purple dye, glass mirrors, spices, and perfumes. Increased safety in travel was a major reason for the booming level of commerce.

By the late 13th century, women were running spinning wheels and dyeing wool into several colors in the newly emerging textile industry. Men operated most of the looms. Women also worked in such trades as shoemaker, tailor, barber, baker, hat maker, harness maker, innkeeper,[52] restaurant proprietor, glove maker, blacksmith, armorer, and silk maker. Women worked in the manufacture and sale of food and beverages including beer. Although many women practiced their husband's trade, others were likely to have one of their own, especially if they were widowed. Women were admitted to guilds as candle makers, weavers, and merchants. Then, as now, women were paid less than men for the same work.

Between the wealthy nobility and impoverished peasantry, therefore, there evolved a new middle class of merchants with different attitudes toward work and different political values. Feudal political institutions thrived when small petty kingdoms consisted almost exclusively of two classes, noble and peasant. When the middle class arrived, it supported rising nation-states and new national monarchies.

The *emergence of nation-states and monarchs* provided centralized political authority and replaced the feudal patchwork of tiny principalities. Under feudalism, a king was nominally in charge of vast areas containing perhaps thousands of manors and villages. In practice, lords exerted considerable independence from royalty.

By the end of the 13th century, England's feudal monarchy had been transformed into a parliamentary monarchy. This meant that councils that advised the king included not only nobles and bishops but also members of the merchant class. Wealth generated by this class added considerably to the tax revenue of the king. During the 13th and 14th centuries, cities and parliaments used this revenue to pay soldiers and civil servants to do tasks that vassals performed under feudalism.

By the 15th century, improved weaponry enabled the king's military forces to deliver protection previously provided by lords of the manor. The longbow, gunpowder, the handgun, and the cannon all neutralized the power of the knight and his sword. Content to pay kings for protection no longer given by the lord, citizens developed strong feelings of nationalism for the first time since the Roman Empire. Europeans finally thought of themselves as citizens of France or Germany or of a city-state like Milan or Florence, rather than simply as residents of a local manor.

New World ventures were fueled by the spirit of exploration and funded in most cases by governments of the new nation-states. Driven by the prospect of financial gain and annoyed by the natural geographic advantage enjoyed by the merchants of Venice, legendary navigators sought new trade routes to the Far East. As early as 1418, Prince Henry of Portugal began exploration of the west African coast. Bartolomeu Diaz rounded the southernmost Cape of Good Hope in 1488 and prepared the way for the 1499 voyage of Vasco de Gama to India. After being rejected by the kings of England, France, and Portugal, Christopher Columbus was finally given financial support from King Ferdinand and Queen Isabella of newly united Spain, which had just defeated the Moors of Granada. Columbus made a total of four voyages to the Western Hemisphere, the first in 1492. He died in 1506, still believing he had reached the east coast of India.

With financial support of Bristol merchants, John Cabot explored Newfoundland and Nova Scotia in 1497. Vasco Nunez de Balboa was the first European to reach the Pacific Ocean in 1513. The fleet of Ferdinand Magellan was the first to circumvent the entire globe in 1519, although Magellan himself died en route. All of these feats were possible because of both individual daring and technological advance in ship design (including better masts, rudders, and sails as well as larger cargo space) and navigational instruments (especially the magnetic compass and more accurate maps). Exploration increased the wealth of sponsoring nations as the volume of trade increased and as colonies were ultimately established. The global outreach mentality of these adventurers was the exact opposite of the inward based feudal manor.

The *substitution of currency for barter* allowed transactions to proceed more smoothly. Serfs who traded bread for ale or eggs for cloth had little use for money; indeed, many serfs had never seen a coin. As fairs and village shops flourished, however, the convenience of money became obvious. Currency also facilitated borrowing for investment purposes, the financing of weaponry for the Crusades and other wars, and the shipping activities of those engaged in international trade. Eventually, use of credit became widespread so that merchants and others did not have to carry large sums of cash, especially bulky coin. The rediscovery of money clearly greased the wheels of commerce and contributed to the breakdown of feudal relationships.

The *enclosure movement* made agriculture more efficient but severely reduced opportunities for serfs to live off the land. Encouraged by the new currency-based economy, lords in the 13th century began to fence (or separate by hedge or ditch) grazing lands that were previously considered the commons. Enclosed pastures would be used to raise livestock, especially sheep, because of the growing demand for wool. As the process continued, the new farming enterprises only vaguely resembled the feudal manor. Empty, dilapidated huts previously inhabited by serfs were perhaps the most visible reminder of what had been.

Lords, in effect, had converted their fiefs into privately held land. Peasants, no longer able to use the commons for their cows and chickens, became displaced and had to pursue opportunities elsewhere. Some labored for money wages in agriculture while others found work either in small rural textile plants or in village shops.[53] The impersonal forces of the market had replaced feudal ties and land had become an important resource for providing not only subsistence but, in the not too distant future, a certain level of prosperity.

Not all of these forces that chiseled away at feudal institutions were equally important in the newly forming European nations. Some monarchies were more aggressive than others in exploration. People in some regions responded more fanatically to the Crusades while other groups were more directly affected by itinerant merchants. Timing was certainly different in each case. By the 14th century, for example, England and France were already modern nations with emerging market economies. Spain, by contrast, did not change from a feudal to a modern state until the late 15th century when the territory today known as Italy was still a collection of powerful city-states.

Individual differences notwithstanding, similarities in the decline of feudalism across regions presented a pattern. By the early 16th century, the basic institutions for a market economy were already in place throughout much of Europe. Attitudes of the population toward the pursuit of wealth had changed and those of the Church would soon adjust with the times. When future innovations in technology materialized, the economic results would be explosive.

Asian and Middle Eastern Feudalism

Although the European experience significantly

influenced American economic thought, important forms of feudalism also developed in nations outside of Europe.

Japan

Feudalism in Japan closely resembled the European model, although each developed independently. Between the 10th and 19th centuries, feudal manors called *shoen* operated primarily in eastern Japan. Shoen consisted of wet rice fields or terraced upland fields but no large pastures for grazing. By the 12th century, these estates were fairly complex organizations. Their farm implements like spades, hoes, and plows were made of iron; carts were pulled by horses and oxen; manure was used as fertilizer; and irrigation systems with dikes and ditches were built.[54] Villages of thatched roof houses and a Buddhist or Shinto temple were located close to the fields. (Shintoism is the native religion of Japan.)

Feudal lords, known as *daimyo,* ran their shoen on an absentee basis. Their vassals were faithful servants called *samurai,* professional soldiers who were generally given money or some type of fief other than land. Below the samurai were the peasant land cultivators called *sakunin.* Better off than the European manorial serf, the sakunin either owned his tract of land which could be passed to his heirs or gave land title to the daimyo in return for protection and immunity from taxes.[55]

At the top of the hierarchy was the *shogun,* a title of imperial military commander given by the emperor. Shoguns were, in effect, heads of government who controlled Japan from the late 12th through mid-19th centuries. The most powerful was the Tokugawa Shogunate which ruled as military dictators between 1603 and 1868 while the emperor was a weak figurehead. The shoguns maintained a rigid feudal system until the Meiji Restoration eliminated shogun rule and returned power as well as fiefs to the emperor.

Japanese feudalism was governed by numerous rights

called *shiki,* which detailed what each person associated with the shoen could expect. Rights of the cultivators, for example, were seldom more than the opportunity to live on the land, to till it, and to consume what was left after higher rights were satisfied. In some cases, however, special privileges like fishing, woodcutting, or hunting were permitted.

Samurai were inspired by the code of *bushido* or the *way of the warrior.* This code stressed personal honor and the ideal of selfless loyalty to the lord. When firearms were introduced into Japan at the close of the 16th century, the samurai still retained his warrior position, unlike the mounted knight in Europe who was displaced. This is largely because firearms were scarce and their use by vassals was discouraged by the shogunate.[56]

During the last years of Japanese feudalism, a number of key developments suggested its impending demise. Commitment to bushido waned as the shogunate grew increasingly corrupt. During extended periods of peace, the samurai became an unruly group of unemployed vagrants who often turned to crime including murder. Ambitious and law-abiding samurai settled into new careers as bankers, merchants, and manufacturers. The Tokugawas resisted change and attempted to isolate the country from foreign influence. Their overthrow enabled Japan to industrialize and enter the modern era.

India

The medieval feudal system in India was also similar in some respects to that of feudal Europe. Indian feudalism was rooted in its caste system, which originated perhaps as early as 1000 BCE. Deeply engrained in Hindu tradition, the caste system established a hierarchy of classes. At the top were the *brahmins,* who were priests or masters of spiritual matters. Next came the *kshatryas,* who were warriors, princes, and great lords. They were followed by the *vaisyas,* who were small land-holding peasants, farmers, breeders of stock, artisans, and merchants. At the bottom were the *sudras,* who originally were native slaves and later serfs.

During the Middle Ages, India was decentralized into numerous regional kingdoms, each headed by a warlord. If a warlord gained supremacy by dominating his neighbors, he was called a *maharaja.* As his kingdom grew, he controlled a larger number of vassals who provided him with additional tax revenue and military service. Like the European system, Indian feudal arrangements varied from place to place and over time.

During the period of Islamic influence beginning in the eleventh century, for example, the Rajput clan system was employed. Lands were granted to vassals who had military obligations as well as tax responsibilities. There is some evidence that these taxes fell fairly heavily on the kshatrya.[57] Later, however, tax-free estates called *jagirs* were granted. This arrangement remained until the 19th century when the British colonists sought revenue from these estates.[58]

Indian merchant guilds regulated international trade. Regional kingdoms traded with China, Southeast Asia, Arab countries, and even some European merchants. Guilds built temples and monasteries, loaned money to maharajas, and increased the wealth of Indian royalty through taxation. Some guilds had their own armies. A combination of Muslim and European invasions ultimately hampered Indian trade and challenged its feudal institutions, although its caste system survived well into the 20th century. Outlawed by the current Indian constitution, the caste system finally is showing signs of breaking down.

The Middle East

Fragments of feudalism were also to be found in the Middle East. Local lords ruled from castles over vassals and peasants in southern Arabia even before the arrival of Islam in the seventh century.[59] In the fourteenth century Ottoman Empire, land was given as fiefs to the military aristocracy, but no feudal nobility developed to counter the power of the monarch.[60] There is even evidence of tribal feudalism among the nomadic population of 14th and 15th century Persia.[61]

Compared to Europe, the medieval Middle East was more advanced in several respects including its architecture, thriving cities, manufacturing and commerce, the arts, mathematics, medicine, and especially science. Islamic scientists preserved knowledge gained from ancient Greece, Egypt, Persia, Babylon, India, and China. In addition, they conducted their own experiments which added to knowledge in several fields of science. Some of these advances found their way to the West through Muslim centers of learning in Spain and Sicily, as well as through translations of original Arabic scientific works into Latin.[62]

An important figure in Islamic scientific history is Taqi al-Din (1526–1585) of Istanbul, who wrote several books on astronomy, optics, and mechanical clocks. He also built an observatory. Equally accomplished in the field of medicine was a Syrian named Ibn al-Nafis who published a theory of the circulation of blood in the thirteenth century, long before the concept was discovered in 1628 in the West.[63] In the 9th century, an Arab mathematician[64] introduced the discipline of algebra. These advances coupled with the early Islamic writings in the field of economics cited earlier document achievements in the medieval Middle East before similar knowledge reached Europe. Such patterns have prompted recent attempts to explain why scientific and economic progress since the Middle Ages has been far more pronounced in the West.

In a landmark book, prominent Princeton University Middle East scholar Bernard Lewis offers several possible explanations. These include fanatical religious authorities (as opposed to Islam per se), the embrace of beliefs and practices that may once have been but no longer are progressive,

Muslim sexism that has negated the talents of half its people, the exhaustion of precious metals at about the same time that Europeans were uncovering similar resources in the Americas, and inbreeding due to marriage between cousins in rural areas.[65] Other possible reasons include the closing of Islam to the outside world and the decline of medieval Islamic philosophy, which eventually became submissive to the literal interpretation of the *Qur'an*.[66] Middle Eastern fundamentalist groups have historically preferred blaming scapegoats such as Westerners and departures from rigid religious principles.

China

A form of feudalism existed in China during the Zhou Dynasty between 841 and 221 BCE. Because the government was weak, power was decentralized in principalities, peasants worked on the lord's estate in return for protection, military plunder was rampant, and vassals re-granted their fiefs to subvassals. Chinese feudal estates, however, were larger and better organized than later European manors. Unlike their illiterate European counterparts, Chinese lords were often well educated. By the third century BCE, China had concluded an economic and political experiment that would not begin in Europe for another ten centuries.

Asian and Middle Eastern experiences inform us that European feudalism was neither unique nor original. Rather, given the uncertainties associated with invading marauders on horseback, feudalism of some type was probably inevitable as a defense against such chaos. Similarities in feudal structures were remarkable, considering that each developed independently during periods in which virtually no communication between distant lands occurred. The differences in various feudal experiments and their impact, however, were often significant.

Although trade was limited during the feudal era in

Europe, it thrived in feudal India. Feudalism led to versions of capitalism in Europe and Japan but it did not immediately produce a similar economic system in China, India, or much of the Middle East. Wherever it occurred during the Middle Ages, however, feudalism set in motion forces that would influence global trading patterns over several centuries. Such patterns could not have been imagined by anyone living on an English manor, a Japanese shoen, or an Indian jagir.

Technology vs. Institutions During the Middle Ages

By any measure, the Middle Ages are a period when institutional resistance to change most dramatically suppressed the advance of technology and contributed to backwardness. Much of what was achieved in antiquity had been lost and had to be relearned. That process of relearning took more than ten centuries! Technology stagnated. Invention was minimal. Human knowledge regressed, largely because of a repressive Church, the only institution whose power grew during this period. The manor, the guilds, and the Church were institutions committed to maintaining the status quo among the general population. For most of this period, they succeeded in doing precisely that.

Superstition, reliance in signs from above, religious ritual, fear of demonic forces, and other forms of ceremonialism guaranteed that progress was miniscule. Inventions like the heavy-wheeled plow, crop rotation, use of iron in hand tools, the horse harness, windmills, watermills, spinning wheels, eyeglasses, wheelbarrows, and mechanical clocks pale in comparison to the fact that most people were illiterate, living standards were pitiful, health care was non-existent, and life expectancy was very short.

The contribution that Scholasticism made to an understanding of economics was minor and would have been even smaller had it not been for the influence of Arab Islamic scholars. The Inquisition guaranteed that new ideas would not be welcome and the mindless bloodshed for which it was responsible destroyed any prospect for human creativity or economic growth. Not until feudal institutions weakened and the medieval mindset was replaced by a quest for reason would the downward spiral into backwardness be reversed.

Summary and Conclusions

Historians still debate the precise boundaries of the Middle Ages. In the history of economic ideas, the medieval period may be considered the thousand-year span between the official fall of Rome (476) and the middle of the Renaissance (about 1500) when humanist writers emerged. Optimistic about personal creativity and economic growth, they challenged feudal attitudes, coined the term Middle Ages, and inspired reform of existing institutions, some of which were beginning to embrace change.

Developed in response to the chaotic and violent state of Europe in the absence of Roman power, feudalism was a decentralized system of government designed for mutual protection of different social classes. The feudal order was based on institutions like vassalage, a contractual agreement between lord and vassal and the fief, a means of livelihood such as a parcel of land. The lord was an overseer of land. The vassal was a nobleman who pledged loyalty and service to the lord in return for protection and the fief. Serfs were peasants who worked the land and performed other types of manual labor. The king–lord–vassal–serf hierarchy was rigid and long lasting, although variations in local custom regarding rights and duties existed.

Economic activity was organized around a manor, a portion of a fief controlled by an individual lord who sought to make it as self-sufficient as possible. Each manor contained demesne land, open fields, and common land. The demesne was tilled by the serf but its product was reserved for the lord.

Open fields were strips of land for use by individual serfs. The commons was primarily pasture land open to all. Medieval villages offered rudimentary living conditions for serf, lord, and clergy, as well as buildings where various items could be produced and stored.

The feudal economy was based on agriculture where technological advance was modest. Innovations outside of agriculture were equally so. The major economic goal was survival. Diets were bland and nutritionally deficient, women had no economic opportunities and limited legal rights, infant mortality was high, life expectancy was low, superstition was widespread, and cities declined in importance up to the tenth century.

The guild guiltlessly guided economic activity as well as political and social life in cities. Merchant guilds regulated international and local commerce while craft guilds set quality standards for products, controlled prices and wages, and determined the amount to be produced. Like manors, craft guilds sought to maintain the status quo and were hierarchical, although some upward mobility from apprentice to journeyman to mastercraftsman was possible. By resisting change and discouraging innovation, guilds limited economic progress.

Economic activity was strongly influenced by the Church, which prospered more than any other medieval entity. Scholasticism sought to unite Christian faith with reason, especially Greek philosophy. Thinkers like Thomas Aquinas argued for a just price, one that did not disturb the social position of buyer or seller, and against usury. The fact that few beyond the clergy were literate helps to explain why medieval society was static and unprogressive. Few non-clerics were equipped to orchestrate major change while the clergy openly resisted change. Path dependency maintained its hold for the better part of a thousand years.

A series of forces eroded feudal institutions and eventually led to collapse of the system. The Crusades sent people of different social classes to the Middle East, where they observed more advanced cultures and sought change when they returned to their drab manors and villages.[67] Traveling merchants brought numerous products to fairs along trading routes from Italy to Flanders. Serfs sold surplus food in local markets, which led to the decline of the manor and the lord–serf relationship. Cities were reborn as improved safety in travel encouraged international trade, women worked with men in several industries, and a new middle class emerged.

The new nation-states and monarchs provided centralized political authority. They were supported by the new merchant class, armies with improved weaponry that delivered protection more efficiently than feudal lords did, and growing feelings of nationalism among the people. New World ventures by explorers such as de Gama, Columbus, and Magellan brought wealth to European nations and were part of an adventuresome spirit that the inward-looking feudal manor lacked. The substitution of currency for barter made transactions easier and broke down feudal relationships based on custom. Finally, the enclosure movement enabled lords to convert their fiefs into privately owned land, increased agricultural productivity, and forced serfs to seek employment for wages wherever they could find it.

Feudalism in Japan and India closely resembled the European experience. The shogun-daimyo-samurai-sakunin hierarchy in Japan and the brahmin-kshatrya-vaisya-sudra hierarchy in India displayed obvious similarities to the king-lord-vassal-serf model in Europe. Parallels may also be drawn between the shoen, jagir, and manor as feudal estates. Middle Eastern and Chinese feudalism involved situations somewhat different from those in Europe but nonetheless exhibited distinct feudal characteristics. The collapse of medieval feudalism in Europe set the stage for a commercial revolution quite unlike any prior change in human history.

Footnotes:

1. To many historians and archaeologists, precise dates of lengthy historical periods are unimportant. For a sample of views, see: John Moreland, *Archaeology, Theory and the Middle Ages: Understanding the Early Medieval Past,* (London: Gerald Duckworth and Co., 2010); Norman Davies, *Europe: A History,* (Oxford: Oxford University Press, 1996), especially pp. 291–292; and Henri Pirenne, *Economic and Social History of Medieval Europe,* (New York: Harcourt Brace, 1956).

2. Simon Esmonde Cleary, *The Roman West, AD 200-500: An Archaeological Study*, (Cambridge: Cambridge University Press, 2013) and Neil Christie, *The Fall of the Western Roman Empire: An Archaeological and Historical Perspective*, (London: Bloomsbury Academic, 2011).

3. Catherine F. Cooper and Julia Hillner, eds., *Religion, Dynasty, and Patronage in Early Christian Rome, 300-900*, (Cambridge: Cambridge University Press, 2007).

4. A. D. Lee, *From Rome to Byzantium, AD 363-565: The Transformation of Ancient Rome*, (Edinburgh: Edinburgh University Press, 2013).

5. By the beginning of the 16th century, humanist philosophers had voiced optimism about human creativity and the potential for progress. As a result, they challenged the complacency and fatalism of medieval life, including its sacred institutions. Drawing on classical Greek and Roman authors, humanist writers emphasized reason over medieval and Church tradition. Some, including Pius II and other popes, were pro-Christian and sought a merging of ideas from Greek scholars such as Plato with Christianity. Others were secular with beliefs ranging from agnosticism to atheism.

Humanists expressed a wide range of political philosophies. Thomas More attacked private property and called for democratic socialism in his *Utopia* (1516), an ideal state reminiscent of Plato's *Republic.* Desiderius Erasmus advocated reform of the Church and society in *Colloquies* (1518) and satirized human nature in *The Praise of Folly* (1509).

The most controversial of the humanists was Niccolo Machiavelli, who advocated any policy, regardless of its ethical or religious effects, that adds to the power of the central government. In *The Prince* (1513), he favored the strong state of a single leader while, in his *Discourses* (1513–1517), he appeared to favor a form of representative democracy. His use of reason, pragmatism, and empiricism has created greater appreciation of his methods than his goals. His possible influence on mercantilism is discussed in Chapter 6. Both More and Erasmus were active in the Catholic Church while Machiavelli was an astute observer of Italian politics.

Humanist optimism spread to a growing segment of the population at the close of the Middle Ages. While early humanists, notably Francesco Petrarch in the fourteenth century, clearly wrote prior to the 1500s, Erasmus is generally considered to be the greatest of the Renaissance humanist scholars. His first book, the *Adages,* an anthology of Greek proverbs, appeared in 1500. Updated several times, this reference work introduced many scholars to ancient Greek thought and demonstrated the insights of a pagan philosophy, which, up to that time, was often dismissed for narrow religious reasons. Other important Renaissance humanists included John Colet, Francois Rabelais, Michel Montaigne, Marsilio Ficino, and Pico della Mirandola.

6. Sean Lafferty, "Law and Society in Ostrogothic Italy:

Evidence From the *Edictum Theoderici*", *Journal of Late Antiquity*, 3, 2 (2010), pp. 337-364. The Ostrogothic Kingdom was established by the Ostrogoths in Italy and neighboring areas. It survived from 493 to 553. The *Edictum Theoderici* was a set of Germanic legal codes designed to settle disputes between the Germans and the Romans.

7. Neil Christie and Paul Stamper, (eds.), *Medieval Rural Settlement: Britain and Ireland, AD 800-1600*, (Oxford: Windgather Press, 2012).

8. Rory Cox, "Asymmetric Warfare and Military Conduct in the Middle Ages", *Journal of Medieval History*, 38, 1 (2012), pp. 100-125.

9. Boris Todorov, "The Value of Empire: Tenth Century Bulgaria Between Magyars, Pechenegs, and Byzantium", *Journal of Medieval History*, 36,4 (2010), pp. 312-326.

10. An interesting history of these concepts is given in Norman F. Cantor, *The Civilization of the Middle Ages,* (New York: Harper Collins, 1993), pp. 195–203.

11. Leonie V. Hicks, "Magnificent Entrances and Undignified Exits: Chronicling the Symbolism of Castle Space in Normandy", *Journal of Medieval History*, 35, 1 (2009), pp. 52-69.

12. Sidney Painter, *Mediaeval Society* (Ithaca, NY: Cornell University Press, 1951), p. 17. Although this statement conveys the spirit of the feudal hierarchy, it is technically inaccurate in that some land remained outside the feudal structure and was held by wealthy landowners who did not grant it to vassals as fiefs. Such land was called *allodial land.* Title of ownership was obtained through inheritance, gift, or purchase, much like private property today.

13. Jonathan R. Lyon, "Fathers and Sons: Preparing Noble Youths to be Lords in Twelfth Century Germany", *Journal of Medieval History*, 34, 3 (2008), pp. 291-310.

14. Such a person has been called "the man of several masters." See Marc Bloch, *Feudal Society,* Vol. 1 (Chicago: University of Chicago Press, 1961), pp. 211–218.

15. John J. Bagley, *Life in Medieval England,* (London: B. T. Batsford Limited, 1960), pp. 26–27.

16. Joseph R. Strayer and Dana C. Munro, *The Middle Ages, 395–1500,* 4th ed. (New York: Appleton-Century-Crofts, Inc., 1959), p. 125.

17. Francis Oakley, *The Medieval Experience: Foundations of Western Cultural Singularity,* (New York: Charles Scribner's Sons, 1974), pp. 84–87.

18. David A. Hinton, "Demography: From Domesday and Beyond", *Journal of Medieval History*, 39, 2 (2013), pp. 146-178.

19. J. M. Roberts, *A Short History of the World,* (New York: Oxford University Press, 1993), p. 246.

20. Jacques Le Goff, *Money and the Middle Ages: An Essay in Historical Anthropology*, (Cambridge: Polity Press, 2012).

21. General works on the economy include Jan Dumolyn, "'Our Land is Only Founded on Trade and Industry': Economic Discourses in Fifteenth Century Bruges", *Journal of Medieval History*, 36, 4 (2010), pp. 374-389; Carlo Cipolla, *Before the Industrial Revolution: European Society and Economy, 1000–1700,* 2nd ed. (New York: W. W. Norton, 1980); and Norman J. G. Pounds, *An Economic History of*

Medieval Europe, (London: Longman, 1974).

22. C. M. Woolgar, "Food and the Middle Ages", *Journal of Medieval History*, 36, 1 (2010), pp. 1-19 and C. M. Woolgar, "Gifts of Food in Late Medieval England", *Journal of Medieval History*, 37, 1 (2011), pp. 6-18. See also Roberts, p. 229 and p. 249.

23. Susan Rose, *The Wine Trade in Medieval Europe, 1000-1500*, (London: Continuum, 2011).

24. Elisheva Baumgarten, "A Separate People? Some Directions for Comparative Research on Medieval Women", *Journal of Medieval History*, 34, 2 (2008), pp. 212-228; Frances Gies and Joseph Gies, *Women in the Middle Ages,* (New York: Thomas Y. Crowell Co., 1978), pp. 27–28.

25. Philip Grace, "Family and Familiars: The Concentric Household in Late Medieval Penitentiary Petitions", *Journal of Medieval History*, 35, 2 (2009), pp. 189-203.

26. Anne Curry and Adrian R. Bell, "Waging War in the Fourteenth Century", *Journal of Medieval History*, 37, 3 (2011), pp. 231-232; Thom Richardson, "Armour in England, 1325-99", *Journal of Medieval History*, 37, 3 (2011), pp. 304-320; and Clifford J. Rogers, "The Development of the Longbow in Late Medieval England", *Journal of Medieval History*, 37, 3 (2011), pp. 321-341.

27. This discussion of time and measurement draws on a perceptive video presentation of the period. See The Annenberg/CPB Collection, *The Western Tradition,* Program 21: "Common Life in the Middle Ages," Santa Barbara, California: Intellimation, Fall 1989.

28. Sheilagh Ogilvie, *Institutions and European Trade:*

Merchant Guilds, 1000-1800, (New York: Cambridge University Press, 2011); Gary Richardson, "Guilds, Laws, and Markets for Manufactured Merchandise in Late Medieval England", *Explorations in Economic History*, 41, 1 (January 2004), pp. 1-25; Gary Richardson, "A Tale of Two Theories: Monopolies and Craft Guilds in Medieval England and Modern Imagination," *Journal of the History of Economic Thought,* 23, 2 (June 2001), pp. 217–242; and Norman Zacour, *An Introduction to Medieval Institutions,* (New York: St. Martin's Press, 1969).

29. Painter, p. 80.

30. Shepard B. Clough, *The Economic Development of Western Civilization,* (New York: McGraw-Hill, 1959), p. 101.

31. Steven Bednarski and Andree Courtemanche, "Learning to Be a Man: Public Schooling and Apprenticeship in Late Medieval Manosque", *Journal of Medieval History*, 35, 2 (2009), pp. 113-135.

32. The classic work on this topic is Stephen T. Worland, *Scholasticism and Welfare Economics,* (Notre Dame, IN: University of Notre Dame Press, 1967). (Worland taught the author his first course in economics at the University of Notre Dame in 1964.) For a more recent view, see Joao Cesar das Neves, "Aquinas and Aristotle's Distinction on Wealth," *History of Political Economy,* 32, 3 (Fall 2000), pp. 649–658.

33. The controversy over whether the just price was based on costs of production or the market price is highlighted in Fabio Monsalve, "Scholastic Just Price Versus Current Market Price: Is It Merely a Matter of Labelling?", *European Journal of the History of Economic Thought*, 21, 1 (2014), pp. 4-20. For an earlier view, see Samuel Hollander, "On the

Interpretation of the Just Price," *Kyklos* 18, 4 (December 1965), pp. 615–634.

34. For a thorough history of the concept of usury, see Charles Geisst, *Beggar Thy Neighbor: A History of Usury and Debt*, (Philadelphia: University of Pennsylvania Press, 2013).

35. Lewis H. Haney, *History of Economic Thought,* (New York: Macmillan, 1933), p. 95.

36. One way of finding out who was literate involved testing people when they served on juries. See William S. Deller, "The Texture of Literacy in the Testimonies of Late Medieval English Proof-of-Age Jurors, 1270-1430", *Journal of Medieval History*, 38, 2 (2012), pp. 207-224.

37. Paul Johnson, *A History of Christianity*, (New York: Simon and Schuster, 1976), especially pp. 116-117.

38. Michael D. Barbezat, "The Fires of Hell and the Burning of Heretics in the Accounts of the Executions at Orleans in 1022", *Journal of Medieval History*, 40, 4 (2014), pp. 399-420.

39. William Manchester, *A World Lit Only By Fire: The Medieval Mind and the Renaissance,* (Boston: Little Brown, 1992), pp. 190-193.

40. This argument has actually been made in selected sources since 1922 but is only recently gaining (reluctant?) acceptance. For a thorough summary of the evidence, see S. M. Ghazanfar, "The Economic Thought of Abu Hamid Al-Ghazali and St. Thomas Aquinas: Some Comparative Parallels and Links," *History of Political Economy,* 32, 4 (Winter 2000), pp. 857–888.

Al-Ghazali was born in 1058 in Khorasan, Iran, was educated in Nishapur and Baghdad, and was later appointed a professor at Nizamiyah University of Baghdad. He left his academic position to pursue a life of solitude but later returned to teaching. He died in Baghdad in 1111 (some accounts list the year of his death as 1128). A prolific author, he also wrote *Kitab Tuhafut al-Falasifa (The Incoherence of the Philosophers), Kimiya-e-Sa'adat (The Essence of Ihya Ulum al-Deen),* as well as a study in astronomy. Al-Ghazali was influenced by several Islamic writers including Ibn Sina (980–1033), who was known as Avicenna in the West, Ibn Rushd (1126–1198), known as Averroes in the West, and Al-Farabi (d. 950).

41. Aquinas's teacher, Albertus Magnus (1201-1280), and his contemporary Raymund Martin (d. 1285) were both strongly influenced by Al-Ghazali. Martin, in particular, could read Arabic and made a thorough study of Al-Ghazali's writings. Aquinas was also exposed to the work of Al-Ghazali through the writing of the Jewish scholastic, Moses Bin Maimonides (1135–1204).

42. Ibrahim M. Oweiss, "Ibn Khaldum, Father of Economics," in George N. Atiyeh and Ibrahim M. Oweiss, *Arab Civilization: Challenges and Responses,* (New York: State University of New York Press, 1988), pp. 112–127. See also Joseph J. Spengler, "Economic Thought in Islam: Ibn Khaldun," *Comparative Studies in Society and History*, 6, 3 (April 1964), pp. 268-306.

Ibn Khaldun was born in Tunis in 1332 and was the descendant of a well-to-do Andulusian (Spanish) family. He was appointed a judge by the Sultan of Egypt and is recognized by some in the Western world as the Father of Sociology. He died in Cairo in 1406.

43. Ibn Khaldun, *The Muqaddimah: An Introduction to History,* (Princeton: Princeton University Press, 1967) (translated by Franz Rosenthal), chapter 2, p. 337. In this work (pp. 273–338), Khaldun also presented a forerunner of the *multiplier principle,* which John Maynard Keynes and others would advance in the 1930s. In addition, Khaldun stated the concept that income equals expenditures, argued that capital accumulation leads to economic growth, encouraged low rates of taxation, presented a modern theory of money, and even developed versions of cost-push and demand-pull inflation.

44. Hamid Hosseini, "Seeking the Roots of Adam Smith's Division of Labor in Medieval Persia," *History of Political Economy,* 30, 4 (Winter 1998), p. 655.

45. Hosseini, p. 679.

46. Susanna A. Throop, "Mirrored Images: the Passion and the First Crusade in a Fourteenth-Century Parisian Illuminated Manuscript", *Journal of Medieval History,* 41, 2 (2015), pp. 184-207; Anne E. Lester, "What Remains: Women, Relics and Remembrance in the Aftermath of the Fourth Crusade", *Journal of Medieval History*, 40, 3 (2014), pp. 311-328; Megan Cassidy-Welch and Anne E. Lester, "Memory and Interpretation: New Approaches to the Study of the Crusades", *Journal of Medieval History*, 40, 3 (2014), pp. 225-236; Marek Tamm, "How to Justify a Crusade? The Conquest of Livonia and New Crusade Rhetoric in the Early Thirteenth Century", *Journal of Medieval History*, 39, 4 (2013), pp. 431-455; and Thomas Asbridge, "Talking to the Enemy: The Role and Purpose of Negotiations Between Saladin and Richard the Lionheart During the Third Crusade", *Journal of Medieval History*, 39, 3 (2013), pp. 275-296.

47. For specific case studies of this period, see Jessica

Dijkman, *Shaping Medieval Markets: The Organization of Commodity Markets in Holland, c 1200- c 1450*, (Leiden and Boston: Brill, 2012); Georg Christ, *Trading Conflicts: Venetian Merchants and Mamluk Officials in Late Medieval Alexandria*, (Leiden and Boston: Brill, 2012); and Daniel R. Curtis, "Florence and its Hinterlands in the Late Middle Ages: Contrasting Fortunes in the Tuscan Countryside, 1300-1500", *Journal of Medieval History*, 38, 4 (2012), pp. 472-499. For a more complete treatment of the merchants and trading patterns, see Robert S. Lopez, *The Commercial Revolution of the Middle Ages, 950–1350,* (Cambridge: Cambridge University Press, 1976).

48. Margaret Hastings, *Medieval European Society, 1000–1450,* (New York: Random House, 1971), p. 83.

49. David Nicholas, *The Medieval West, 400–1450: A Preindustrial Civilization,* (Homewood, IL: Dorsey Press, 1973), p. 162.

50. These markets are discussed in detail in William N. Parker and Eric L. Jones, eds., *European Peasants and Their Markets: Essays in Agrarian Economic History,* (Princeton, NJ: Princeton University Press, 1975).

51. For background to these developments, see Tom Scott, *The City-State in Europe, 1000-1600*, (Oxford: Oxford University Press, 2012) and Richard Hodges, *Dark Age Economics: The Origins of Towns and Trade, A.D. 600–1000,* (New York: St. Martin's Press, 1982) as well as the classic Henri Pirenne, *Medieval Cities: Their Origins and the Revival of Trade,* (Princeton, NJ: Princeton University Press, 1952 (1925)).

52. John Hare, "Inns, Innkeepers and the Society of Later Medieval England, 1350-1600", *Journal of Medieval History*,

39, 4 (2013), pp. 477-497.

53. Mark Bailey, *The Decline of Serfdom in Late Medieval England: From Bondage to Freedom,* (Woodbridge: Boydell Press, 2014). For discussion of the effects of the enclosure movement, see J.R. Wordie, "The Chronology of English Enclosure, 1500–1914," *Economic History Review,* 36, 4 (November 1983), pp.483–505.

54. David J. Lu, *Japan: A Documentary History,* (London: M. E. Sharpe, 1997), p. 82.

55. Steven Warshaw, *Japan Emerges,* (Berkeley, CA: Diablo Press, 1993), p. 33.

56. George B. Sanson, *Japan: A Short Cultural History,* (Stanford, CA: Stanford University Press, 1978/1931), p. 422.

57. Francis Watson, *India: A Concise History,* (New York: Thames and Hudson, 1974), p. 90.

58. Stanley Wolpert, *A New History of India,* 5th ed., (Oxford: Oxford University Press, 1997), pp. 111–112.

59. Bernard Lewis, *The Arabs in History,* (Oxford: Oxford University Press, 1993), p. 20.

60. Peter Mansfield, *A History of the Middle East,* (London: Penguin Books, 1991), pp. 28–29.

61. Nikki R. Keddie, *Roots of Revolution: An Interpretive History of Modern Iran,* (New Haven, CT: Yale University Press, 1981), pp. 12–13.

62. Bernard Lewis, *What Went Wrong? The Clash Between Islam and Modernity in the Middle East,* (New York: Oxford

University Press, 2002), pp. 78–79.

63. Lewis, pp. 79–81.

64. Philip K. Hitti, *The Arabs: A Short History,* (Washington, DC: Regnery Publishing, 1996), pp. 146–147.

65. Lewis, pp. 156–160. The argument has also been made that, except for Turkey, "predominantly Muslim societies are ruled by a wide variety of authoritarian, autocratic, despotic, tyrannical, and totalitarian regimes." See Bernard Lewis, "Islam and Liberal Democracy: A Historical Overview," *Journal of Democracy,* 7, 2 (1996), pp. 52–63.

The list composed by Lewis includes traditional autocracies such as Saudi Arabia and the Gulf sheikhdoms; modernizing autocracies like Jordan, Egypt, and Morocco; Fascist style dictatorships like Saddam Hussein's Iraq and Bashar Assad's Syria; radical Islamic regimes such as Iran and the Sudan; and former Soviet republics of central Asia such as Azerbaijan and Kyrgyzstan (who are struggling between secularization and Shari'a). Considering lists such as these and the fact that the Organization of the Islamic Conference (OIC) officially lists 53 predominantly Muslim states, only one of which (Turkey) may be considered democratic, it may be quite reasonable to ask: Are democracy and Islam logically inconsistent?

The alternative view is presented in Fatema Mernissi, *Islam and Democracy,* (Cambridge, MA: Perseus Publishing, 2002). For a slightly different perspective that addresses a similar question, see Amy Chua, *World on Fire: How Exporting Free Market Democracy Breeds Ethnic Hatred and Global Instability,* (New York: Doubleday, 2003).

66. Robert Spencer, *Islam Unveiled: Disturbing Questions about the World's Fastest Growing Faith,* (San Francisco:

Encounter Books, 2002), chapter 7, especially pp. 120–126. The philosopher who defended orthodox Islam against the philosophical advances of writers like Ibn Sina (Avicenna) was Abu Hamid al-Ghazali, mentioned earlier for influencing both Thomas Aquinas and Adam Smith. Al-Ghazali even concludes his classic work by raising the question of whether the philosophers of his day who do not strictly adhere to Islamic law should be killed for being infidels. See Abu Hamid al-Ghazali, *The Incoherence of the Philosophers,* translated by Michael E. Marmura, (Provo, Utah: Brigham Young University Press, 2000), p. 226.

67. The Crusades also had the effect of permanently increasing animosity between the Christian and Islamic worlds. Many in the Middle East today still view the inhumane atrocities of numerous Crusaders as a major source of disdain for the "infidel" West and an inspiration for renewed holy war. It should be kept in mind, however, that the Crusades were a response to violent acts of barbarism committed in the name of Islam between 636 and the 11th century. Those who were conquered by Islamic armies during this period were often indiscriminately raped and/or murdered. Those who survived were generally given the option of conversion to Islam or death, which is precisely the type of religious fascism preached by Islamic fundamentalists today. For some of the more gruesome accounts of this early *jihad,* see Spencer, *Islam Unveiled,* chapter 8; Bat Ye'or, *The Decline of Eastern Christianity under Islam: From Jihad to Dhimmitude,* (Rutherford, NJ: Fairleigh Dickinson University Press, 1996); and Paul Fregosi, *Jihad in the West: Muslim Conquests from the 7th to the 21st Centuries,* (Amherst, NY: Prometheus Books, 1998).

Chapter Six

Mercantilism, Science, and the Industrial Revolution

The industrial revolution followed upon a revolution in scientific method. But it is taking the revolution many centuries to produce a new mind.

John Dewey

The liberation of women from exclusive domesticity... is a straightforward consequence of the industrial revolution of two hundred years ago.

Barbara Bergmann

What was the good of industrial development if, after half a century, the condition of the masses was still just as miserable as before?

Thomas Piketty

While the Renaissance clearly ignited a cultural revolution in literature and art, it also gave birth to new ideas about human potential. Its humanist writers broke the medieval intellectual stalemate that had bowed, at times unconditionally, to religious authority. Rejecting this static moral code, humanists encouraged individual freedom and rational thought. Their message was that competent and creative people could influence the direction of future events, generate progress, and improve the quality of life.

In its attempt to merge faith with reason, scholasticism had emphasized preparation for life in the next world. Humanism, by contrast, drew upon the secular thought of the ancient Greeks and Romans to address practical concerns about life in this world. As the humanist perspective spread, the medieval virtues of humility and self-restraint gave way to confidence in ability and unrestrained achievement.

Humanists rose to positions of prominence as respected authors and advisors to governmental leaders. Their influence in unleashing human energy was arguably greater than the accomplishments of New World explorers. As the renowned philosopher Will Durant has written, "It was the humanists, not the navigators, who liberated man from dogma, taught him to love life rather than brood about death, and made the European mind free"[1]. Riches in the Americas awaited exploitation but the power of ideas would prove to be more significant and longer lasting. Both religious and economic thought were about to experience monumental change.

The Protestant Reformation

Corruption and controversy within the medieval Church set in motion a series of reforms. The growing wealth and political power of bishops, the blatant sexual escapades of individual priests, the presence of as many as three rival popes at the same time, the nepotistic practice of appointing relatives to key positions, and the selling of indulgences all tarnished the reputation of Church authority. Indulgences, according to official religious teaching, reduced the amount of time a soul spent in purgatory before entering heaven. They were granted for reciting prayers and performing charitable acts but were also sold for cash payments to the Church.

The latter practice inspired a break from Church teaching, led by a monk named Martin Luther (1483–1546). When he nailed his Ninety-five Theses to the door of the Wittenberg castle in 1517, Luther launched an official religious dissent that would ultimately split Christendom. Because he and his numerous followers protested against

Church dogma, they became known as Protestants. Their movement and later separation from the Church of Rome was called the *Protestant Reformation,* an umbrella term that eventually applied to all reformers, not just those who became Lutherans.

The theology of Lutheranism, which emphasized individual religious conviction and the right to read as well as interpret the Bible without the assistance of clergy, gained widespread appeal. In addition, Protestant ideas could be easily disseminated because of the recent invention of printing. Converts among the nobility seized Church property and eliminated Church taxes. The latter action halted the outflow of money from German towns to Rome.

Luther's writings and speeches denouncing poverty caused him, at least initially, to be revered among the masses. No doubt encouraged by his success, they launched a Peasants' Revolt in 1524. A religious reformer but not a revolutionary, Luther sided with the nobility, which violently suppressed the peasant uprising the following year. Individual initiative, resistance to outside (papal) authority, and order imposed by the state were among the principles advanced by early Protestantism. All would play a part in the economic surge that soon followed.

The Reformation enjoyed its greatest early success in Germany, Scandinavia, England, and Holland. Its growth was stimulated by a French theologian, John Calvin (1509–1564), whose major efforts were based in Geneva, Switzerland. Inspired by Luther, Calvin preached a more rigorous theology that stressed predestination, or the belief that divine authority had already decided who would be saved and who would be condemned in the next world. His followers often looked for signs of their destiny; the most visible sign of salvation, they believed, was earthly success.

Calvin preached strict discipline in both daily life and in commercial dealings. Unlike Catholic theologians, however, he did not object to the pursuit of gain. His economic views, therefore, were consistent with the behavior of the new merchant class which was disciplined and acquisitive. Those who believed that their material success was a sign from above often felt an inner confidence that became crucial to the entrepreneurial drive.

The new religious acceptance of economic advance may well have been the final piece of the puzzle that sealed the fate of feudalism and fueled an early merchant capitalism. After centuries of religious disapproval of the drive for wealth, devout believers could now embrace a religious philosophy that blessed their hard work, self-sacrifice, and success. In his classic *The Protestant Ethic and the Spirit of Capitalism* (1904), German sociologist Max Weber argued that Protestantism, especially Calvinism, gave capitalism an important impetus.[2] The *Protestant ethic* implies that "God helps those who help themselves." Divine sanction of efficiency, frugality, and business ventures enabled merchants to function with authoritative approval of their activity.

Major Principles of Mercantilism

As cities, trade, money, nations, and the ethic of personal gain all grew in importance, mercantilism gradually replaced the declining feudal order. Although precise dates may again be disputed, this new system thrived roughly between 1500 and the 1770s. *Mercantilism,* as it was practiced during this period, was a philosophy of national wealth and power. It glorified the merchant, encouraged nation building and the spirit of nationalism, and advocated strong central government direction of the economy. Although its principles were not uniform in all countries, some common threads of mercantilist doctrine may be outlined.[3]

The early mercantilists embraced *bullionism,* the belief that a country's wealth was measured by its stock of precious metals (i.e., its gold and silver bullion). Nations with few mines acquired bullion by either trade or colonization.

For goods sold in international markets, payment was frequently made in precious metals. Mercantilists reasoned, therefore, that the stock of bullion would increase if a nation maintained a *favorable balance of trade,* or an excess of exports over imports. When accounts were settled, more gold and silver would flow into rather than out of a country.

To assure this result, mercantilist governments restricted imports (especially of luxury goods), discouraged domestic consumption (so more would be available for exports), and prohibited the outflow of bullion. The penalty for exporting gold or silver from Spain was death! To keep manufacturers well supplied with resources, governments also regulated the export of raw materials. England, for example, passed a law preventing the export of live sheep. First offense was punishable by loss of property, imprisonment, and amputation of the left hand. Second offense was punishable by death![4] Mercantilists enforced their principles ruthlessly.

The concepts that a large inflow of specie might cause inflation and that both parties might gain from trade were not fully grasped by early mercantilist writers. Rather, they believed that, when trade occurred, one side gained while the other lost. Since both sides sought the upper hand, achieving an advantage was easier when a powerful nation traded with its colony.

Overseas colonies were valuable markets for the export of manufactured goods as well as the import of both raw materials and bullion itself. Given mercantilist philosophy, the gold mines of Brazil, the silver mines of Mexico, and other nations' ships were irresistible targets. Some statesmen hired pirates to claim their specie from rival ships on the open seas. This strategy was easier and often more effective than forcing slaves to mine precious metals in the New World.

Governments either limited or prevented manufacturing in their colonies, restricted colonial imports from and exports to other nations, and required that goods be transported only in ships of the mother country. Provisions such as these were part of the British Navigation Acts and Staple Acts, both passed during the mid-seventeenth century. Combined with other exploitive policies, these laws helped fuel the American Revolution.

The mercantilists believed in a strong central government that intervened in several ways in the private economy. Some industries were protected from competition by high tariffs on imported goods. Firms that produced for foreign markets were often granted monopoly power. Government subsidies to selected industries and projects such as the building of canals were common. To encourage exports, tolls on the internal transportation of goods and taxes on firms were kept to a minimum. To assure quality as well as the nation's reputation overseas, the production of goods for foreign markets was closely regulated. At times, rules bordered on the absurd.

According to French weaving regulations of 1718, for example, yarn in five separate districts near Burgundy had to contain precisely 576, 1,216, 1,344, 1,376, and 1,408 threads, respectively. White cloth in one district had to have exactly 2,368 threads. Rules governing the process of dyeing were even more thorough. Penalties for failure to comply included confiscation or destruction of fabric, fines, and permanent cancellation of weaving rights.[5] Not unlike current Internal Revenue Service tax forms, these requirements were ridiculously specific and discouraged productive effort.

Finally, the mercantilists favored a growing population that displayed a strong belief in nationalism. Such a policy assured an ample supply of soldiers when governments inevitably became militaristic. It also guaranteed a large supply of workers, which kept wages and therefore export prices low. To remain powerful, nations had to compete in international markets, defeat enemies in wars, and maintain subservient colonies. A large, energetic, and patriotic citizenry was essential in realizing these objectives.

Some Important Mercantilists

The mercantilists were hardly a unified group. Many were merchants themselves. This explains the positive light in which their occupation was often portrayed in their writings. Others were government officials who had a strong vested interest in seeing their nation prosper. Still others were pamphleteers caught up in the excitement of a prosperous age.

This threefold division was not mutually exclusive. Some who wrote and distributed pamphlets on burning economic issues of the day were either merchants or government officials. In addition, some who were merchants early in their careers later worked for government. Therefore, motives for advocating specific policies varied. Who were the leading architects of these sometimes logical and often flawed principles?

Diverse mercantilist thinkers included Niccolo Machiavelli, Antonio Serra, Antoine de Montchretien, Thomas Mun, and Jean Baptiste Colbert. Machiavelli was a major proponent of the powerful state. Serra wrote the first formal work of mercantilism, which provided arguments for the export of manufactured goods. Montchretien was the first to use the term *political economy* and to challenge the traditional mercantilist view that wealth consisted of gold and silver bullion. Mun advocated the export of bullion if the goods acquired could be re-exported at a profit. He also developed an advanced accounting system for calculating the balance of payments. French finance minister Colbert pursued extreme government control of industry and military ventures, both of which alienated citizens and nearly bankrupted the national treasury. France was eventually to produce a more progressive economic philosophy, which would be influenced by, among other things, advances in the physical sciences.

The Rise of Scientific Discoveries

During the seventeenth century, European philosophers increasingly believed that, through reason, the human race could discover the truth about itself and the universe that it inhabits. Over time, this idea spread. Especially in eighteenth-century France and England, there occurred a questioning of authority and tradition, a search for empirical fact as opposed to mere belief, an emphasis on critical thought, and a secular individualism based on human control over its own destiny. This change in attitudes and ongoing quest for a rational understanding of the human condition became known as the *Age of Reason* or the *Enlightenment.*

The great works of such giants as Descartes, Voltaire, Rousseau, Montesquieu, Hobbes, Locke, and others were all part of this era. Perhaps most significantly, however, the Enlightenment led to advances in scientific thought. Although discoveries were many, two were especially noteworthy for their ultimate impact on the soon-to-emerge discipline of economics. These were the concept of the sun-centered universe and the law of gravitation.[6]

The belief that the earth was the center of the universe was part of the astronomy of Claudius Ptolemy, the Greek scientist whose *Almagest* in 140 CE outlined the motion of heavenly bodies. His explanation was accepted by the scientific community until the sixteenth century. It was the Polish astronomer Nicolaus Copernicus (1473–1543) who advanced the argument that the sun was the center of the universe while Earth, like all other known planets, orbited the sun.

After the invention of the telescope in 1608, astronomers such as Galileo Galilei (1564–1642) were able to confirm the arguments of Copernicus, build on his view of the universe, and discover additional planets. Both Copernicus and Galileo became the center of much controversy because their scientific achievements challenged established Church teaching. Their work did not impress a succession of popes but both men inspired the person who was to become the foremost scientist in the world, Isaac Newton (1642–1727).

In his *Principia* (1687), Newton depicted the universe as a mechanism that was understandable and potentially reducible to mathematical laws. His law of gravity stated that heavenly bodies remain in motion because of forces that prevent them from colliding. As a result, much like the spring of a clock, the universe functions smoothly and continuously in endless harmony. Its complex precision was the work of a skillful, artistic Creator who, upon completing his project, left it alone to run itself. The perfection of this mechanism was due to laws of nature that, Newton believed, applied not only to the Cosmos but to the smallest of entities within it.

Attracted to the novelty and logic of Newton's arguments, many people sought to adapt them to areas outside of physics. As the eighteenth century began, leading European thinkers became increasingly enamored of Newton's mechanistic view and of the prospect of *scientific measurement.* The task of humanity, many reasoned, was to assure that all activity was consistent with this natural law. Virtually no one questioned the legitimacy of applying principles that govern inanimate objects to living human beings. So impressive were Newton's analyses that extending them wherever possible simply seemed like the correct thing to do.

Natural law led to the concept of a natural economic order. If a Supreme Being created a magnificent universe with all its components functioning so efficiently that further intervention was unnecessary, what possible justification could there be for interfering with the natural operation of the economy? (Logically dubious) questions like this would inspire new economic philosophies destined to challenge the active role played by government in mercantilism. Armed with the new successes of science, a possibly more rational explanation of the origin of the universe than that provided by Genesis, and a desire for relief from oppressive government policies, economic theorists were about to enter the scene. Their story begins in France.

Physiocracy: The First Attack on Mercantilism

Over the span of 131 years, France was ruled by only two monarchs, Louis XIV (1643–1715) and Louis XV (1715–1774). During both reigns, wars were common, royal lifestyles became increasingly extravagant, colonies such as Canada and India were lost, and economic hardship for the masses occurred all too frequently. All of these factors ultimately contributed to the French Revolution of 1789.

Throughout this troubled period, agriculture remained the backbone of the French economy. Despite numerous fertile growing regions, French peasantry enjoyed few economic successes because of a prohibitively high tax burden. Industry did not prosper because of the huge web of regulation resulting from mercantilist policies. As early as the 1750s, much-needed new ideas for managing the French economy were beginning to emerge. Their targets were the outmoded philosophy of mercantilism and a corrupt government that still exhibited some aspects of feudalism.

The new school of thought in France was called *physiocracy,* a term that literally meant rule of nature. Its arguments were the first formal critique of mercantilism.[7] Although their primary influence lasted for only about two decades, the physiocrats inspired later thinkers, especially the classical economists whose day in the sun would be much longer and brighter. The physiocrats were also significant because they were the first group who actually called themselves economists.

Strongly influenced by developments in physical science, physiocracy was based on conformity with natural law. Members of this school believed that the greatest economic benefit accrued to those who complemented the natural order. According to this view, people deserved reward for hard work as long as the rights of others were not violated in the process. Each individual knew his or her interests best and also knew that to act contrary to natural law would be self-destructive. The purpose of human laws was merely to protect liberty and property.

Belief in a natural order was easily translated into a belief in minimal government intervention in the economy. The French economists called this *laissez faire,* which literally meant to let go or to leave alone. People should be free, they argued, to choose their occupation, to work and live where they like, to use their property as they see fit, and to pursue financial gain. As a result, the physiocrats opposed most government restrictions on private individuals and businesses on grounds that such policies interfered with natural law. They were especially critical of mercantilist efforts at directing the economy, granting monopoly privileges, and regulating minute details of production.

The physiocrats believed that merchants, craftsmen, and manufacturers were *sterile* because they only repackaged what they used up in raw materials and labor. As a result, these trades did not generate a surplus or net product. According to physiocracy, the only true source of wealth was land. When seeds were planted, crops, which were many times the original value of the seeds, were created. When animals reproduced, the value of the livestock increased. When farmers produced agricultural surpluses, they provided food for merchants and craftsmen. The latter two groups, by contrast, could not survive without special assistance from mercantilist governments.

Although physiocrats claimed their doctrines were based on scientific principles, their writings supported French agriculture. In the eighteenth century, the old landed elite still exerted potent influence on government policy in France, much more so than in neighboring countries. The physiocrats did believe, however, that only landowners should pay taxes, since agriculture alone generated surpluses. The landed gentry was in the privileged position of collecting rent on their land while essentially doing nothing. Taxing this rent was a popular strategy to all except kings and clergymen. Since all other taxes interfered with the natural order, the physiocrats felt they should be repealed.

Finally, physiocracy made crude but insightful attempts to model the economy. The school's founder was a prominent physician named François Quesnay (1694–1774). Impressed by William Harvey's discovery of the circulation of blood, Quesnay developed a similar approach to analyzing the flow of economic variables. His classic *Tableau Economique* (1758) constructed a circular flow of goods and money in a competitive economy. A modern version of his diagrams, which shows how businesses and households interact in contemporary markets, is still used in many economics textbooks today. An early scientific discovery continues to influence the methods of the profession.

As personal physician to Louis XV, the wealthy Quesnay believed that products and blood both circulated according to natural law. The challenge was to understand each mechanism as well as human reason was capable of doing. His original diagrams showed the flow of goods and money between landlords, farmers, and the *sterile class* (merchants, craftsmen, and manufacturers).[8] His early efforts to calculate the aggregate value of production in France inspired later work in this area by quantitatively oriented economists.[9]

Two other men figured prominently in physiocratic thought. Pierre Samuel duPont de Nemours (1739–1817), who barely escaped death by guillotine when the French Revolution succeeded in a (for him most) timely manner, was the first to use the term physiocracy.[10] DuPont held a number of important positions with the French government, including president of the National Assembly. After migrating to Delaware, he was asked by President Thomas Jefferson to design a model for the U.S. educational system. His descendants would later achieve great wealth in the American chemical and automobile industries.

Anne Robert Jacques Turgot (1727–1781)[11] was a civil servant who in 1774 became minister of finance, the same position held by Colbert a century earlier. Unlike the dictatorial Colbert, the reform-minded Turgot economized by slashing government spending. He also eliminated the guilds and trading monopolies, abolished forced labor of peasants, improved tax collection, and implemented free trade of domestic grain. Hated by the privileged wealthy who opposed his reforms, Turgot was relieved of his duties by a reluctant Louis XVI, who was under pressure from special interests, including Marie Antoinette. Some historians feel that government unwillingness to accept Turgot's reforms was a factor that led to the French Revolution.

Their blind faith in agriculture and their transfer of natural law concepts to the economic realm generally earn the physiocrats the label of *naive,* or at least misguided. In their day, however, agriculture was quite productive, while manufacturing industries were rather inefficient, even if not sterile. The bias of the physiocrats, therefore, was not entirely unjustified. Their concerns with aggregate production flows and with the question of who bore the tax burden were clearly forward looking. So was the philosophy of laissez faire which would command increasing respect when output exploded during the following decades.

The Industrial Revolution

No single event has had as dramatic and permanent an impact on world economic history as the *Industrial Revolution.* First used by nineteenth century historian Arnold Toynbee, the term refers to the substitution of machine technology for human labor in the production process. Initially evident in the mid-eighteenth century, the change in manufacturing methods occurred slowly but persistently and has continued to the present.

Some economic historians prefer to enumerate a series of stages, beginning with the mid-to-late-eighteenth-century revolution in textile machinery and steam power.[12] According to this view, a second Industrial Revolution occurred during the mid-nineteenth century when improvements in steel production boosted the railroads and agricultural machinery. A third stage developed in the early twentieth century with the gasoline-powered automobile and electricity.

Post–World War II advances in electronics, space travel, and nuclear technology constitute a possible fourth stage, while the Information Revolution spawned by the computer gave birth to a fifth, which is ongoing. Although stages such as these clearly have merit, the mid-18th century to present schematic emphasizes the continuous nature of this stream of ideas, inventions, and results.

Early results were nothing short of spectacular. Between 1780 and 1830, for example, England experienced enormous increases in the production of coal, copper, iron, and cotton fabrics. The number of patents granted soared as technological innovation reached a furious pace. It would be some time before gains would spread to much of the population. Lifestyles for all, however, would rapidly change in unforeseen ways.[13]

The Unique Role of England

Many reasons have been offered why industrialization occurred first in England.[14] Some of the more perceptive arguments include the following. First, the British were well endowed with both natural resources and acquired wealth. The country possessed large deposits of coal and iron, numerous rivers for water power and natural harbors for shipping, and a mild but damp climate suitable for textile manufacturing. Its colonization, trade, warfare, and even piracy during the previous century brought wealth not only to its nobility but also to its newly established middle class.

Second, England was blessed with large supplies of both capital and inexpensive labor.[15] Merchants had prospered, banks thrived, and guild restrictions had diminished. Investing in the ventures of others had, therefore, become an acceptable and lucrative practice. The enclosure movement had forced workers off the land but it also had encouraged labor mobility. People were willing to work wherever opportunities surfaced. Advances in food production, sanitation, and medicine promoted population increase. In other words, capitalism was well established and poised for further growth.

Third, both domestic and foreign markets were fairly mature. On the eve of mass production, many consumers were willing and able to pay for new products. The number of potential buyers grew as the British middle class expanded and as overseas colonies prospered. In addition, England was geographically isolated from the European continent which, hampered in its own development by wars and Napoleon's dreams of conquest, actively sought British manufactured goods.

Fourth, government created an environment conducive to the growth of British industry. Its legal system provided patents[16] and property rights along with low taxes on industrial profits. Nobility on the continent still harbored occasional resentment for the merchant class, a character trait largely abandoned by rulers in the British Isles. Scientific inquiry was encouraged as organizations such as the Royal Society of London were established as early as 1660. The general population ultimately proved to be more fascinated than threatened by the outpouring of new inventions.

Finally, often overlooked agricultural factors contributed greatly to Britain's industrial success.

Improvements in agricultural productivity enabled the feeding of an increasingly urban nation. As early as 1701, an English farmer named Jethro Tull invented a drill which planted evenly spaced seeds and reduced the amount of seed needed. In the early eighteenth century, Charles Townshend and Robert Bakewell developed new methods of crop rotation and selected breeding of livestock, respectively. When the American Cyrus McCormick invented the reaper in 1834, it was quickly imported by England, where it gave agriculture yet another boost. Without these advances, fewer resources would have been available for urban industrial pursuits and the pace of change would have been much slower.

Textiles

Prior to the Industrial Revolution, small-scale production such as spinning and weaving activities was performed in the home. The terms *cottage industry* and the *putting out system* were used to describe this domestic manufacturing. Merchants provided raw materials and sold the final products. Women and children combed raw cotton with brushes and spun it on a foot-propelled wooden spinning wheel. Men would then weave the spun cotton on a hand loom. The process allowed women to work at their chosen pace in their homes where they could also care for children and perform other household tasks.

The major limitation in such a system was the inability to produce a wide range of goods in large quantities. Although some men were involved in cottage industries, others worked as artisans in city shops where they were members of guilds. The Industrial Revolution relocated workers from their homes and shops into large factories where they operated machines capable of mass production. As a result, large markets could more easily be served and a traditional way of life was changed forever.

A series of eighteenth-century inventions increased

productivity in the textile industry. As early as 1733, John Kay invented the flying shuttle, which mechanized a portion of the process, saved labor, and increased the speed of weaving. Spinning now had to catch up. The spinning jenny, invented by James Hargreaves in 1764, enabled a number of threads to be spun simultaneously, unlike the home spinning wheel which could spin only a single thread at a time. Spinning output soon increased eight times over previous levels.

The water frame, invented by Richard Arkwright in 1769, was the first textile industry technology to be powered by water instead of by hand. As a result, spinning was no longer done at home and the thread produced by the water frame was stronger. Arkwright's mill in Darbyshire opened in 1771 and became a model factory that was imitated elsewhere. The spinning mule, invented by Samuel Crompton in 1779, eventually replaced both the spinning jenny and the water frame. Crompton's mule enabled Britain to compete with calico and muslin cloth produced in India.

The power loom, invented by Edmund Cartwright in 1785, further mechanized the weaving process and was the forerunner of the modern loom. The cotton gin, invented by the American Eli Whitney in 1794, separated cotton fiber from seeds. The combined effect of all of these innovations included huge increases in the amount of raw cotton imported from America and similarly large exports of British cotton products.

Coal and Iron

The eighteenth century also witnessed productivity gains in the coal and iron industries. As the century began, iron ore was smelted with charcoal, a process that was rapidly depleting the available supply of wood. In 1709, Abraham Darby began smelting iron using coke made from coal. Since coke produced more oxygen than charcoal did, smelting with coke resulted in a higher-quality iron at lower cost. Eventually, cast-iron stoves for heating, large iron pots for cooking, and iron wheels for carts in coal mines came into widespread use. In 1750, machines made of iron were introduced into the textile industry.

Later technological developments included the invention of the blast furnace by John Smeaton in 1760, the introduction of puddling (a process that removed carbon and, therefore, produced a higher-quality iron) by Henry Cort in 1783, and the opening of the world's first iron bridge in 1781 at Coalbrookdale, England where it still stands today. In 1815, Sir Humphry Davy invented the safety lamp, which vastly improved working conditions in coal mines. Two later innovations enabled steel to replace iron. In 1856, William Siemens invented the open hearth process, and in 1859, Henry Bessemer invented a refining process that was named for him.

Steam Power and Printing

Some historians believe the invention that had the most profound effect on the Industrial Revolution was steam power. Others claim it was printing. Both were important. Although knowledge of the potential for steam can be traced to Greece in the second century BCE, the first primitive steam engine used to pump water from mines was invented by Thomas Savery in 1698. The Savery engine was quite inefficient in its use of fuel and could only raise water about two feet but it inspired a number of improvements. In 1712, Thomas Newcomen improved the steam engine so that deeper mines could be pumped. Because it too required large amounts of fuel, this engine was used primarily where coal was inexpensive.

Fortunately for all concerned, a Newcomen engine needing repair was taken to an instrument maker named James Watt in 1763. Fascinated by the machine, Watt separated its heating and cooling functions, which reduced the amount of fuel it required, and added further refinements later. He is generally credited with having invented the first practical steam engine.

Because of Watt's invention, factories no longer had to be located close to a source of water power. They could now be built anywhere that an ample supply of coal existed. The first textile factory powered by steam began operation in 1785. The steam engine was destined to have its biggest impact, however, in the area of transportation.

While observing horses pull wagons on rails near coal mines, Watt and others envisioned a potential role for steam power. After years of experiments, the first steam locomotive was built by Richard Trevithick in 1802. William Hedley followed with his *Puffing Billy,* which hauled eight coal wagons at nearly 5 mph in 1813. The first practical steam locomotive was developed in 1825 by George Stephenson on Britain's Stockton and Darlington rail line. Four years later, his *Rocket* reached the astounding speed of 29 mph. During the 1830s and 1840s, a railroad boom occurred in England, Germany, France, and the United States.

Steam power had been adapted to water transportation much earlier. In 1788, a steamboat built by an American named John Fitch made a 20-mile journey from Philadelphia to Burlington. In 1807, Robert Fulton's *Clermont* traveled 150 miles along the Hudson River. Especially in England and the United States, canals soon provided competition for overland transportation. By 1838, steamships were crossing the Atlantic.

Movable type in printing had actually been invented in 1041 by Bi Sheng in China. Knowledge of this technique was probably brought into Europe during the Mongol invasions exactly two centuries later. Because the Chinese language contains thousands of characters, use of the new invention was more practical in transcribing the limited number of letters contained in European languages.

In 1440, the German inventor Johannes Gutenberg

built a slightly different printing press that for the first time enabled the mass production of printed books. His movable type used oil-based inks and was made from metal molds and alloys. A similar machine at about the same time was built by Laurence Koster of Haarlem, Netherlands but Gutenberg is generally credited as the original inventor of the modern printing press.

Gutenberg initially printed copies of papal indulgences for the Church and a decade later began printing multiple copies of the Bible. By the early 19th century, the mechanics of the hand-operated press had changed little, although printed books in numerous languages were now widely circulated throughout Europe and elsewhere. In 1811, steam power was applied to the printing process with the result that industrial printing presses became capable of producing wide circulation newspapers. Using the new technology, numerous businesses at this time thrived and contributed to increased literacy. Gutenberg, by the way, had been a poor businessman and profited little from his major invention.

Other Noteworthy Inventions

Introduced into British factories by William Murdoch in the 1790s, gaslighting quickly challenged the candle and oil lamp as major sources of artificial light. The first photograph was taken by Frenchman Nicephore Niepce in 1826. He soon collaborated with Louis Jacques Mande Daguerre, who in 1837 invented daguerreotype, a process for developing images using mercury and iodine. Two years later, Englishman William Fox Talbot developed the negative, which made multiple prints possible. The modern science of photography was born. Diverse artificial lighting schemes would continue to play a role in photography until the invention of the flashbulb in 1925.

As early as 1764, an experimental electric telegraph was used in Geneva by George Louis Lesages. A single-wire telegraph, designed by Englishman Francis Ronalds, initially appeared in 1816. The world's first commercial telegraph was invented by Charles Wheatstone and William Cooke in 1837, when it was tested on a London to Birmingham rail line. Two years later, the telegraph was installed for permanent use on the Great Western railroad. Although he began experimenting with telegraphy in 1832, the American Samuel F. B. Morse did not send his famous message from Washington to Baltimore until 1844. He did develop the Morse Code to standardize the system in 1838 and later collaborated with Cyrus Field in laying the first transatlantic cable in 1866.

A number of other scientific advances during the Industrial Revolution set the stage for later technological breakthroughs. In 1831, British physicist Michael Faraday discovered electromagnetic induction, a principle that led to development of the electric generator. During the 1830s, Cambridge University mathematician Charles Babbage developed the principles of the mechanical computer but failed in his attempts to construct the machine. Babbage was truly more than a century ahead of his time.

In 1838, German astronomer Friedrich Bessel was the first to measure the distance of a star from Earth. This feat encouraged others to look beyond the known solar system. Eight years later, the planet Neptune was discovered by another German astronomer, Johann Galle. The use of anesthesia began in 1842 when American surgeon Crawford Long operated on a patient who had been given ether. It is difficult to imagine the status of electric power, computer technology, astronomy (as well as space travel), and surgery today without these early contributors.

Considered the world's workshop during the nineteenth century, England enjoyed an early advantage in the export of manufactured goods. The United States and nations of the European continent would eventually compete in world markets. The economic progress of Europe, however, proceeded at an uneven pace. Belgium, France and Germany industrialized during the second half of the nineteenth century. Italy,[17] Holland, and Switzerland soon followed, but Spain, Portugal, and Russia moved very slowly along the industrial path.

The Industrialization of Asia

Most of the nations of Asia, Latin America, and Africa remained agriculturally based economies well into the twentieth century. Japan, however, underwent a significant industrial transformation in the nineteenth century.

Lingering Feudalism in Japan

The transition from feudalism to merchant capitalism to industrial capitalism took place in England between the late fifteenth and early nineteenth centuries. Throughout this period, Japan remained largely feudal.[18] Some artisans produced goods such as silk and porcelain for the ruling elite and some merchants, called *chonin,* engaged in internal trade, primarily of rice.

From 1603 until 1868, the Tokugawa shogunate pursued policies of economic isolation and resistance to foreign ideas. Consequently, Japan learned little during this time from the European experience. Because change was discouraged, neither an innovative impulse nor a strong sense of nationalism emerged. Some merchants prospered but most of the increase in wealth found its way into the hands of the ruling class.

By the middle of the nineteenth century, pressure for change mounted. Corruption among (and therefore dissatisfaction with) the shogun grew. External influences also intensified. Upon his arrival in Tokyo in 1853, U.S. Navy Commodore Matthew Perry told Japanese leaders he would attack the city if it did not begin trading with the West. Lacking military might and frightened by Perry's four steamships (the technology was unknown in Japan), the shogun was forced to comply.

A resurgence of both Shintoism, the ancient religion that reserved a prominent place in society for the emperor, and nationalism occurred during the following decade. With surprisingly little violence, the Tokugawa shogunate relinquished power to the emperor during the Mejii Restoration of 1868.

The Zaibatsu

The circumstances leading to Japanese industrialization, therefore, were quite different from those in England. The results, however, were ultimately more impressive. Once the process was begun in Japan, it took just three decades for a modern industrial economy to replace a decentralized feudal society. Drawing on mercantilist philosophy, Mejii rulers advocated strong government intervention in a nationally self-sufficient economy. In pursuit of a powerful state, they officially abolished feudalism in 1871 and promoted economic growth and military strength.

The early evolution of capitalism in Japan was potentially awkward since few entrepreneurs with adequate financial resources existed. To fill the void, government built and operated factories. It also subsidized them after they were sold to private investors in the 1880s. Ownership was dominated by four families: Mitsui, Yasuda, Sumitomo, and Mitsubishi. Known as the *zaibatsu,* which literally meant *money clique,* these families quickly became the primary force in the Japanese economy. Their heirs, especially the Sumitomos and Mitsubishis, remain a major economic force today, despite the attempt by American occupation forces to dismantle the zaibatsu after World War II.

Virtually no new technology originated in nineteenth century Japan. After their frequent visits to the West, Mejii leaders adopted the industrial, organizational, and financial techniques of several countries. The silk industry imported its equipment from France. The Japanese army was modeled after that of Prussia while its navy followed the lead of Britain. The banking system drew its early inspiration from the Civil War–era national bank of the United States but was later based on the central bank of Belgium.

Modern European farming methods enabled Japanese agriculture to become the base upon which its industrial effort was built. Silk, tea, and rice exports earned foreign exchange which helped to fund early industrialization. Cotton did not become an important export until 1900. Heavy industries such as iron, steel, and chemicals eventually thrived, largely because of the combined efforts of government and the zaibatsu.

Japan adopted Western industrial technology but remained unimpressed with its democratic political institutions. Once the Japanese manufacturing sector was built, however, the country did acquire the Western propensity to wage war. Using modern weapons, Japan defeated China in 1895 in a battle over Korea. Japan thus gained control of Korea, Taiwan (which it renamed Formosa), and the Liaotung Peninsula. In 1905, the Japanese army soundly crushed the forces of czarist Russia.

Japan's military victories, made possible by its new industrial strength, opened many eyes across the globe. While its growing need for land and raw materials would eventually lead to increasing militarism and humiliation in World War II, growth in its heavy industry early in the twentieth century was impressive. An island nation with limited natural resources, few entrepreneurs, and questionable export potential was destined to become a major force in the Industrial Age.

China

The road to industrialization in China, India, and other Asian countries was much slower.[19] China is a perplexing case. It eliminated its rudimentary form of feudalism more than two centuries before the birth of Christ. Virtues like hard work, frugality, and creativity have long been part of its social ethic. Inventions were common early in its history. China was the first country to manufacture silk cloth during the time of the ancient Romans. The Chinese invented porcelain, paper, printing, and the magnetic compass.[20] Despite such feats, neither merchant capitalism nor large-scale industrialization took root.

Feudalism was displaced in most countries by an emerging merchant class. Merchants, however, were held in low esteem throughout China where a hierarchical, bureaucratic government replaced the decentralized feudal order.[21] When crafts developed, Chinese peasants were simply too poor to provide the necessary large market that might have stimulated additional production. When iron was initially produced, it was used for weaponry and artwork, but not to build tools.[22]

Early in the fifteenth century, China traded with other Asian countries, in some cases even using Chinese ships. In 1433, however, the emperor issued a decree prohibiting such trade and inaugurating a long period of isolation. Anti-foreign sentiment has limited economic progress at several key points in Chinese history.

Railroads, shipyards, and munitions plants were built by the government in the 1860s. The textile industry, especially the spinning and weaving of cotton, was an important sector of the Chinese economy by 1900. Less than 2 percent of China's total factory system, however, had mechanical power by 1912.[23] During the 1920s, electricity powered a growing number of factories and some light industry developed in coastal cities. Heavy manufacturing industries were introduced into Japanese-occupied Manchuria during the 1930s.

Throughout the first half of the twentieth century, industrialization in China lacked direction and was not self-sustaining. The nation's huge population undoubtedly made labor-saving machinery appear to be a mixed blessing. More importantly, however, China simply did not have the strong government leadership and political stability that Japan enjoyed during its Mejii era.

Although China's dynamic ruler, Sun Yat-sen, encouraged both nationalism and development of industry during the early part of the century, civil war erupted in the 1920s. The nationalist government of Chiang Kai-shek was challenged by communist leader Mao Zedong. When Japan invaded China in 1937, Chiang and Mao united to fight the invaders. After the Japanese defeat in World War II, civil war resumed in China until the communist victory in 1949. Socialist planning achieved limited results in mobilizing the Chinese economy. Despite China's communist government, there is likely more capitalist activity there today than at any previous point in the nation's history. The country currently has the highest rate of economic growth in the world, although that growth has slowed slightly since 2010.

India

India was a colony during the European mercantilist era. Portugal arrived in the early 1500s and was followed by Holland as the century was drawing to a close. By the early 1600s, France and England had chartered monopolies that would oversee most of India's trade. As France faded from the scene, England established political and economic control which it maintained for the most part from 1750 until Indian independence in 1947. Especially during the early part of this period, India was a classic colony in that it imported British manufactured goods and exported cotton as well as other raw materials to England.

Although newly independent India possessed adequate railroads and a modern communications network, industrialization proceeded haphazardly.[24] Agriculture has employed fairly primitive technology. Early government planning emphasized irrigation and development of electric power as well as the iron, steel, aluminum, chemical, paper, and cement industries. In recent years, economic growth has been more pronounced, as an increasingly educated workforce has found opportunities, particularly in technology based industries.

The Asian Tigers

Since World War II, industrialization has produced near-miraculous results in Singapore, Taiwan, South Korea, and Malaysia. Originally a major participant in this economic advance, the British colony of Hong Kong became part of China in 1997 and has contributed substantially to the continued growth of its economy. Taiwan and South Korea have been especially strong in their information technology sectors. Singapore and Hong Kong initially prospered as international financial centers before diversifying into several manufacturing ventures. While specific development strategies have varied among the so called Asian Tigers, production of goods for export has been a major goal.

A mix of entrepreneurial finesse and central government direction (notably public investment in education and in building of infrastructure) has proven to be quite effective in all of these economies. All have also rebounded well from the global financial crises of 1997 and 2008. Less impressive yet still noteworthy growth has occurred in Indonesia, Thailand, and the Philippines. Although relatively late entries into high-technology products and other manufactured goods, all of the above East Asian countries provide further evidence that the Industrial Revolution is ongoing and that its effects continue to multiply.

Technology Finally Overcomes Ceremonialism

Renaissance humanists, some Christian while others either agnostic or atheistic, provided the mental energy to challenge the intellectual lethargy of the medieval period. The Enlightenment advanced the case for reason above restrictive religious dogma. Its successes were numerous, most notably in the field of science. Scientific achievements provided new ways of observing the universe along with a desire to expand the quest for new knowledge.

Mired in its numerous sex and financial scandals, the best that the institution of religion could accomplish was a reform movement with new attitudes about the pursuit of wealth. This was a belated response to its disgraced position in the eyes of its followers and allowed its newly fragmented structure to maintain some degree of moral authority in an only slightly more secularized world. In the realm of commerce, a new merchant class emerged and enjoyed some amount of economic success.

The eighteenth century Industrial Revolution was the single most important triumph of technology over established ways of doing things in the history of the world up to that time. While many economic historians enthrone steam power as the most important invention of the period, a stronger case can be made for the invention of printing, for at least two reasons. First, the rapid spread of the written word in an inexpensive form caused an equally rapid growth in literacy. This, in turn, enabled instructions for the operation of the new machinery to be communicated effectively to a required newly trained labor force. The improvement in communication that literacy achieved in the workplace and in home life cannot be underestimated. As a result, businesses functioned more smoothly and idle curiosity among the population at large expanded, enabling further advances in knowledge at a later date.

Second, the Church vehemently opposed the use of printing (even the printing of the Bible), as it had most other inventions, and for good reason. The argument is made most succinctly by Ayres:

> It is easy to maintain sacred fictions in a community to whom every letter is an occult symbol; in a community to whom the printed word has become a common tool, no fiction is shielded from the scrutiny of the people…[25]

The Bible had been a sacred mystery for hundreds of years. Church leaders could easily select which of its many contradictory statements to declare reverent to an unsuspecting faithful in search of life guiding principles. Once available to a population now capable of reading *all* of its passages, the Bible could now be subjected to critical evaluation.

To be sure, other forms of ceremonialism remained while religious institutions continued to exert some degree of power. Their most popular and somewhat clever defense involved declaring from time to time that harsh-sounding biblical passages were merely allegories with disguised messages that were never intended to be taken literally. The hidden meaning behind directives to stone women who are not virgins and to murder heretics along with slaves who are not docile is apparently still tied up in some theological committee.

Summary and Conclusions

Optimistic about the potential of ideas and reason, Renaissance humanism tackled worldly problems with enthusiastic confidence. Critical of dogma on many fronts, the Protestant Reformation challenged the official church attitude toward material pursuits. The Protestant ethic gave religious approval to the disciplined, success-seeking activity of the merchant class. Theologians such as Martin Luther and John Calvin were particularly influential in advancing this perspective.

From about 1500 until the 1770s, a philosophy of national wealth and power called mercantilism was practiced by several European countries. Among other things, mercantilists advocated a favorable balance of trade to increase the stock of precious metals, maintenance of overseas colonies, strong government intervention in the economy, and a spirit of nationalism. Mercantilist thinkers included Niccolo Machiavelli, Antonio Serra, Antoine de Montchretien, Thomas Mun, and Jean Baptiste Colbert.

The seventeenth century Enlightenment questioned many existing patterns of European thought, perhaps most dramatically in the physical sciences. Drawing on the work of Copernicus and Galileo, Isaac Newton argued that the complex universe was left alone by its Creator to run itself according to natural law. Many who followed Newton attempted to apply natural law to all human behavior, including an assumed natural economic order where outside government interference was deemed unnecessary.

In mid-18th century France, the physiocrats, influenced by natural law concepts, challenged mercantilism, advocated laissez faire policies, and argued that land was the only true source of wealth. The founder of this group, the physician François Quesnay, built a flow model of economic variables which was inspired by the discovery of the circulation of blood. Other leading physiocrats included Samuel duPont de Nemours, a prominent French government official who later emigrated to America, and Anne Robert Jacques Turgot, French minister of finance whose reforms were opposed by wealthy special interests.

Beginning in the late eighteenth century, the Industrial Revolution substituted machines for human labor, caused unprecedented increases in production, and created irreversible lifestyle changes. England industrialized first because of large amounts of natural resources and acquired wealth, adequate supplies of capital and inexpensive labor, mature domestic and foreign markets, a legal environment conducive to industrial growth, and advances in agricultural productivity.

Spinning and weaving were part of a cottage industry until early inventions like the flying shuttle, spinning jenny, water frame, spinning mule, power loom, and cotton gin relocated workers in large factories where mass production began. The coal and iron industries were aided by such innovations as smelting with coke, the blast furnace, puddling, the safety lamp, and the open hearth and Bessemer refining processes.

The most important inventions of the Industrial Revolution were steam power and improvements in printing. The former enabled factories, steamships, and railroads to be built and operated in diverse locations. As a result, manufacturing and transportation became increasingly efficient. The latter spawned an entirely new industry and increased the level of literacy. Other noteworthy inventions included gaslighting, photography, telegraphy, electromagnetic induction, and anesthesia. During the 1830s, the principles of the mechanical computer were developed even though the machine itself would not be effectively assembled for more than a hundred years.

Some European nations industrialized faster than others in the nineteenth century. France, Germany, and Belgium followed most rapidly on the heels of England. Elsewhere, Japan was transformed from a feudal society into a modern industrial economy during only three decades in the late 1800s. The circumstances of Japanese industrialization were vastly different from those in England.

China, India, and other Asian countries modernized at a much slower pace. The case of China is especially puzzling because so many prerequisites appeared to be in place at various points in its history. Much of Latin America and Africa employ fairly crude technologies even today. A number of Pacific Rim nations, on the other hand, show signs of becoming major industrial competitors as the twenty-first century progresses.

The 18th and early 19th century European experience was destined to stimulate new thinking about economic performance. With only a few traces of feudalism remaining and with mercantilism increasingly disputed, a more mature economic system of industrial capitalism was emerging. The Industrial Revolution, however, was about to require new explanations of what it was doing for and to the human race.

Footnotes:

1. Will Durant, *The Renaissance: A History of Civilization in Italy from 1304–1576 A.D.,* (New York: Simon and Schuster, 1953), p. 86.

2. Max Weber, *The Protestant Ethic and the Spirit of Capitalism,* (London: George Allen and Unwin Ltd, 1904) and Richard H. Tawney, *Religion and the Rise of Capitalism,* (New York: Harcourt, Brace, and World, 1926).

3. Bruce Elmslie, "Early English Mercantilists and the Support of Liberal Institutions", *History of Political Economy,* 47, 3 (September 2015), pp. 419-448; Philip J. Stern and Carl Wennerlind, *Mercantilism Reimagined: Political Economy in Early Modern Britain and Its Empire*, (Oxford: Oxford University Press, 2013). How mercantilism evolved is discussed in the following three sources: Spencer Dimmock, *The Origin of Capitalism in England, 1400–1600,* (Leiden & Boston: Brill, 2014); Christiane Eisenberg, *The Rise of Market Society in England, 1066–1800,* (New York and Oxford: Berghahn Books, 2013); and Martha C. Howell, *Commerce Before Capitalism in Europe, 1300-1600*, (New

York: Cambridge University Press, 2010).

4. Stanley L. Brue, *The Evolution of Economic Thought,* 5th ed., (Fort Worth, TX: Dryden Press, 1994), p. 19.

5. Eli Heckscher, *Mercantilism,* Vol. 1 (London: George Allen & Unwin Ltd, 1935), pp. 160–164.

6. E. Ray Canterbery, *The Making of Economics,* 3rd ed., (Belmont, CA: Wadsworth Publishing, 1987), pp. 23–32.

7. Some transitional thinkers (Sir William Petty, Sir Dudley North, and David Hume) challenged specific mercantilist principles. North and Hume were outspoken proponents of free trade. Because they disagreed with certain mercantilist ideas, Sir Josiah Child and Richard Cantillon might be regarded as transitional thinkers. Physiocracy was a more fundamental attack on mercantilism. Petty and Cantillon had distinct mercantilist tendencies; the same cannot be said for any of the Physiocrats.

8. Vardi Liana, *The Physiocrats and the World of the Enlightenment*, (Cambridge: Cambridge University Press, 2012); Gianni Vaggi, *The Economics of François Quesnay,* (Durham, NC: Duke University Press, 1987); and Las Herlitz, "The Tableau Economique and the Doctrine of Sterility," *Scandinavian Economic History Review,* 9, *1* (1961), pp. 3–55.

9. Walter Eltis, "How Quesnay's Tableau Economique Offered a Deeper Analysis of the Predicament of France," *Journal of the History of Economic Thought,* 24, 1 (March 2002), pp. 39–53 and H. Spencer Banzhaf, "Productive Nature and the Net Product: Quesnay's Economies Animal and Political," *History of Political Economy,* 32, 3 (Fall 2000), pp. 517–552.

10. DuPont's ideas may be found in J. J. McLain, *The Economic Writings of DuPont de Nemours,* (Newark: University of Delaware Press, 1977).

11. Peter Groenewegen, "Turgot's Place in the History of Economic Thought," *History of Political Economy,* 15, 4 (Winter 1983), pp. 585–616 and Anthony A. Brewer, "Turgot: Founder of Classical Economics," *Economica,* 54, 4 (November 1987), pp. 417–428.

12. See, for example, Robert Heilbroner, *The Making of Economic Society,* 9th ed., (Englewood Cliffs, NJ: Prentice Hall, 1993), p. 93.

13. Emma Griffin, *Liberty's Dawn: A People's History of the Industrial Revolution,* (New Haven: Yale University Press, 2013); Peter M. Solar, "Opening to the East: Shipping Between Europe and Asia, 1770-1830", *Journal of Economic History,* 73, 3 (September 2013), pp. 625-661; and Jan Luiten van Zanden, *The Long Road to the Industrial Revolution: The European Economy in a Global Perspective, 1000-1800,* (Leiden: Brill, 2009).

14. Joseph E. Pluta, "The Industrial Revolution and Modern Global Business", *Perspectives in Business,* 4, 2 (Fall 2007), pp. 9-16. See also Gregory Clark, Kevin H. O'Rourke, and Alan M. Taylor, "Made in America? The New World, the Old, and the Industrial Revolution." *American Economic Review,* 98, 2 (May 2008), pp. 523–528.

15. For one reason why labor was inexpensive, see Jane Humphries, "Childhood and Child Labour in the British Industrial Revolution", *Economic History Review*, 66, 2 (May 2013), pp. 395-418.

16. Sean Bottomley, "Patenting in England, Scotland and

Ireland During the Industrial Revolution, 1700-1852", *Explorations in Economic History*, 54, 4 (October 2014), pp. 48-63.

17. Carlo Ciccarelli and Allesandro Nuvolari, "Technical Change, Non-Tariff Barriers, and the Development of the Italian Locomotive Industry, 1850-1913", *Journal of Economic History*, 75, 3 (September 2015), pp. 860-888.

18. Steven Warshaw, *Japan Emerges,* (Berkeley, CA: Diablo Press, 1993).

19. Karel Davids, *Religion, Technology, and the Great and Little Divergences: China and Europe Compared, 700-1800*, (Leiden: Brill, 2013); Prasannan Parthasrathi, *Why Europe Grew Rich and Asia Did Not: Global Economic Divergence, 1600-1850*, (Cambridge: Cambridge University Press, 2011); and Carol H. Shiue and Wolfgang Keller, "Markets in China and Europe on the Eve of the Industrial Revolution", *American Economic Review*, 97, 4 (September 2007), pp. 1189-1216.

20. Rondo Cameron, *A Concise Economic History of the World: From Paleolithic Times to the Present,* 2nd ed., (New York: Oxford University Press, 1993), p. 83.

21. Lucian W. Pye, *China: An Introduction,* (Boston: Little, Brown and Co., 1972), pp. 3, 37, and 352.

22. Cameron, p. 84.

23. Walt W. Rostow, *The World Economy: History and Prospect,* (Austin: University of Texas Press, 1978), p. 526.

24. Sumit K. Majumdar, *India's Late, Late Industrial Revolution: Democratizing Entrepreneurship,* (Cambridge:

Cambridge University Press, 2012).

25. Clarence E. Ayres, *The Theory of Economic Progress*, 2nd ed., (New York: Schocken Books, 1962), p. 150. Elsewhere in this chapter, Ayres also argues that printing contributed to literacy which aided mechanical operations in the factory.

Chapter Seven

Adam Smith and Friends

When the regulation is in support of the workman, it is always just and equitable; but it is sometimes otherwise when in favour of the masters.

Adam Smith

The interest of the landlord is always opposed to the interests of every other class in the community.

David Ricardo

Who can tell how many of the most original thoughts put forth by male writers belong to a woman by suggestion? If I may judge by my own case, a very large proportion indeed!

John Stuart Mill

The original writings of Adam Smith, David Ricardo, Thomas Malthus, Jeremy Bentham, John Stuart Mill, and others have come to be known as classical economics. Classical ideas continue to influence the world today. Many contemporary economists believe the profession formally began with Smith.

Classical economics exerted *the* major impact on *macroeconomic* thinking from roughly the 1770s until the 1930s. *Selected* classical ideas were refined and made more precise by neoclassical writers during the nineteenth century. These refinements have continued to the present and form the basis of mainstream *microeconomic* thinking. Evolutionary economics emerged more than a century ago as a dissent against the mainstream. The current mainstream/evolutionary controversy, therefore, can be fully appreciated only if the early classical origins of mainstream thought are clearly understood.

Mercantilism and the Classical Dissent

Classical economics was, in part, a dissent against mercantilism, which, as we have seen, guided economic policy in several European nations for roughly the 275 years after 1500. Smith and others were especially critical of the mercantilist beliefs in bullionism and in their type of government intervention that supported special interests, including monopoly firms.

According to the classicals, the mercantilists overemphasized the importance of precious metals as a measure of national wealth. The classical argument was that the wealth of nations was determined, not by *monetary* factors, but by *real* factors. These included improved technology and a larger amount of productive resources, both of which enabled more goods and services to be produced. Money, their argument continues, serves only as a medium of exchange and has value because of what it can purchase, not because of its intrinsic worth. Put somewhat differently, the trade so venerated by the mercantilists is feasible only if there is something to trade. Wealth and power, according to the classical economists, result from the ability to produce goods and services, not from the mere holding of gold and silver bullion.

Adam Smith and his early followers saw mercantilist use of government as primarily benefiting large firms in their trade with other countries. To Smith and others, this frequently resulted in more harm than good. They pointed out, for example, that government under mercantilism was counterproductive because at times it discouraged the production of real goods and services. By supporting bullionist policies of questionable value, government actually diverted resources that could have been used to produce something. Faced with such government direction, which obviously limited economic growth, it was quite logical for Smith and his classical counterparts to reason that greater reliance on the market was more conducive to the attainment of both individual interests and the common good. In other words, they saw the culprit as not being government per se, but rather specific misguided government policies under the prevailing practice of mercantilism.

The Wealth of Nations

By the 1770s, the Industrial Revolution was beginning to have an impact in England. Large-scale economic growth was occurring as commerce expanded, the population grew, agriculture and manufacturing became more mechanized, and a mature banking system developed. Within the next few decades, the effects would spread to much of the European continent. In short, England and other countries were emerging as industrial market economies. Yet, in one sense, this was a success story in search of an explanation.

Clearly, the reasons for this economic advance were not to be found in the dated arguments of mercantilism. Most countries, for example, had long since abandoned their mindless stockpiling of gold and silver bullion. The explanation finally came when Smith published *The Wealth of Nations* in 1776.

Widely recognized as the founder of modern economics, Smith taught such varied subjects as literature, logic, ethics, jurisprudence, and moral philosophy at his alma mater, Glasgow College in Edinburgh.[1] There he befriended James Watt, whose early experiments with steam greatly interested Smith. A stimulating lecturer, Smith attracted students from as far away as Switzerland and Russia. But he never formally taught a course in economics which would remain a branch of philosophy long after his death.

Although he never married and little is known of his romantic interests, Smith was very extroverted and sociable. He was also a bit clumsy and absentminded to the point of occasionally walking great distances while still in his pajamas! In addition to teaching, he worked as commissioner of customs and as tutor to the stepson of Britain's chancellor of the exchequer. The latter financially lucrative position took him to France where, somewhat bored, he began writing his magnum opus "in order to pass away the time."[2]

As the title of his classic book suggests, Smith was searching for the causes of national wealth. Rejecting the mercantilist form of government direction and its emphasis on monetary factors, Smith argued that wealth was caused by a chain of events that began with the principle of the *division of labor.* This now well-accepted notion states that more output can be achieved if workers specialize than if they perform all tasks of producing a good from start to finish.

In today's economy, this principle can easily be seen in the automobile assembly line where one worker installs the doors, another the bumpers, a third the tires, and so on. Through such specialization and the use of capital equipment (including robots), many automobiles can be produced in a single day. If each worker tried to do it all, output would be much lower. In Adam Smith's day, factories were already using this principle with much success. Each worker became highly skilled at some small but important phase of the production process and much time was saved as workers did not have to move about the factory.

The chain of events suggested by Smith proceeded as follows.[3] Division and specialization of labor led to increased labor productivity, greater output, higher wages to reward that productivity, higher per capita incomes, higher levels of consumption, and greater wealth of the nation. Although division of labor started the growth process, capital accumulation was necessary for growth to continue.

The money needed to purchase machines came from thriftiness (saving). In other words, employers or those from whom they borrowed had to refrain from current consumption. As saving grew, more funds became available for capital accumulation. When more machines were purchased and installed in the workplace, an even greater division of labor was possible, the growth process was nurtured, and the chain of events began all over again.

Laissez Faire and the Invisible Hand

Contrary to the ideas of the mercantilists (and others before them) that one person's gain was another's loss, the classical notion of growth meant that all could gain as the size of the economic pie grew. But how was this growth to occur without the guiding hand of government deemed so necessary by the mercantilists? In the view of Smith and other classical writers, the market economy was, for the most part, capable of regulating itself.

Classical economics, therefore, has come to be associated with the notion of *laissez faire* advanced earlier by the physiocrats. Both schools questioned those government policies proposed and pursued by the mercantilists. The classical economists, however, ultimately advocated a limited form of laissez faire in which the economy was primarily, but not exclusively, guided by competition rather than government.[4] To illustrate how this was possible, Smith advanced the principle of the *invisible hand.*

This metaphor states that each individual in pursuit of his or her own self-interest automatically guarantees that the general good is served. It is as if an unseen hand in the marketplace, as opposed to the regulatory hand of government, guided such an outcome. The motivating force, in Smith's view, was self-interest.

People in business produce goods for reasons other

than benevolence or public-mindedness. Rather, it is in their best interest to do so; that is, they are attempting to earn a living. Potential producers are naturally attracted to those goods that provide them with the largest reward. Goods that are in greatest demand by consumers tend to be the most profitable for producers. Therefore, the interaction of buyers and sellers in the marketplace guarantees that producers make what consumers want. In this sense, the market regulates itself and no guiding or "visible" hand of government is necessary to assure that the common good is served.

According to the classical economists, therefore, what role should government play in economic affairs? Smith *begins* his discussion of this issue by stating that government must address "three duties of great importance."[5] These include national defense, the administration of justice (that is, protection of private property from internal threat), and those goods that would not be provided under the profit motive. This last area includes education and basic public works such as roads and bridges.

Entrepreneurs do not find it profitable to offer such services as police protection and highway maintenance. Nevertheless, it is certainly in the interest of society to have these things. The classical economists argued, therefore, that government could supplement private-sector output without directly competing with private businesses.

Many economists today misrepresent Smith's views to advance their own agenda of limited government. *Smith never stated that all government intervention beyond the three functions he emphasized produced negative results. Rather, he argued that specific government policies pursued under mercantilism were misguided.* Without question, for example, he maintained that government's role in establishing and revising a legal system was an evolutionary process that would need to adapt as circumstances changed. In the interest of expediency, he saw government as an active player in this process.[6] Those who claim that Smith believed government should be restricted only to the three functions just listed selectively cite a single passage from the *Wealth of Nations* and ignore what he had to say elsewhere. His call for public education that will reach people of all social classes, especially those who are employed in boring factory jobs that stunt their creative development, is anything but an argument for "limited" government.

Say's Law

Noticeably absent from Adam Smith's list of appropriate functions for government was a role in providing for full employment. The classical economists were concerned about unemployment, which more than occasionally was present in their day. They argued quite explicitly, however, that prolonged unemployment (recession) was unlikely. Temporary unemployment, in their view, would be cured by mechanisms at work within the private sector of the economy, not by government intervention.

To understand how such an argument could be made, a concept developed by a French economist, Jean-Baptiste Say (1767–1832), must be examined.[7] Rising output levels in the late eighteenth century caused many people to be concerned about the possibility of unemployment caused by overproduction. Put simply, the supply of goods might outpace their demand. For the first time in history, manufacturers appeared capable of generating goods in such quantities that consumers at some point might become saturated with them.

If businesses provided more than people wanted, inventories of unsold goods would build up and firms would respond by reducing production and employment. Popularizing an idea that actually was advanced by others before him, J. B. Say reasoned that such a "general glut" was impossible because "supply creates its own demand." This apparently simple yet insightful statement came to be known as *Say's law.*

What is actually being proposed here is that money earned from production (supply) provides individuals with the means to purchase (demand). Stated somewhat differently, every act of production creates income and, therefore, demand equal to the value of that production. A farmer's supply of corn, for example, creates income so that the farmer can satisfy his demand for clothing, shelter, and books. The weaver's supply of clothes creates purchasing power so that he or she can demand the farmer's corn and other goods as well. If this example is extended to include all participants in the economy, it is logical to conclude that, so long as all of the income generated by the production of output is spent, this output (supply) would create its own demand.

Because the classical economists believed that money had value only as a medium of exchange, money was considered useful only as a means of acquiring goods and services. A strict interpretation of this view would suggest that people would not hold money for any extended period of time. Therefore, once they were paid, individuals would almost immediately spend money on goods and services.

What if people elected to save some portion of their income instead of spending it all? Would this saving cause overproduction and unemployment and render Say's law invalid? And if unemployment occurred, shouldn't government do something about it? The classical economists argued that, even if saving caused temporary unemployment, the private sector of the economy contained a mechanism that would restore full employment. This mechanism was flexible interest rates.

The Classical Theory of the Interest Rate

In the classical view, saving would not produce a lack of demand because the amount of saving would automatically be transformed into investment by business firms. If saving took money (demand) out of circulation, investment put it back in. So long as saving and investment were equal, supply still created its own demand and full employment was maintained. But what guaranteed this equality? The answer, according to the classical perspective, was the interest rate.

The classical economists argued that saving was the source of funds that would eventually be loaned to borrowers. Acts of saving on the part of households and lending on the part of banks took place in something called the *market for loanable funds* (or, more simply, the market for money). When people placed their unspent money in banks, these deposits became the supply of loanable funds. People would be inclined to save, the classical economists reasoned, only if they were paid to refrain from consuming. This payment was the interest rate; the higher it was, the more people would save.

Businesses, by contrast, viewed the interest rate as a cost of borrowing funds, the price they had to pay for the use of money. The amount of business investment, therefore, was inversely related to the interest rate. The classical economists viewed business investment as the demand for loanable funds. Therefore, the interest rate (or the price of money) was determined where saving equaled investment (or, put somewhat differently, where the supply of loanable funds equaled the demand for loanable funds).

How does this interest rate mechanism guarantee that saving equals investment and that Say's law remains valid? First, if saving were momentarily greater than investment, money would be in relatively plentiful supply. Its price (the interest rate) would, therefore, fall. Whenever something is abundant relative to the desire of people to have it, its price falls. Exactly the opposite would happen if money were relatively scarce, in which case the interest rate would rise.

Second, suppose people became more thrifty—that is, they decided to save more. The relatively abundant supply of loanable funds would make it difficult for banks to loan it all out. To encourage additional borrowing, bankers would lower interest rates. The prospect of obtaining money at a lower price would encourage business owners to increase investment until saving and investment were again equal at the new, lower interest rate. Flexible interest rates in the loanable funds market guaranteed that saving equaled investment and that Say's law was upheld.

Price-Wage Flexibility

According to classical economics, overproduction and unemployment could not occur for yet another reason: flexible prices and wages. These additional mechanisms in the private economy operated in a manner similar to that of flexible interest rates.

Consider the market for a typical agricultural product (say, corn) and the market for labor needed to produce corn. Suppose corn in the late eighteenth century sells for 5¢ per bushel and people who work as laborers on farms receive a wage of 60¢ per week. Now suppose consumer demand for corn declines considerably. Fewer workers are now needed to meet this smaller demand for corn. Would this cause unemployment to occur and Say's law to become invalid?

The classical economists argued that any such unemployment would only be temporary. Unemployed workers would compete for existing jobs which would put downward pressure on wages. Workers would be willing to work for lower wages because they would be better off doing so than if they were not working at all. Further, if prices fell, workers might not be worse off at these lower wages.

When wages fall, production costs to the firm are lower and businesses can charge lower prices and still earn a profit. As prices fall, more corn is demanded by consumers. In response, production is stepped up, eliminating some of the temporary unemployment. Eventually, the price of corn falls to 3¢ per bushel and the wage paid to workers who produce corn falls to 40¢ per week.

Compared to the situation we started with, the quantity of corn bought and sold will be lower, as will the number of workers needed on farms that grow corn. What happens to these workers who have lost their jobs in the corn industry? The answer is that they find employment in other industries that are experiencing an increase in the demand for their products. The classical economists argued that a decrease in demand in one sector of the economy (here corn) would be offset by an increase in demand in other sectors (perhaps wheat, clothing, or shoes). A general deficiency of demand (and, therefore, prolonged unemployment) was impossible because perfectly flexible prices and wages would guarantee the existence of full employment and the validity of Say's law.

Determinants of Output and Employment

In the classical view,[8] the output of goods and services depended on four factors: labor or the level of employment, the capital stock (that is, factories and equipment), the level of technology, and natural resources. An increase in any one of these factors would increase the volume of output. The level of employment is determined where the demand for labor and supply of labor are equal. The classical economists argued that this point corresponded to a position of full employment. In other words, if a going wage of 60¢ per week resulted in two million workers finding jobs, full employment was defined at this level.

Two million workers, combined with a given capital stock (factories and machines), the existing level of technological knowhow, and a fixed amount of natural resources such as land and mineral wealth, would produce a specific volume of output. This output of goods and services might be thought of as the *aggregate* amount supplied. Output in the classical system was completely supply determined.

The classical economists did not believe that output was affected by changes in the level of demand. This view resulted directly from their faith in Say's law. If a person believed that supply created its own demand, there was little reason to be concerned about the level of demand.[9] Although aggregate demand had no impact on output in the classical system, it did influence the price level. This was done through the amount of money in circulation.

In the mercantilist era, countries that encouraged the inflow of gold and silver experienced an important byproduct of their pursuit of national wealth via bullionism. That byproduct was inflation. The wealthy classes of Spain, for example, because of their rising stock of precious metals, increased their demand for goods produced throughout Europe and, therefore, bid up the prices of these goods. The volume of goods produced, however, did not rise because the inflow of bullion did nothing to increase the real resources of the economy or promote technological advance.

The classical economists, therefore, devoted relatively little attention to the demand side of the economy. Influenced by the experience of mercantilism, they believed that money in circulation alone determined the overall level of demand. Expansion of the money supply increased aggregate demand and the price level. Increases in aggregate demand, however, had no effect on output, which could change only because of changes in aggregate supply.

With such a perspective, it is easy to see why the classical economists would downplay the importance of aggregate demand. Money supply increases, which boosted aggregate demand during the mercantilist era, caused severe inflation—hardly a welcome development. Classical economics, however, attempted to explain the monumental economic growth in Europe brought on by the Industrial Revolution. Its emphasis on aggregate supply appeared far better suited to provide this explanation.

Economic Growth

According to the classical economists, advances in technology affect the economy when major inventions (such as steam power) are adapted for use in the factory. The stock of capital grows when business firms invest more in new industrial plants and equipment. The building of new factories or the expansion of existing facilities are cases in point. The discovery of additional iron ore deposits enhances the potential for natural resource use in the production process. Any of these changes would raise the level of total output or aggregate supply.

Better technology, more machines, and more natural resources would also have a second effect: increasing the demand for labor. More efficient equipment, for example, makes labor more productive. As a result, more output is produced, workers receive higher wages, and incomes rise. Knowing that consumers now have enhanced purchasing power, managers of firms invest further. Funds for this new investment come from increased consumer saving, made possible by their higher incomes, and from higher profits. New investment brings on a second wave of more efficient equipment, and the cycle repeats itself.[10]

Some workers feared that introduction of labor-saving machinery made them expendable. Retraining of workers would, of course, be necessary so that the new machinery could be operated effectively. Temporary loss of jobs might occur as workers relocated. The long term effect of technological change, however, has been to create more jobs as both output and average income levels have risen.

One classical perspective was (and is) that economic growth bestows widespread benefits. Business owners clearly gain as their firms become larger and more profitable. Armed with growing incomes, consumers stand ready to purchase the vast array of goods that producers have so efficiently placed at their feet. Compared to life in the Middle Ages, prospects for improvement in living standards for much of the population appeared within reach.

This was (and still is) an optimistic view. Its interpretation of the invisible hand argument suggested a harmony of interests between various participants in the economic game: producers and consumers, factory owners and their workers, the wealthy and those less fortunate, and so on. Not all classical economists shared this optimism. Smith himself was aware of the simplistic nature of such a view and remained cautious as he observed the industrial process during his later years.

Although economic advancement did improve the lot of many, industrialism also had a negative side. Its immediate effects were most easily seen in unhealthy working conditions, pollution, child labor, and the rise of assorted urban problems. The transformation from a rural, agricultural society into an industrial, machine-oriented factory system was not to be accomplished without personal stress and uncertainty. Serious assessment of these issues would occur when classical prestige waned during the second half of the nineteenth century. A more somber tone emerged even earlier, however, during the height of classical prominence.

Expansion of the Classical School

A number of people contributed to the development of this thinking but primary attention here will focus briefly on three people: David Ricardo (1772–1823), Thomas Malthus (1766–1834), and John Stuart Mill (1806–1873). In marked contrast to the optimistic interpretation of Smith, both Ricardo and Malthus held somewhat more pessimistic views of the world and of the economic system that functioned within it. Mill went so far as to advocate social reforms and a larger role for government, positions some earlier writers would have considered unnecessary and undesirable. Ricardo, Malthus, and Mill probed more deeply into the structure of society to identify potential difficulties not entirely evident to many of their immediate predecessors.

David Ricardo

First and foremost a practical man, David Ricardo was very involved in the business and public affairs of his day.[11] He was a stockbroker who amassed a considerable fortune by the age of forty and later became a member of Parliament. There he advocated several controversial reforms, including a tax on wealth and greater religious freedoms, such as the end of discriminatory laws against Roman Catholics.

Ricardo was the third of seventeen children born to Spanish Jews who had emigrated to London from Holland. His family's size contributed to the dire Malthusian population forecasts that will be discussed momentarily. Ricardo had no formal education beyond the age of fourteen. When he turned twenty-one, he married a Quaker woman and converted to the Anglican Church. Quite by accident, at age twenty-seven he came upon a copy of Adam Smith's *Wealth of Nations* while on vacation in the town of Bath. The book fueled his interest in both the theoretical and practical aspects of political economy. Ricardo died of an ear infection at the age of fifty-one.

Perhaps Ricardo's most significant contribution to the field of economics was his analytical ability. Some of his early writing was on the role of money in the economy. He formally stated the principle of comparative advantage as the basis for international trade. When the issue became controversial, he emerged as a strong defender of Say's law.

Ricardo placed greater emphasis than most classical economists on the question of income distribution: who gets what share of the nation's income. Devoting more attention than Smith to the potential conflict of interest between landowners, business owners, and workers, Ricardo described the efforts of each group for shares of the economic pie.

Wages were received by workers, profits by business owners, and rent by landowners (interest, the return to capital was combined with profits).

Ricardo viewed rent as essentially unearned income or payment received simply because the landlord was fortunate enough to own the soil. Stated bluntly (and borrowing a phrase from Smith), Ricardo believed the landlord reaped where he did not sow. Moreover, he argued that rising rents and wages squeezed the profits of the business owner. This was an unfortunate and inappropriate consequence in his view since the entrepreneur was the risk taker responsible for economic growth. Ricardo devoted much of his professional life to the successful repeal of special-interest legislation that favored the landlords.

Rising food prices during the Napoleonic wars prompted Parliament to pass an updated version of Britain's infamous Corn Laws in 1815. (The British called wheat and other grains *corn,* while corn grown in American colonies was called *maize.*) To protect against a possible postwar fall in agricultural prices, the Corn Laws imposed tariffs on the import of all grains (wheat, oats, rye, and barley). The legislation benefited landlords (many of whom were members of Parliament) who could now count on the virtual elimination of foreign competition in grain markets. This made it easier for landlords to raise rents, especially on the most fertile land. Landlords, in effect, were granted a degree of monopoly power.

In Ricardo's view, rent permitted landowners to live off the labor of others. By supporting this arrangement through the Corn Laws, government had created a landed aristocracy that enjoyed an easy path to wealth because of its privileged position in society. Entrepreneurs who made production decisions took risks in hiring labor and machinery and, therefore, *earned* profits if their operations were successful. Workers who actually tilled the soil performed strenuous tasks each day and clearly *earned* their wages. The landlords, however, did virtually nothing but still *received* rent for use of their land. Ricardo, therefore, considered rent to be an unearned, unnecessary, and unproductive cost of growing food.

To analyze the issue,[12] he offered one of the first clear explanations of the *principle of diminishing returns.* In the short run of any production process, some resources such as labor and machinery may be thought of as variable. This means they can be added or reduced as needed. At least one resource, however, is fixed; only so much of it exists even if more is needed. In geographically compact England, land is the obvious fixed resource.

According to the principle of diminishing returns, as increasing amounts of variable resources (say, labor and machinery) are added to a fixed resource (land), eventually *increases* in output will become smaller. Output (of say, wheat) still grows but at a diminishing rate as each new worker or machine is hired. The result: both owners of machinery and workers receive smaller and smaller increases in output produced by their efforts.

Ricardo believed that wages tended toward a basic subsistence level, just high enough to provide food and shelter and to allow families to reproduce. If wages are at or near subsistence, entrepreneurs earn profits which allow them to invest in new machinery. As population grows, the demand for food and the price of food both rise. Wages must now increase just to maintain subsistence. As land becomes increasingly scarce, landlords charge higher rents which drive food prices still higher. The higher rents squeeze profits while the higher food prices squeeze wages.

In other words, the productive members of society see their returns reduced because of higher returns to unproductive members. If profits fall to zero, new investment ceases and the economy stops growing. Progress brought about by the Industrial Revolution is now replaced by a tendency toward stagnation and subsistence. Ricardo used the term *stationary state* to describe this no-growth economy.

Influenced by such arguments, business owners and workers, normally at odds, united against landlords in opposition to the Corn Laws. The owners of manufacturing firms opposed these tariffs on grounds that they raise food prices and wages, thereby reducing profits and decreasing exports of manufactured goods. Workers felt that rising rents threatened their job security.

Largely through the efforts of Ricardo, who was now a member of the House of Commons, the Corn Laws, one of the most blatant examples of special-interest legislation in world history, were repealed in 1846. Ultimately, this action proved to be more than merely a cut in production costs or even the victory of business and labor over the idle landed elite. By repealing the Corn Laws, free trade became a cornerstone of British policy and free market capitalism officially replaced mercantilism. The stage was now set for the development of British manufacturing whose export possibilities were enhanced by reduced trade restrictions. Mutual benefits of free trade were soon to be realized.

Adam Smith and many government policy makers believed that the basis for trade was *absolute advantage.* Formally defined, absolute advantage is the ability of a nation to produce *all* goods more efficiently (more cheaply) than any other nation with which it might trade. Because of superior technology and natural resource endowments, for example, an industrialized nation may be in such a position compared to a resource poor country with limited technology.

If one country had an absolute advantage over another in the production of all goods, Smith believed there was no reason for trade to occur. According to Ricardo, however, trade between two countries was still feasible based on the concept of *comparative advantage.* Formally defined, comparative advantage is the ability of a nation, compared to nations with which it trades, to produce *some* goods *relatively* more efficiently (more cheaply) than others.[13] In other words, two countries are both made better off by specialization and trade even if one has an absolute advantage in producing both goods.

Suppose, for example, that nineteenth century Britain and Italy both produce steel and coal. Steel costs $100 per ton to produce in Britain and $600 per ton to produce in Italy. Coal costs $100 per ton to mine in Britain and $200 per ton to mine in Italy. Britain definitely has an absolute advantage in the production of both goods. Britain is six times as efficient as Italy in the production of steel and twice as efficient in the production of coal. According to the principle of absolute advantage, there is no reason for trade to take place between the two countries.

In a relative sense, however, Britain has an advantage over Italy only in the production of steel. Italy has a relative advantage over Britain in the production of coal. This is because Britain is six times more efficient in producing steel but only twice as efficient in producing coal. In Britain, one ton of steel can be traded for one ton of coal. In Italy, six tons of steel can be traded for two tons of coal. Producing steel in Italy costs three times as much as mining coal. Both countries would benefit if Britain specialized in the production of steel and Italy specialized in the production of coal.

If Italy transfers the resources used to produce one ton of steel into the mining of coal, the country will get three tons of coal. At home, Britain can trade one ton of steel for one ton of coal. So Britain is better off if it can trade one ton of steel to Italy for any amount more than one ton of coal. Italy would be willing to send Britain anything less than three tons of coal for one ton of steel because it must give up three tons of coal for one ton of steel at home. Trade, therefore, makes both countries better off. By specializing and trading, the total amount of output would be higher than if each country tried to be self-sufficient in both products. This is the essence of the principle of comparative advantage.

A second example involves popular fictional

characters. Originally a comic book creation and later a television series, Superman was finally immortalized on the big screen in the 1980s. Not only was he "more powerful than a locomotive" and "able to leap tall buildings in a single bound," but he was arguably the most productive person on the planet. In other words, he had an absolute advantage over everyone else in the production of just about everything.

Suppose a natural disaster hits Metropolis, causing mass destruction. According to Smith's notion of absolute advantage (and the producers of the film), everyone else should become spectators while Superman rebuilds bridges and tall buildings. This is because he could perform both jobs more efficiently than anyone not from the planet Krypton. The script would be different, however, if it were written according to the principle of comparative advantage. Ricardo and all present-day economists would want both Superman and the rest of the cast to participate in the rebuilding effort.

A team of volunteers from the *Daily Planet* newspaper (including Jimmy Olson and Lois Lane but not Clark Kent, who has mysteriously disappeared) would still be relatively more efficient than Superman in one of the tasks.[14] By specializing, total output would increase, despite the fact that Superman could outperform these bumbling, physically inferior but hard-working reporters in both jobs. The fact that Jimmy Olsen and Lois Lane in hard hats might not create the most exciting of plots is irrelevant.

Ricardo was living proof that abstract ideas in economic theory were capable of influencing economic policy. His use of the principle of diminishing returns to describe income distribution issues led to repeal of the Corn Laws. His encouragement of free trade, guided by comparative advantage, would enable nations to grow and standards of living to reach levels that would have made mercantilists extremely envious. For his analytical insights, Ricardo is sometimes considered to have been the most important of the classical economists.

Thomas Robert Malthus

Born into a prominent family, Thomas Robert Malthus received private tutoring as a child. At the age of twenty-two, Robert (the name he preferred) graduated from Cambridge University and became an ordained minister in the Church of England, although his activities as a clergyman were limited. He eventually pursued a teaching career at Haileybury College where, as professor of history and political economy, he was the first to be officially recognized as an academic economist. The witty, generally cheerful professor practiced the restraint he publicly advocated by delaying marriage until age thirty-eight and fathering only three children.

Early intellectual inspiration came from his eccentric father, Daniel, and from the overly optimistic philosophy of William Godwin and Marquis de Condorcet. Both writers believed in the ultimate attainment of human perfection and the achievement of a world where war, crime, disease, psychological disorders, and petty human bickering would be eliminated. Daniel Malthus was impressed with this view; his son vehemently disagreed. Godwin's daughter, Mary, who rebelled when she ran off to wed the poet Percy B. Shelley, apparently also questioned human perfection prospects when she authored the classic *Frankenstein.*

The younger Malthus was especially troubled by Godwin's argument that population growth in England was extremely beneficial. His reply would bring him both fame and ridicule, would shatter many diverse utopian dreams, and would modify the positive outlook of other classical economists.

Malthus was also influenced to some degree by religious millennialist fanatics, some of whom forecast the end of the world as early as the conclusion of the eighteenth century.[15] Perhaps these views, along with his own observation of human deprivation, may have at least partially guided his critical perspective.

Although his contributions to the field of economics were many, Malthus is best remembered for his *theory of population* in which he argued that the human race would reproduce faster than its ability to feed itself.[16] In support of this proposition, Malthus used population figures from Britain's former American colonies provided by Benjamin Franklin and argued that population grows in a geometric progression: 2, 4, 8, 16, 32, 64, 128, 256, etc. The food supply, by contrast, increases only in an arithmetic progression: 2, 4, 6, 8, 10, 12, 14, 16, etc.

In a geometric progression, each number after the first is obtained by multiplying the preceding number by a constant—in this case, the number 2. In an arithmetic progression, each number after the first is obtained by adding a constant to it, in this case, again 2. No matter how well supplied with food at the start, the population after a time would face rather bleak consequences because of the interaction of the two progressions, unless population growth was somehow slowed.

Checks to population growth include those that increase the death rate (plagues, famine, and war) and those that reduce the birth rate (birth control, postponed marriages, etc.). Malthus realized, of course, that high death rates during certain periods reduced the impact of his geometric progression. Half the population of Europe died during a five-year period in the mid-1300s, for example, as a result of the bubonic plague.

Among those policies capable of reducing the birth rate, Malthus rejected birth control (and certainly abortion) on moral grounds. He advocated fewer marriages, postponed marriages, and abstinence from sex, although he was aware of the limited potential of such pleas, especially the last one. Not unexpectedly, his critics have occasionally complained that he was more of a whining, namby-pamby moralizer than an analytical social scientist.

The only checks likely to affect population growth in

the Malthusian view, therefore, were plagues, wars, famines, and natural disasters. In addition, Malthus believed that increases in the standard of living of the poor merely encouraged them to have more children. This would increase the population further and reduce living standards back to subsistence levels.

Faced with the seemingly logical conclusion that the human race was doomed to live in a state of perpetual poverty, it is small wonder that the outlook Malthus took was pessimistic. It is also little surprise that the noted historian Thomas Carlyle, on reading Malthus's essays on population, dubbed economics "the dismal science," a caricature that has persisted to the present.

Is there reason for the pessimism of Malthus on the population versus food issue in today's world? Clearly, in the industrialized nations Malthus observed and for which he expressed concern, the fatal impact of his progressions has not come to pass. In these nations, as in the United States, declining birth rates and technological advance have delayed and perhaps permanently prevented the serious outcome Malthus offered.

New techniques of cultivation, fertilization, and irrigation have allowed American agriculture, for example, to produce an abundance of food despite a rapid decline in the number of farmers. Technological improvements in other industries and the development of new products have created opportunities for higher living standards. As a result, larger numbers of Americans have been able to enjoy the bountiful harvests and other products as well.

In the so-called developing nations of the world, however, economic conditions all too frequently resemble the forecasts of Malthus. In certain regions of Africa and Latin America, death by starvation is often a harsh reality, as population growth openly conflicts with limited resource capabilities.

Western technology in the form of medical science has

increased life expectancy in a number of nations but cultural taboos often prevent birth-control measures from slowing population growth. Technology in developing countries has not produced the necessary gains in agricultural and industrial output to match Western living standards. The long term prospects for many nations approach the same condition of permanent poverty forecast by Malthus.

A second and lesser-known contribution of Malthus was his criticism of Say's law.[17] Stressing the possibility of an overproduction of goods, Malthus argued that a glut of many commodities (but never of food) could occur. In this argument, emphasis was placed on the likelihood of unemployment due to a deficiency of aggregate demand. At one point, he even advocated government spending for public works to provide temporary employment.

Forward looking, perhaps, but he failed to impress most of his contemporaries with these arguments. Some economists today, however, view him as a critic within the classical school who anticipated the arguments another famous economist, John Maynard Keynes, was to make a full century later. Was Malthus the first Keynesian?

John Stuart Mill (and Jeremy Bentham)

The eldest of nine children, London native John Stuart Mill learned Greek at the age of three (this is not a typo!). By the time he was eight, he had read Plato, Xenophon, and other classic authors *in Greek* and had begun studying Latin. Before he was twelve, he had read Aristotle, had learned algebra and geometry, and had begun studying calculus, chemistry, and physics.

For fun, he read history (including the works of Plutarch) and taught Latin to his younger siblings. James Mill, his father and respected economist himself, was the cause of this most unusual educational experiment. When John turned thirteen, his father pronounced him ready for the economics of Smith and Ricardo. After studying for a year in France, where he met J. B. Say, the younger Mill began his thirty-five-year career with the East India Company at the ripe old age of seventeen.

Shortly after turning twenty, Mill realized he had been robbed of both his youth and his capacity to experience human warmth. While growing up, he had had neither friends, nor toys, nor holidays. His father was demanding and sarcastic while his mother was cold and unloving. Distraught, he suffered a nervous breakdown and seriously considered suicide. He found new meaning, however, in the poetry of Wordsworth, Coleridge, and Goethe. Then, his depression virtually vanished during his more than twenty-year friendship with a married woman, Harriet Taylor, whom he finally married after the death of her first husband.

Mill's major writings include *A System of Logic* (1843), *Principles of Political Economy* (1848), *On Liberty* (1859), and *The Subjection of Women* (1869), the latter inspired by his wife. Building on the ideas of Ricardo, Mill supported Say's law and disagreed with Malthus that there could be a deficiency of aggregate demand. Mill turned many of Ricardo's obscurely written concepts into readable prose. His *Principles* was the leading textbook in the field for over forty years.[18] Like Ricardo before him, Mill was briefly a member of Parliament.

When Mill was sixteen, he became enamored with the economics of Jeremy Bentham (1748–1832). The following year, Mill even founded a group that studied and interpreted Benthamite ideas. By the time he was thirty (that is, after his life had taken a more humane and romantic turn), his writing was openly critical of Bentham. What was this economic philosophy that so influenced Mill and ultimately caused him to be one of its most vocal critics?[19]

Bentham drew on an ancient Greek principle called *hedonism,* which emphasized that people seek to maximize pleasure while avoiding pain. Bentham modified the extreme individualism that hedonism implied. His revamped philosophy was called *utilitarianism* and it promoted the greatest happiness for the greatest number of people. Neither of these philosophies meant total anarchy. People were restrained in their pursuit of pleasure, for example, by fear of punishment imposed by society through laws or by religion in its promise of an afterlife. Bentham, therefore, saw desire for individual gain as normal and as taking place within an orderly framework.

Measuring happiness, pleasure, or satisfaction was not an easy task. To sidestep the issue, Bentham invented the concept of *utility,* or want-satisfying power. Utility was a characteristic supposedly possessed by all goods. The total amount of satisfaction received by consuming a good was called *total utility.* The additional amount of satisfaction or utility received by consuming additional amounts of a good was called *marginal utility.*

Bentham argued that all goods were subject to the *principle of diminishing marginal utility.* This meant that the more of a good one consumed, the smaller the additional satisfaction derived from each consecutive unit. On a hot day, the first can of Coke is wonderful, the second is still great, the third pretty good, and the fourth only so-so. Goods such as ice cream cones, glasses of beer, and even money are subject to this principle. Each successive unit adds smaller and smaller amounts to total utility.

Bentham's ideas had many policy implications. If a government program benefited many people and harmed only a few, it should be enacted. Since the marginal utility of a dollar to a rich man was smaller than the marginal utility of a dollar to a poor man, one could argue that money should be redistributed from rich to poor. Robin Hood apparently operated on this very principle, although Bentham himself doubted such redistribution would be effective. Bentham's greatest happiness for the greatest number philosophy caused him to champion democracy, oppose the elite British monarchy, and support legal and educational reforms. He was especially interested in prison reform, suffrage for women, and legalization of unions.

Since he agreed with Smith that people were motivated by self-interest, Bentham was attempting to quantify the human motivations that propel Smith's invisible hand. What Bentham sought was a type of social arithmetic. For calculations to be accurate, however, utility had to be measurable. This was a major problem, although the utilitarians tended to ignore it. Their followers were apparently quite impressed by the fact that such a system of social accounting was even remotely possible.

Although deadly serious about the validity of his undertaking, Bentham himself was something of an eccentric. His entire estate was willed to the University of London (which he founded) with one stipulation, that his earthly remains be present at all future board meetings. To this day, his (nicely dressed) skeleton is displayed in a glass case on campus and he has yet to miss a meeting. In more ways than one, Bentham's influence has been lasting.

Early in his life, Mill was impressed with the scientific precision of utilitarianism. Later, however, he found Bentham too narrow and too dogmatic. Surely, Mill finally recognized, people were motivated by more than pleasure. What about the pursuit of the finer things in life such as quality, creativity, and art? Ultimately, utilitarian rigidity was simply too stifling to Mill whose ever-inquisitive mind was always open to new ideas. Mill, therefore, became critical of Bentham's methodology but continued to be influenced by his penchant for reform.

Mill is sometimes accused of being effective at synthesizing the thought of others but having few original ideas. This is a highly inaccurate assessment. He was the first to argue clearly (using words, not graphs) how prices are determined for products in international markets. He shows how tariffs and transportation costs affect both prices and the patterns of trade between countries. In his analysis of production, Mill was a major contributor to the classical theory of economic growth discussed earlier.

In his concern with both theory and policy, Mill was an advocate of social reform,[20] especially on such issues as rights of workers and consumers, redistribution of wealth, and the economic position of women. When the economy stopped growing, Ricardo argued it had reached a stationary state that, in his view, was cause for concern. Mill reasoned that the stationary state was not necessarily bad. As long as a certain level of affluence was achieved at this point, government could now take steps to redistribute wealth and create greater opportunities for those with modest incomes.

Although he generally adhered to the principles of laissez faire, Mill believed that government could play an important role in environmental issues, consumer protection, and public utility regulation. In a number of these areas, he foresaw future directions that various Western democracies would take.

Mill preferred proportional to progressive income taxes so as not to penalize *earned* income. Using the same logic, he favored progressive inheritance taxes because they were levied on *unearned* income. *Proportional taxes* take the same percentage from everyone regardless of income although Mill proposed that the very poor pay no income taxes whatsoever.

In his writing, Mill displayed a level of humanity and compassion that was unusual in an emerging discipline intent on cold, scientific precision. In advocating use of government policy, however, he sought a balance between aid for the indigent, especially the physically handicapped, and incentives for those who were unemployed but physically capable of work. Mill, therefore, explicitly rejected several principles of socialism (especially its negative views of private property and competition) but supported public education for the poor, which he saw as a long-term investment in human beings.

Perhaps Mill's most forward-looking ideas concerned the economic and social position of women. As early as 1851, he maintained that society loses when talented women cannot work in occupations reserved for men only. He argued later (1869) that men would be more productive in the workplace if they had to compete with women.[21] Mill, therefore, favored a gender-blind hiring policy long before the notion of equal rights for women became fashionable. Although his position fell on deaf ears for some time, he was clearly the first economist to write a detailed analysis of this issue.

Technology (Including Human Know How) vs. Institutions

In its endeavor to describe and model the economy, classical economics clearly represented an advance in economic thought over earlier efforts, including physiocracy. *The Wealth of Nations* elicited wide support in part because mercantilism was already long past its heyday. A well reasoned explanation of how the Industrial Revolution was affecting millions of lives was long overdue. Adam Smith's often optimistic portrayal of events likely minimized dissent in his day and for some time afterward.

David Ricardo's call for repeal of the Corn Laws clearly met with opposition from those, namely the landlords, who had benefited from that special interest legislation. His analytical insights were also challenged and most of the recognition he received came only belatedly. In many ways, his perceptive contributions faced greater scrutiny than those of Smith and Say.

Cultural taboos in developing countries, especially those concerning birth control, have slowed the acceptance of Malthusian warnings there. That path dependency has led to sluggish economic growth and has kept alive the possibility that his dismal population forecasts may still prove true in some places. John Stuart Mill's suggested reforms, especially those involving equal rights for women, were only partially and reluctantly implemented because of longstanding limited openness to women's issues.

Other proposals to come from members of the classical school have been debated over the years, not so much because tradition has refused to accept new ways of thinking but rather because their accuracy was challenged. This is not institutional resistance to change. It is instead a part of the normal evolution of ideas as some stand the test of time while others fail to do so and are replaced.

The classical notion that the economy naturally tends toward a position of full employment, on the other hand, has repeatedly been proven false and has prompted further debate on policy choices when unemployment persists. Doing nothing in response to widespread unemployment, however, is a stance that still has its advocates. Many people today see this passive strategy as firmly rooted in a distant and even a distorted nostalgic past. A similar argument may be made about Jeremy Bentham's concept of utility and the reluctance of some economists today to relegate this dated fantasy to the trash bin of economic thought.

Footnotes

1. Some of the more recent readable works on Adam Smith include Maria Pia Paganelli, "Recent Engagement With Adam Smith and the Scottish Enlightenment", *History of Political Economy*, 47, 4 (September 2015), pp. 363-394; John Creedy, "Adam Smith and All That," *Journal of the History of Economic Thought,* 24, 4 (December 2002), pp. 479–489; John E. Elliot, "Adam Smith's Conceptualization of Power, Markets, and Politics," *Review of Social Economy,* 58, 4 (December 2000), pp. 429–454; Elias L. Khalid, "Making Sense of Adam Smith's Invisible Hand: Beyond Pareto Optimality and Unintended Consequences," *Journal of the*

History of Economic Thought, 22, 1 (March 2000), pp. 49–63; and Keith Tribe, "Adam Smith: Critical Theorist?" *Journal of Economic Literature,* 37, 2 (June 1999), pp. 609–632.

2. The statement was made in a letter to his friend, David Hume. See E. C. Mossmer and I. S. Ross, eds., *The Correspondence of Adam Smith,* (Oxford: Clarendon Press, 1977), p. 102.

3. This chain effect is described in Robert B. Ekelund Jr. and Robert F. Hebert, *A History of Economic Theory and Method,* 4th ed., (New York: McGraw Hill, 1997), p. 118.

4. For a thorough review of the concept of laissez-faire, see: Jacob Viner, "The Intellectual History of Laissez-Faire," *Journal of Law and Economics,* 3, 3 (October 1960), pp. 45–69.

5. Adam Smith, *The Wealth of Nations,* (Indianapolis: Liberty Press, 1981 (1776)), Vol. I, p. 687. Many sources analyze Smith's alleged views on limited government. A sample of the more readable of these include George C. Stigler, "Smith's Travels on the Ship of State," *History of Political Economy,* 3, 3 (Fall 1971), pp. 265–277; Donald Winch, "Science and the Legislator: Adam Smith and After," *Economic Journal,* 93, 3 (September 1983), pp. 501–520; and H. H. Song, "Adam Smith as an Early Pioneer of Institutional Individualism," *History of Political Economy,* 27, 3 (Fall 1995), pp. 425–448.

6. Warren J. Samuels and Steven G. Medema, "Freeing Smith from the 'Free Market': On the Misperception of Adam Smith on the Economic Role of Government," *History of Political Economy,* 37, 2 (Summer 2005), pp. 219–226. See also Mats Forsgren and Mo Yamin, "A Commentary on Adam Smith and International Business", *Multinational Business Review,* 18, 1, 2010, pp. 95-112 and Duncan Foley, "The Theology of

Economics", *Challenge: The Magazine of Economic Affairs,* 49, 6 (November-December 2006): pp.103-112. Foley argues that mainstream economics today is inconsistent with the original purposes of the classical economists, including Smith, Ricardo, and Mill. Adam Smith's alleged religious beliefs are also questioned by a number of scholars.

7. For background on Say's law and the life of J. B. Say, see Evert Schoorl, *Jean-Baptiste Say: Revolutionary, Entrepreneur, Economist,* (Abingdon: Routledge, 2013); Evelyn L. Forget, *The Social Economics of Jean-Baptiste Say: Markets and Virtue,* (London: Routledge, 1999); Philippe Steiner, "J. B. Say and the Political Economy of His Time: A Quantitative Approach," *Journal of the History of Economic Thought,* 21, 4 (December 1999), pp. 349–368; Philippe Steiner, "The Structure of Say's Economic Writings," *European Journal of the History of Economic Thought,* 5, 2 (June 1998), pp. 227–249; and Mark Blaug, ed., *Jean-Baptiste Say,* (Brookfield, VT: Edward Elgar, 1991).

8. Several authors present basic classical macroeconomic positions including: Richard T. Froyen, *Macroeconomics: Theories and Policies,* 10th ed., (New York: Macmillan, 2012), chapter 3; James L. Cochrane, *Macroeconomics before Keynes,* (Glenview, IL: Scott, Foresman: 1970), especially chapters 1, 3, and 5; and Robert V. Eagly, *The Structure of Classical Economic Theory,* (London: Oxford University Press, 1974).

9. During the 1980s, a pseudo school of economic thought called "supply side economics" emerged and received much popular attention. It was even heralded by some as the basis for the economic policies of the Reagan Administration. Many of its proponents labeled these ideas as largely new and even revolutionary. In fact, most of the propositions it advocated were a simplistic rehashing of selected classical

principles. It could rather easily be argued that, instead of originating in the 1980s, the first supply side economists were the classical economists some two centuries earlier.

10. Discussion of Adam Smith's original concept of economic growth may be found in Walter Eltis, *The Classical Theory of Economic Growth,* 2nd ed., (New York: Palgrave, 2000) and Joseph J. Spengler, "Adam Smith's Theory of Economic Growth," *Southern Economic Journal,* 25, 2 (April 1959), pp. 397–415.

11. For different perspectives of Ricardo, see: Neri Salvadori and Rodolfo Signorino, "Defense versus Opulence: An Appraisal of the Malthus-Ricardo 1815 Controversy on the Corn Laws", *History of Political Economy*, 47, 1 (March 2015), pp. 151-184; William Dixon, "Ricardo: Economic Thought and Social Order", *Journal of the History of Economic Thought*, 30, 2 (June 2008), pp. 235-253; Sergio Cremaschi, "Ricardo and the Utilitarians," *European Journal of the History of Economic Thought,* 11, 3 (September 2004), pp. 377–403; Mark Blaug, ed., *David Ricardo, (*Brookfield, VT: Edward Elgar, 1991); Samuel Hollander, *The Economics of David Ricardo,* (Toronto: University of Toronto Press, 1979); and Kenneth J. Arrow, "Ricardo's Work as Viewed by Later Economists", *Journal of the History of Economic Thought,* 13, 1 (Spring 1991), pp. 70–77.

12. This concept actually was advanced earlier by Jacques Turgot, one of the French physiocrats.

13. Roy J. Ruffin, "David Ricardo's Discovery of Comparative Advantage," *History of Political Economy,* 34, 4 (Winter 2002), pp. 727–748.

14. Similar arguments could be made using other fictional superheroes.

15. George Soule, *Ideas of the Great Economists,* (New York: Mentor Books, 1952), pp. 46–47.

16. Thomas R. Malthus, *An Essay on the Principle of Population,* (London: J. Johnson, 1798). Over the next 30 years, the book went through six editions. For recent interpretations, both favorable and critical, see Gregory Clark, Joseph Cummins, and Brock Smith, "Malthus, Wages, and Preindustrial Growth", *Journal of Economic History*, 72, 2 (June 2012), pp. 364-392; David N. Weil and Joshua Wilde, "How Relevant is Malthus for Economic Development Today?" *American Economic Review*, 99, 2 (May 2009): pp. 255-260; David Collard, "Malthus, Population, and the Generational Bargain," *History of Political Economy,* 33, 4 (Winter 2001), pp. 697–716; David M. Levy, "How the Dismal Science Got its Name: Debating Racial Quackery," *Journal of the History of Economic Thought,* 23, 1 (March 2001), pp. 5–35; John Pullen, "The Last Sixty-Five Years of Malthus Scholarship," *History of Political Economy,* 30, 2 (Summer 1998), pp. 343–352; and Samuel Hollander, *The Economics of Thomas Robert Malthus,* (Toronto: University of Toronto Press, 1997).

17. James Bonar, C. R. Fay, and John Maynard Keynes, "A Commemoration of Thomas Robert Malthus," *Economic Journal,* 45, 2 (June 1935), pp. 221–234 and Salim Rashid, "Malthus' Model of General Gluts," *History of Political Economy,* 9, 3 (Fall 1977), pp. 366–383. The original statement of these views may be found in Thomas R. Malthus, *Principles of Political Economy,* 2nd ed. (London, 1836). The first edition of this book was published in 1820.

18. For recent work on Mill, see: Shiri Cohen Kaminitz, "J. S. Mill and the Value of Utility", *History of Political Economy*, 46, 2 (Summer 2014), pp. 231-246; Nathalie Sigot and Christophe Beaurain, "John Stuart Mill and the Employment

of Married Women: Reconciling Utility and Justice", *Journal of the History of Economic Thought,* 31, 3 (September 2009), pp. 281-304; Rudi Verburg, "John Stuart Mill's Political Economy: Educational Means to Moral Progress," *Review of Social Economy,* 64, 2 (June 2006), pp. 225–246; Amos Witztum, "Economic Sociology: The Recursive Economic System of J. S. Mill," *Journal of the History of Economic Thought,* 27, 3 (September 2005), pp. 251–281; Donald Winch, "Mill as Romantic Idealist", *Journal of the History of Economic Thought,* 26, 4 (December 2004), pp. 543–555; Hans E. Jensen, "John Stuart Mill's Theories of Wealth and Income Distribution," *Review of Social Economy,* 59, 4 (December 2001), pp. 491–507; and Oskar Kurer, "John Stuart Mill: Liberal or Utilitarian?" *European Journal of the History of Economic Thought,* 6, 2 (June 1999), pp. 200–215.

19. For an evaluation of Bentham and his contributions, see Edwin G. West, "The Benthamites as Educational Engineers: The Reputation and the Record," *History of Political Economy,* 24, 3 (Fall 1992), pp. 595–622. For older yet perceptive accounts, see Jacob Viner, "Bentham and J. S. Mill: The Utilitarian Background," *American Economic Review,* 39, 1 (March 1949), pp. 360–382 and P. A. Palmer, "Benthamism in England and America", *American Political Science Review,* 35, 4 (October 1941), pp. 855–871.

20. Robert B. Ekelund and Robert D. Tollison, "The New Political Economy of J. S. Mill: The Means to Social Justice," *Canadian Journal of Economics,* 9, 2 (May 1976), pp. 213–231.

21. Stanley L. Brue, *The Evolution of Economic Thought,* 5th ed., (Fort Worth: Dryden Press, 1994), pp. 150–151.

Chapter Eight

Broad Challenges to an Increasingly Narrow Mainstream

All I know is I'm not a Marxist.
Karl Marx

A drunkard in the gutter is just where he ought to be...we can only, by interfering with (the law of the survival of the fittest), produce the survival of the unfittest.
William Graham Sumner

The most valuable of all capital is that invested in human beings.
Alfred Marshall

There is the economic life process still in great measure awaiting theoretical formulation.
Thorstein Veblen

For the discipline of economics, the voyage from the time of the classical economists to the twenty-first century has been anything but smooth. During that period, economic principles have been praised, rebuked, revised, discredited, buried, and resurrected. Mainstream thought has fueled dissent that has offered fresh perspectives but has penetrated traditional approaches only to a limited degree. Some important historical events have tarnished the image of economists and cast serious doubts on their ability to predict. And yet, despite the difficult journey, many of the ideas of Smith, Ricardo, Bentham, Mill, and even Malthus have arrived more or less intact. This chapter sets the stage for the direct confrontation between the mainstream and evolutionary views. It also highlights some of the major differences in the dissents of Marx and Veblen.

Our story begins in mid-nineteenth century. The Industrial Revolution had progressed to the point that new inventions proliferated in both Europe and America. Although the standard of living for industrial workers was finally beginning to rise somewhat, the gap between rich and poor remained wide. Astute observers of the industrial scene viewed Adam Smith's harmony of interests vision as a nostalgic fiction. The harsh reality of the times was that life remained difficult for most people, despite the steady flow of new technology. Smith's laissez-faire policies were beginning to be seen as a dubious response to the brutal living and working conditions experienced by factory workers worldwide.

Major contributions of the more pessimistic classical economists were also being questioned. Despite population growth, average incomes were rising, while acute food shortages did not materialize, so Malthus was challenged. Agricultural productivity was rising despite the law of diminishing returns, so Ricardo was challenged. Mill, the last surviving member of the classical school and clearly the most respected economist of the period, had already rejected the eccentric Bentham but was himself wavering between capitalism and some moderate versions of socialism.

Mill's tax reform proposals and encouragement of British trade unions met with some success. His other reform positions, however, especially his support of women's rights and income redistribution, elicited at best a lukewarm response. While established economic principles were accurately describing some circumstances of the day, they were missing badly on others. New and different points of view were inevitable and probably overdue.

Marxism

The greatest challenge to the discipline of economics and to the system of capitalism itself came from the dissident philosopher Karl Marx (1818–1883). Accepting virtually all of the premises of classical economics, Marx argued that the capitalist system held within itself the seeds of its own destruction. He accepted the principles of self-interest and capital accumulation as driving forces behind economic activity, he was impressed with the ability of technological innovation to increase production of goods, and he used the classical labor theory of value but with different results.

Family and Personal Life

Marx,[1] the oldest surviving son among nine children, was born into a wealthy Jewish family in the Prussian community of Trier near Koblenz in the industrialized German Rhineland. Although there were many rabbis in the extended family, his father, Hirschel, converted to Lutheranism, the official state religion. He also changed his first name to Heinrich in order to enhance his legal career with the government and avoid the rising tide of anti-Semitism in Prussia.

The younger Marx studied at universities in Bonn and Berlin, initially pursuing law to appease his father, but soon he became more interested in philosophy and political activism. He received a doctorate at age twenty-three, which was impressive, from the University of Jena whose academic reputation was not as great as that of more prestigious European universities. He married two years later but could not obtain a university position in philosophy because of his atheism and radicalism. Rejected by academia, he turned instead to journalism, editing a Cologne newspaper and later serving as European correspondent for the *New York Daily Tribune.*

His political views forced Marx to move often, first to Paris, then to Brussels, and finally to London where he did much of his research and writing at the British Museum. His wife, Jenny von Westphalen, was an aristocrat who became an accomplished socialist writer under male pseudonyms. Eventually, however, Marx fathered a son, Frederick, with their long-time household servant, Helene Demuth, while Jenny was enduring her fifth pregnancy. From then on, their family life, already scarred by disease and poor nutrition, deteriorated and Jenny's written support of left-wing causes diminished.

Marx and Jenny had seven children of their own, including a son and daughter who died in infancy, a second son who died at age eight, and a third son who was stillborn. The family lived much of their life in poverty and received considerable financial support from Marx's collaborator, Friedrich Engels (1820–1895), son of a successful German textile industrialist. Among other things, Engels even claimed to be the father of Marx's illegitimate child in order to protect the family. On his deathbed (more than a decade after Marx and Jenny had died), Engels belatedly informed Marx's daughter, Eleanor, of her father's infidelity.

Prominent among fellow radicals and feared by government officials who considered him dangerous, Marx was largely unknown to others. Although he was a contemporary of John Stuart Mill, for example, the two never met even though both resided in London at the same time. Marx hoped that *Das Kapital* would bring both notoriety and much needed income. Volume I sold only 1,000 copies, prompting him to comment that his royalties did not even pay for all the cigars he had smoked while writing the book. Marx suffered from poor health, including liver problems and digestive/gastro-intestinal ailments, during much of his adult life. His death was most likely due to a lung abscess.

The Stages Theory of History

Marx was strongly influenced by the German philosopher Georg W. F. Hegel (1770–1831) who viewed society as governed by a *dialectic:* When an idea gains acceptance (a thesis), it is destined to be challenged by a counterargument (its antithesis). From this conflict emerges a new idea (a synthesis), which enhances the state of knowledge and becomes the basis for the cycle repeating itself. Marx applied the dialectic to economic concerns and called his version *dialectical materialism.* He would argue that feudalism (thesis) was countered by the market (antithesis) and that the outcome of this clash of forces was capitalism (synthesis).

To Marx, history is constantly influenced by the interplay of dialectical interaction.[2] Unlike the classical economists, who appeared to praise *capitalism* (a term actually invented by Marx) as the ultimate triumph over mercantilism, Marx believed a new dialectic was taking shape. Capitalism (thesis) was destined to be challenged by socialism (antithesis), the final outcome of which would be communism (synthesis).

To back this argument, Marx offered a theory of history based on six stages: 1) primitive (tribal) economies, 2) slavery, 3) feudalism, 4) capitalism, 5) socialism, and 6) communism. Marx believed that a form of communism existed in tribal societies, such as the nomadic hunting and gathering cultures of prehistory, because land was not privately owned and people worked together to assure the survival of the group. This observation caused Marx to believe that communism was the natural form of economic organization to which the world must one day return.

Slavery, such as in ancient Greece and Rome, crudely upset the idyllic setting of tribal cultures and forced some people to work for others. Marx saw feudalism as a more subtle form of slavery, with the nominally free serf replacing the slave but still living under bondage. Capitalism, he believed, represented the height of a class struggle between the capitalist (bourgeoisie) and the workers (proletariat), a struggle that essentially had been present ever since slavery replaced tribal communism.

Marx argued that, because of the internal contradictions inherent in capitalism, it would be replaced by socialism, a stage where monetary incentives remained and government still played a key role. Ultimately, communism emerged in a final stage during which people supposedly would work to satisfy higher ideals than private accumulation of wealth. The state, no longer necessary to redirect the incentive structure, would "wither away." How did Marx use serious economic analysis in pursuit of what many people would regard as an idealistic fantasy?

Alienation and Surplus Value

Adam Smith argued that the division of labor enabled huge increases in production but he was also aware that performing boring, repetitive tasks each day would cause workers, in his words, to "become as stupid and ignorant as it is possible for a human creature to become."[3] Marx called this dehumanizing result of specialization in the workplace *alienation*. The worker, he said, was divorced from the final product because the he created only a minute portion of it.

The craftsman even in late medieval times could create a beautiful and functional piece of furniture out of raw wood. Upon completion of the task, he could look upon the result with pride. The industrial factory worker, however, was robbed of his or her creativity and made to perform monotonous tasks by the owners of capital. The division of labor, therefore, is yet another concept in the arsenal of the classical economists that Marx used to produce a polar opposite conclusion. To Smith, the result was huge increases in output; to Marx, the result was an underpaid class of workers increasingly alienated by what work had become.

To develop the analysis further, Marx used the classical labor theory of value. Like the classical economists, Marx believed that the value of a product depended on the amount of labor time required to produce it. But, said Marx, a product is sold for more than its *labor value*. Marx called the selling price of a good its *exchange value*. The difference between exchange value and labor value Marx called *surplus value*. Capitalists were obviously motivated to increase surplus value. One way they could do this was by lengthening the workday. Since workers at the time were paid a daily wage rather than an hourly wage, requiring them to work more hours enabled them to produce more without being paid more. A better way to achieve the same result was increasing the use of technology that reduced the amount of labor time needed.

Increasing surplus value by using more technology was the motive behind the accumulation of capital. Marx, therefore, used the labor theory of value to show that the factory owner had a natural incentive to keep (daily) wages low, force workers to work long hours, and substitute capital for labor whenever possible.

Business Cycles and Revolution

Marx was one of the first economists to study business cycles. The typical business cycle has a growth phase or boom, a peak, a recession phase or downturn, and a trough or low point, after which the cycle repeats itself. If aggregate income is measured over time, cycles may look like a series of waves on the ocean. Marx was quick to point out, however, that the cycles were not of even duration like the waves on a relatively calm sea. Rather, each boom was bigger than the previous growth spurt, while each downturn was more severe, much like the ocean's waves just prior to a storm.

Capitalists were able to meet demand during boom

periods because of a fairly large pool of abundant labor. Marx called this group the *industrial reserve army.* During recessions, this group was unemployed. As each downturn became more severe, however, more workers were released from their jobs and the industrial reserve army grew larger.

The day of reckoning occurred when a downturn became so prolonged that unemployed workers, who now constituted a rather large group, had no choice but to revolt. The first step in the transition to socialism, therefore, involved the *dictatorship of the proletariat* when workers seized and managed factories themselves. The capitalist was no longer needed, the capitalist class was in effect eliminated, and the revolution was moving toward the establishment of a classless society.

Assessment

To summarize, Marx believed that the pursuit of surplus value resulted in the exploitation of labor as well as the need both to accumulate capital and to substitute it for labor whenever possible. Faced with a declining rate of profit during economic downturns, some firms left the industry, causing a trend toward monopoly and a concentration of wealth in the hands of fewer and fewer capitalists. While workers experienced alienation in the workplace, their low wages and higher unemployment rates during increasingly severe business cycle downturns caused greater misery among the proletariat and a growing industrial reserve army. Under such conditions, revolution of the masses was assumed to be inevitable.

Marx's descriptions of life for workers under capitalism were more accurate than his predictions of its ultimate demise. His model of capitalism was 1840s Prussia, where working conditions were appalling, living conditions for industrial workers were worse, and government was corrupt and undemocratic. Factory owners there (and elsewhere) did exploit workers, alienation was widespread, business cycle downturns did contribute to the increasing misery of the proletariat, and the drive for capital accumulation knew few boundaries. Class conflict in such a setting probably provided a more accurate framework for analysis than Smith's harmony of interests model.

However, with the exception of Europe early in the twentieth century, class conflict in industrialized nations has never reached the crisis proportions Marx suggested. In economically advanced countries, a solid middle class composed of small business owners, professionals, teachers, sales personnel, and even blue-collar wage earners has emerged. In many cases, the state itself has intervened to produce social services, regulation of public utilities and assorted business practices, programs to stabilize business cycles, and laws favoring organized labor.

Since long-term unemployment problems have been rare, the industrial reserve army has failed to materialize and wages have risen, certainly for skilled workers. New technology has increased the productivity of machinery and slowed the falling rate of profit so essential in Marxist analysis. Of course, the labor theory of value proposed by Marx was as inaccurate as similar efforts by his predecessors because the costs of other resources such as machines and raw materials contributed to the value of manufactured goods.

Rising living standards—whose benefits have spread over much of the population, including workers—are generally seen as proof of Marx's predictive failure. Further, the embrace of Marxist ideology by totalitarian regimes in the former Soviet Union, China, the former East Germany, North Korea, and Cambodia have tarnished Marx's image, although Marx himself would have been astounded at the atrocities committed in his name. The collapse of communism in Eastern Europe and its replacement by young capitalist economies is seen by many as evidence of a flawed economic system, even though their formerly socialist economies only vaguely resembled the Marxist prescription.

While leaders in all of the above countries used Marxist slogans when it was convenient for them to do so, theirs were clearly bastardized versions of Marxism at best. Pol Pot in Cambodia, for example, oversaw the murder of over two million of his own people in the infamous killing fields of the 1970s. Nowhere in the writings of Marx is anything so despicable even remotely advocated. North Korea under a succession of Kim family despots today resembles more of a religious cult than anything Marx would have championed.

Clearly the ideal state envisioned by Marx would have been difficult to achieve, however, even under less despotic rulers. Some jobs under capitalism are still boring but neither Marx nor his followers have ever been able to demonstrate how menial tasks could be made more exciting under socialism.

The strongest defense of Marxism may be the claim that capitalist exploitation has shifted to impoverished nations where people still live and work under wretched conditions despite, in some cases, working for multinational corporations. To modern Marxists and to others who speak for the disadvantaged, the social revolution, led by a discontented third world, may yet come. Although Marx did foresee the trend toward monopoly, the difficulty capitalist economies still face in combating the business cycle, and continuing income inequality even in wealthy nations, most historical evidence has shown his catastrophic forecast to be far short of inevitable.

Social Darwinism

The performance of industrial economies in the latter half of the nineteenth century almost appeared to mock the analysis of Marx. Despite periodic economic downturns and seriously evident income inequality, economic growth was impressive and living standards rose for a growing number of people. In the United States, steel manufacturing boomed, agriculture set production records, railroads covered the landscape opening new markets, and new retailing outlets reached millions of consumers. Factories thrived, new inventions as well as new products appeared, and a mentality of progress prevailed. In part, the optimistic mindset was fed by new literature, not all of which was of the highest quality. The message of many writers during this era, whether articulately presented or not, promoted the values of an emerging business civilization.

Shallow "Literature"

Arguably one of the least talented but still popular authors of the period was Horatio Alger. Occasionally one of his books may be used in a literature class today as an example of trash that sells. The storyline in all of his work is pretty much the same. A young boy rises from rags to riches by skillfully combining the virtues of hard work and good luck. Interestingly enough, the advantages of drive, honesty, and thrift take Alger's heroes only so far. At a critical juncture, marrying the boss's daughter or stumbling (while sober, of course) upon a rich benefactor provides that final boost to financial success. Such serendipities only happen to (male) aspirants already walking the righteous path.

Targeted at a mass audience, these novels appealed to those who possessed similar qualities and dreamed of comparable results. Their titles were especially enticing. Who could resist such brief adventures as *Do and Dare, Sink or Swim, Risen from the Ranks, Strive and Succeed, Work and Win,* or the uniquely unsubtle *Facing the World?* Rumors circulated that a given reader actually knew someone who made his fortune after reading one of these inspiring tales. And so the legend grew.

Enough Americans of previously modest means were achieving some amount of economic success over the course of a lifetime, filled with effort and maybe a break or two, that readers became hooked. If the myth became reality for some, who could argue that a larger audience, if amply motivated, might not eventually join the ranks? The Alger stories were popular because a growing number of Americans wanted to believe their message. When some workers received promotions or observed their children becoming upwardly mobile, they saw their dreams fulfilled and identified with one or more of the fictitious plots.

The Misapplication of Darwin

A larger theme was at work here and its origin was rooted in a far more controversial theory. In 1859, biologist Charles Darwin, influenced to some degree by Malthus, published his *Origin of Species.* Its thesis was that, in the world of nature, humans evolved from lower animal forms because they adapted best to changing conditions and survived to become dominant.

Led by English philosopher and sociologist Herbert Spencer (1820–1903), a group called the Social Darwinists argued that social progress resulted from the competitive struggles of human beings in the free market economy. By indiscriminately applying Darwin's principles of biological evolution to society, Spencer offered support to those who believed in laissez faire doctrines. Biologists balked and argued that this was a misguided attempt to infer common patterns in biological and economic trends. Many in business paid little attention to this newfound approval of their actions. The marriage of the physical and social sciences, while not perfect, drew widespread applause from much of the general population.

The phrase "survival of the fittest" was invented by Spencer; it was never used by Darwin. According to Social Darwinism, government interference would upset the natural order. Social programs, in particular, were condemned because they would reward the unfit. Spencer opposed public health measures such as sanitation because it offered unnecessary protection to weaker members of the species. For similar reasons, he also objected to public education, relief for the poor, and regulation of business.[4]

On one occasion, John D. Rockefeller, an avid churchgoer, proudly boasted that God had given him his money. Those millions of Americans who believed him evidently equated godliness with riches. Clergymen of the era routinely preached that poverty was due to the fault and even the sinfulness of the poor. Those who accepted this argument equated wickedness with poverty.

Spencer's American counterpart was Yale University philosopher and sociologist William Graham Sumner (1840–1910). Their combined defense of laissez faire assured their many followers that radical ideas for reform of the economic system were unnecessary at best and outwardly damaging at worst. To Sumner, somehow Darwinian natural selection, the Protestant ethic, and classical economics all contained the same message. Darwin, Ricardo, Mill, and Martin Luther all would have been appalled.

Gilded Age Reality

Although the virtues of laissez faire were praised in public, most corporate executives despised competition and did whatever they could to eliminate it. Their hypocrisy was also evident in their calls for no government assistance at the same time that their mouths were firmly affixed to the federal breast. Railroad entrepreneurs received over 200 million acres of free federal land plus over $64 million in federal loans. High tariffs, which protected American firms from foreign competition, were much in evidence in the late nineteenth century. The Supreme Court, along with state courts, consistently ruled in favor of business and against the interests of organized labor. Apparently, when God gave wealthy businessmen their money, he instructed the federal government to drive the delivery truck.

The period between the assassinations of two presidents, Abraham Lincoln in 1865 and William McKinley in 1901, is often called the *Gilded Age*. The name was penned by humorist and satirist Mark Twain, who used it to describe the society in which he lived: glitter on the outside but base metal underneath.[5] The Gilded Age was a time of considerable industrial growth but also of speculation and corruption. The railroad industry was the primary engine of the former. Regrettably, several of its leaders contributed substantially to the latter.

The term *robber baron* originally described a feudal lord who stole from those who innocently attempted passage through his territory. During the late nineteenth century, it referred to those captains of industry who stole from the public in a more subtle manner using methods of dubious legality. Many business leaders accurately fit the image; perhaps the most noteworthy included railroad tycoons and rogue financiers Jay Gould, Jim Fisk, and Daniel Drew. High on most lists of robber barons would also be the names of Cornelius Vanderbilt and John Pierpont Morgan.[6]

Gould and Fisk once involved a gullible President Ulysses S. Grant in a scheme to drive up the price of gold the duo was hoarding. Hundreds of businessmen, especially importers, lost huge sums of money as a result. Gould, Fisk, and Drew were also notorious for *stock watering,* overcapitalizing firms by selling shares of stock in excess of their true value. In the process, Fisk gained the reputation of being "first in the pockets of his countrymen" while of Gould it was once said, "His touch is death."

Gould was especially adept at acquiring unprofitable railroads, initiating cosmetic changes, funding personal speculation and bribery out of corporate treasuries, and selling at a profit. His victims included four previously reputable railroad lines: the Erie, Union Pacific, Wabash, and Texas

Pacific as well as telegraph line Western Union. While Gould was either destroying or ruining the reputation of a variety of corporations, he was amassing a personal fortune of over $100 million.

The major rival of the Gould-Fisk-Drew trio-owned Erie was Vanderbilt's New York Central, a railroad he built by merging a number of smaller lines into a single entity and watering its stock. In a major price war between the Erie and New York Central, the former was so severely damaged that it ultimately failed to pay a dividend between 1873 and 1942. Vanderbilt had hoped to force the Erie into bankruptcy and acquire it at a deflated price. His strategy was unsuccessful, however, because Erie issued new stock faster than Vanderbilt could buy it. Angered at the outcome, he reportedly erupted: "It never pays to kick a skunk." Dozens of smaller rivals lost millions and consumers ultimately had to face near monopoly conditions. The quotable Vanderbilt, when questioned about the legality of one of his later business dealings, replied: "Law! What do I care about law? Hain't I got the power?"[7]

J. P. Morgan made a fortune during the Civil War by buying rifles from and later selling them back to Union forces for six times their original value. He was also able to speculate in gold based on how the war was going, since he had the first telegraph wire installed on Wall Street and could instantly receive news from the front. Patriotism to Morgan simply meant another profit opportunity. Morgan himself ultimately gained control of several prominent railroads, some by dubious investment strategies.

This was how the "survival of the fittest" world of Spencer and Sumner operated behind the scenes. While not a pretty picture and while these as well as other robber barons were publicly despised, the philosophy supporting wealth acquisition remained strong. Whether intentionally or not, it was soon to get a boost from the economics profession.

Neoclassical Economics

By the 1870s, the policy prescriptions of classical economics were increasingly questioned, especially in Europe. In addition to several long-standing disputes over fine points in classical theory here and there, the major policy issue remained income inequality and the inability of classical economics to address the matter in a theoretically sound and consistent way. To confront this problem more directly, some Europeans embraced the socialism of Marx or some variant thereof. Others promoted the union movement in its effort to secure better wages and working conditions. A third response called for government regulation and social programs to redistribute income. All three approaches defied mainstream classical thought.

The stage was set for one of two possible developments. One might have been a modified, more liberal economics built on the thought of John Stuart Mill who accepted many of Adam Smith's original ideas about growth and technological advance but favored reforms in several areas. A second option would have been a sharpening of classical arguments to justify and provide a more conservative defense of the status quo.

The Marginalists and Demand

As the story unfolded, the second outcome was achieved, although its prescriptions would generate yet more controversy. Initially called the *marginalist* school, this new approach would eventually become part of a larger neoclassical economics. Its leaders would ultimately resurrect and refine classical ideas, make them more theoretically precise, and provide ideological arguments that rejected socialism and fit nicely with the increasingly popular Social Darwinism.

The original name stems from the group's emphasis on

reasoning at the margin. In focusing on the individual consumer and business firm, the marginalists argued that most critical decisions were marginal decisions. These included a firm raising or lowering either price or output by small amounts and a consumer choosing to buy slightly more or less of multiple goods.

The marginalists were attracted to the rigorous analytical approach of David Ricardo and his principle of diminishing (marginal) returns. They were similarly influenced by the hedonistic approach of Jeremy Bentham and his principle of diminishing marginal utility. Both provided crude but potentially valuable concepts that the marginalists would embellish in their reinforcement of mainstream classical ideology.

Diminishing marginal utility tells us, you will recall, that the more of a good one consumes, the smaller the additional satisfaction derived from each consecutive unit. Bentham used this principle to argue for, among other things, reform programs that redistributed income from rich to poor because the former placed a smaller value on an extra dollar than the latter. Given their distaste for such government involvement in the marketplace, the marginalists used Bentham's principle for different purposes.

Like the classical economists, the marginalists were seeking a theory of value, an explanation of what determined the value (or price) of a good. Since marginal utility fell with each additional unit consumed, the only way a firm could sell more was to lower its price. The principle of diminishing marginal utility, in other words, explained why price and quantity demanded were inversely related, a relationship which would soon become known as the *law of demand.*

The marginalists argued that price was set by the value the consumer placed on the last unit which he or she purchased. The role of the consumer in determining price showed that the concept of consumer sovereignty was alive and well, a position that, although deduced by different methods, would have made Adam Smith proud.

While the classicals focused almost exclusively on supply, the early marginalists, in particular, paid almost total attention to demand. Their views, however, coincided strongly with their classical predecessors in support of individualism.

Who were these diverse thinkers who, despite working separately in different countries, developed remarkably similar analytical approaches and came to surprisingly similar conclusions? Early marginalists included Hermann Gossen (1810–1858) of Germany,[8] Carl Menger (1840–1921) of Austria, Leon Walras (1834–1910) of Switzerland, and William Stanley Jevons (1835–1882) of England. All made significant contributions by the early 1870s, primarily in the areas of utility and demand.

The Marginalists and Supply

Supply or production issues were more closely addressed by later marginalists. The *law of diminishing returns* states that, as increasing amounts of a variable resource (say, labor) are added to a fixed resource (land), eventually increases in output become progressively smaller. Ricardo used this principle to explain rents that landlords charged for use of land and to argue against the privileged position of landlords. Marginalists, especially the American John Bates Clark (1847–1938), used it to justify the existing distribution of income.[9]

Marginal product is the change in output that results when an additional worker is hired. Workers allegedly are paid according to their marginal contribution to the firm's output. A salesperson who sells four times as much as a fellow worker should be paid four times as much. A manager of a firm should be paid more than a worker on the assembly line because the manager presumably adds more to output than his or her subordinate. Hard-working, highly productive workers were paid more than lazy, incompetent workers. The Social

Darwinists could not have said it better.

According to the law of diminishing returns, therefore, all receive what they contribute based on productivity and, therefore, what they deserve. In other words, the marginal productivity theory shows that there can be no exploitation of labor. This view, of course, was not universally shared. Critics quickly contended that it was difficult, if not impossible in practice, to separate the contribution of the worker from that of machinery. Even though the problem remains to this day, the marginal productivity theory still constitutes a vital part of the theory of the firm.

Alfred Marshall

When supply and demand considerations are brought together, neoclassical economics becomes firmly established. The major figure in this synthesis and the most eminent neoclassical economist is Alfred Marshall (1842–1924), who combined the best work of the classical economists with the new techniques of the marginalists.[10] His path-breaking *Principles of Economics* was published in 1890.

Marshall grew up in the London suburb of Clapham and was encouraged by his parents to prepare for the ministry. Instead, he was drawn to more analytical pursuits, especially mathematics, which he eventually taught at Cambridge University. Two of his most famous students there were John Maynard Keynes and Joan Robinson.

In 1877, Marshall married one of his students, Mary Paley, and was therefore forced to seek employment elsewhere because of university rules that faculty maintain celibacy. He then moved to the University of Bristol and later taught at Balliol College, Oxford.

Throughout their marriage, the couple remained childless. A number of well-reasoned arguments have been offered as explanations. Among them: sterility and/or impotence on his part, infertility on her part, his frequent bouts with poor health requiring long periods of convalescence, and a two career marriage at a time when this was uncommon.[11] Their relationship was complex. They had many happy moments and shared many professional interests. Their differences on women's education caused considerable friction in their personal life, especially when both spoke publicly on the matter.

Daughter of a minister and eight years younger than her husband, Mary was barred from graduation at Cambridge because she was a woman. She eventually became a lecturer in economics at Newnham College and was a co-author of some of her husband's work. Marshall himself became involved in the ensuing controversy, ultimately taking a rather precarious stance. Although he claimed that he was not against the education of women per se, he objected vehemently to the assimilation of women into an educational system designed for men.

During most of his professional life, Marshall maintained an ambivalent attitude toward women. He believed universities should "open their doors to women" but he opposed Cambridge granting them degrees and allowing them to teach men. His stance on this latter issue was vocalized rather precisely: "Public lecturing to largely male audiences was unsuitable for a woman and would damage her character".[12]

In his well known books, he argued that women should stay at home and he even equates the skill of women in factories with that of children.[13] Through it all, even though she once confided to Keynes "what a jealous and selfish intellectual wretch Alfred had been",[14] Mrs. Marshall remained married to her husband and was generally supportive of his work. Some of their joint writing occurred when the couple vacationed either on the south coast of England, in the Tyrol of Austria, or during lengthy stays in America. When her husband died in 1924 and after she donated his papers and collection of books to Cambridge

University, Mary was unceremoniously granted the title of honorary librarian at the school's library.

To summarize, Alfred Marshall was in favor of women attending universities as long as they were not awarded degrees. It was acceptable for women to teach as long as they did not teach men. It was okay for women to co-author books with men as long as men got primary credit for the effort. The woman's most important place was in the home. And women were intellectually inferior to men. Several of his close male friends did not agree with him. On this issue, the only thing that could possibly be said in his defense is that his views were similar to those of the majority of men in Victorian England. He was not a reformer but he was a man of his times

Equilibrium

The graphical analysis of supply and demand, so widely used in economics courses today, was in its early years called the Marshallian cross.[15] To Marshall, the debate over whether price is determined by cost and supply or by utility and demand was much like arguing which blade of scissors cut a piece of paper. Just as the combined work of both blades ultimately produce the final outcome, so too does the combined effect of supply and demand determine price.

Marshall built this analysis around the concept of *equilibrium*,[16] a position that economic forces tend toward and from which there is no tendency to move. In astronomy, clearly such a balancing of forces is at work to assure that planets maintain their orbits. In chemistry, equilibrium is a state in which a chemical reaction occurs at the same rate as its reverse reaction, resulting in no net change in the amount of each compound. In physics, a pencil resting on a table is in equilibrium, the result of the effects of gravity that restores this position of rest even if it is momentarily disturbed.

An enormous leap of faith is required to apply this

concept to the behavior of human beings and humanly created institutions. And yet, this leap from the physical sciences to the social sciences occurred with unquestioned ease. Neoclassical economists happily argued with a straight face that a market is in equilibrium when the forces of supply and demand are in balance, that a business is in equilibrium when it maximizes profit, and that a consumer is in equilibrium when he/she maximizes utility subject to a budget constraint. Newtonian calculus, which enables one to find maximum and minimum values, was uncritically used to suggest that people should logically behave in this (maximizing/minimizing) manner. Equilibrium, therefore, was borrowed, some would say stolen, from the physical sciences.

Similar equilibria would eventually be invented in psychology, ethics, political science, and other social sciences that sought to become more scientific. It was almost as if social scientists mysteriously began suffering from a serious group inferiority complex and chose to ape the methods of physical science instead of developing their own analytical techniques. Such was the overwhelming influence of Isaac Newton then and, to a surprising degree, even now.

Pursuit of Precision

Equilibrium in economics is clearly less cosmic than equilibrium in astronomy. Nevertheless, the concept added to the perceived scientific precision of a young discipline, bestowed an allegedly greater rigor upon the haphazardness of market interaction, and provided ideological support for the benevolence of market outcomes. Government interference, of course, upsets market equilibrium. The concept, therefore, provides yet another reason why such intrusion is both unnecessary and undesirable.

In all fairness, many have argued that Marshall was not attempting to justify the existing social order, although he did often side with the philosophical positions of his classical precursors. More than most of his contemporaries, Marshall was genuinely seeking a more humanitarian economics. His followers, however, tended to place his admittedly minor attempts at reform in footnotes while emphasizing his analytical insights into market behavior. It is for these advances in mainstream thinking, therefore, that he is most remembered. In his original work, for example, Marshall placed supply and demand diagrams in footnotes. His followers, however, made these diagrams the main body of their writing, a position where these graphs have comfortably remained for more than a century.

Marshall was a man of the Victorian era in which he lived. Prim and proper, his dapper appearance, as well as the vast majority of his analytical conclusions, mirror views of the world offered by much of the period's popular literature. The novels of Jane Austen, for example, describe idyllic households where custom and formality produce a calm reserve and inner peace only rarely interrupted by minor interference from outside world misadventures. Romantic poet Robert Browning concludes one of his verses with the line "All's right with the world."[17]

Marshall's ideas downplayed class distinctions that preoccupied much of the analysis of Ricardo, Mill, and Marx. Instead, Marshall emphasized the roles played by "typical" (not actual) consumers and firms. In this way, he represented traditional economic orthodoxy and was quite consistent with the social philosophy of Spencer and Sumner.

Marshall and the marginalists who immediately preceded him narrowed the scope of economics and made the discipline more specialized. Their preoccupation with microeconomic matters guaranteed that macroeconomics remained largely unchanged between 1850 and the 1930s. Most economists during this period were more concerned with establishing economic laws than with offering policy recommendations. They sought precision in their models of human behavior, business strategy, and market performance.

Institutionalism

Serious dissent from mainstream economics was not limited to Marx. A uniquely American critique was led by the economist and satirist Thorstein Veblen (1857–1929). Just as Marx was the first to use the term *capitalism* before offering his critique of it, Veblen coined the term *neoclassical economics* and then punctured holes in its very foundations. His conclusions, however, are totally at odds with those of Marx.[18]

Early Life of Veblen

By most accounts, Veblen possessed a unique personality. He has been described as irreverent, eccentric, cynical, withdrawn, solitary, elusive, critical, skeptical, and otherworldly. But he was also humble, polite, humorous, and amazingly witty. He dressed like a tramp in seemingly unmatching hand-me-down clothes held up in crucial places by safety pins. He was a perpetual outside observer because, wherever he went, he often appeared not to fit in.

Born to Norwegian immigrants in Cato Township, Wisconsin, Veblen was the sixth of twelve children. When he was eight, the family moved to Wheeling Township in Minnesota which was then near the frontier. His older brother Andrew eventually became an accomplished mathematician. Although his polysyllabic writings were brilliant social criticism, the younger Veblen's academic career was tainted by his disinterest in teaching, disrespect for both university administrators and established norms generally, and alleged though unproven (and very likely non-existent) extramarital affairs. (On this last point, see the Epilogue at the conclusion of this book.) Although he held positions at the University of Chicago, Stanford, Missouri, and the New School for Social Research, he was unceremoniously nudged out at each place and never attained the rank of full professor.

Having spoken Norwegian and English as a child, Veblen entered Carleton College Academy at age seventeen, already possessing bilingual skills that would aid him in one day becoming an accomplished linguist capable of writing and speaking several languages. Veblen studied under John Bates Clark at Carleton College and William Graham Sumner at Yale where he earned a Ph.D. in philosophy in 1884. Unable to secure an academic position largely because of his agnostic views, he returned to the rural Midwest where he spent the next seven years reading and thinking but otherwise in virtual idleness.

When once questioned about his religious preference, Veblen replied that he was a follower of the Lutheran church. When asked why, he said, “Because there is no Lutheran church nearer than 50 miles.” He added, however, that as long as science remained in such disarray, he believed in “some kind of omnipotent Providence.”[19] He disliked farm work and cleverly avoided it, although he did invent assorted agricultural implements but was too late to patent them.[20]

While at Carleton, Veblen wrote papers defending cannibalism and drunkenness, both of which practices were equally offensive at a fundamentalist religious school. His most intriguing undergraduate classmate was Ellen Rolfe, daughter of a railroad magnate and niece of the Carleton College president. When they eventually married in 1888, her father planned to secure Veblen a position as an economist for the Santa Fe railroad. Financial difficulties in the company, however, prevented this from happening. Still unable to find gainful employment as his wife’s family wealth dwindled, Veblen enrolled at Cornell as a graduate student in economics. When one of its leading faculty members moved to the newly established University of Chicago, he persuaded its administration to allow Veblen to accompany him. It was there that the Veblen legend began.

Fundamental Dissent

Veblen rejected Adam Smith's notion of the invisible hand and argued that, even though the discipline was built on this principle, it was merely accepted but never formally tested. The metaphor basically stated that each individual in pursuit of his or her own self interest automatically guaranteed that the public good was served. In other words, making goods and making profit justifiably went hand in hand. Based on his observation of the robber barons, Veblen argued that each individual pursuing his self-interest automatically guaranteed *only* his self-interest. Making money, in other words, was distinctly different from making goods.

Large corporations were not interested in achieving greater efficiency and were most certainly not attempting to promote competition, the self-regulatory feature of the invisible hand. Instead, they sought monopoly power, which enabled them to restrict the output of goods to smaller levels than would be realized under competitive conditions. Lower output and corresponding higher prices make society worse off, not better off. The pursuit of profit by financial manipulation even set in motion forces which sabotaged the making of goods leading to a declining business cycle and ultimately to depression and unemployment.

Veblen criticized neoclassicals for building the discipline on unscientific and woefully deficient theories of human nature and consumer behavior. Hedonistic psychology, which viewed humans as pleasure-maximizing, pain-minimizing machines, had long since been discredited by the psychology profession. Veblen contended that neoclassical economists were ignorant of advances made in the disciplines of psychology, anthropology, and sociology. Because of their faulty assumptions, in other words, the neoclassicals built a logically correct and scientifically precise theory of human behavior based on an artificially constructed human person.

Thinking, feeling, and spontaneous human beings, however, were left out of their analysis.

Veblen did not want to shore up or make minor refinements in existing economic orthodoxy. Instead, he rejected all of neoclassical economics as not addressing issues of importance. Veblen disliked the concept of equilibrium because it implied something positive that might not be so; the market solution produced a result, he argued, that may or may not benefit society as a whole. He had trouble, in other words, with the inference that equilibrium somehow meant "good".

To achieve a neoclassical equilibrium price, for example, a number of factors such as consumer tastes, technology, and various institutions were assumed to be fixed. And yet, Veblen maintained, these are exactly the factors that were changing and merited serious study. Furthermore, they were more interesting than whether a market at a point in time was in competitive equilibrium.

Instincts and the Dichotomy

In place of the Benthamite conception of an always-rational pleasure-maximizing, pain-minimizing mechanistic economic man, Veblen argued that human beings behave according to underlying traits called *instincts*. Resulting from human interaction with the surrounding culture, these instincts produced patterns of human response that have themselves become institutions. Having adopted the older psychology of hedonism, the neoclassical economists were apparently unaware of or chose to ignore the more recent instinct psychology. In his numerous writings, Veblen identified and described at least four major instincts: the parental bent, workmanship, idle curiosity, and the acquisitive drive.

The *parental bent* is a concern for family, the human race, and, in a word, others. The *instinct of workmanship* is the pride one takes in one's work along with the quest to produce high-quality products efficiently and to admire the skills of others. *Idle curiosity* is the search for knowledge for knowledge's sake or the desire to seek answers to questions that interest us. Finally, the *acquisitive drive* negates the parental bent in that it is self-seeking rather than a concern for the well-being of a larger group. Veblen saw the historical evolution of society as a collision of forces involving the first three instincts against the fourth.

Because of the interest that Veblen and his followers showed for the study of institutions, the school of thought which he founded is often called *institutionalism*, although Veblen would have preferred the term *evolutionary economics*.[21] According to the Veblen-Ayres dichotomy in institutionalist theory, two conflicting forces have dominated all cultures and the economies which operate within them. One force is technology, which broadly defined includes all tools and knowledge (mental skills). This force is dynamic, progressive, open to change, cumulative (one discovery leads to another), continuous, and forward looking. It arises not because of the profit motive but rather because of the combined effects of the parental bent, the instinct of workmanship, and, most importantly, idle curiosity.

The second force is institutions which are groupings of people with some common behavior patterns. This force is static, past binding, resistant to change, authoritative (even dictatorial), ceremonial, and past-glorifying. It is the sum total of all customs, habits, myths, rituals, traditions, mores, and taboos which result in conformity of behavior. Similar to the notion of cultural lag in sociology,[22] the rigidity of these "imbecile institutions" slows the speed with which new technical knowledge is introduced.

An institution such as a large corporation may be reluctant to introduce new technology until it gets maximum use out of its existing machinery. Although neoclassical economists saw the pursuit of profit as the source of economic growth, Veblen saw the acquisitive instinct as a key form of habitual behavior. As an example, he cited the creation of institutions such as absentee ownership and the corporate trust as vehicles for restricting competition in order to protect the *vested interests.*

The robber barons were clearly more interested in making money than making goods. Their rapacious ways slowed progress by diverting funds that could have been used to develop new ways of doing things into their own pockets.

Conspicuous Consumption

An even more attractive target for Veblen's biting wit was the spending habits of the idle rich. His 1899 classic *The Theory of the Leisure Class* is still in print and is enjoyed today for both its penetrating insights and unique writing style. A similar claim can be made for only a few 19th-century authors and no other 19th-century economist. The book illustrates Veblen the phrase maker at his best. In it, he introduces terms like *conspicuous consumption, conspicuous leisure, conspicuous waste,* and *pecuniary emulation.*

Veblen lambasted those who need not work and who acquire goods merely to impress those who cannot afford them even though they do work. Especially prestigious is outwardly wasteful consumption. Although people of lesser means clearly would be wise to avoid such expenses, they often follow the lead of the leisure class in their desire to emulate them. Fashionable styles displayed by women advertised to the world that they were obviously supported by men of substantial means. Enormous yachts, luxury automobiles, mansions, and designer clothes were and are examples of such conspicuous waste. Although such goods are produced because (some) consumers want them, their purchase contradicts classical consumer sovereignty, which alleged that the well being of society as a whole is maximized when consumers call the shots.

Veblen even challenged the neoclassical law of

demand, at least for certain types of goods. Consistent with his notion of conspicuous consumption, he argued that, when a snob effect exists, people will buy more, not less, of a good at a higher price. A popularly priced automobile, for example, has no snob appeal and, therefore, will not be purchased by those who seek status. More expensive cars of distinction, such as Jaguars and Rolls Royces, however, command higher prices and will be bought by those seeking to impress others. Alternatively, you cannot be taken seriously at a country club with clothes from Target. Goods in which price and quantity demanded are directly related have come to be known as *Veblen goods.*

Effects on Policy

Veblen objected to neoclassical economics offering an apology for the unequal distribution of income when most large incomes resulted from financial manipulation and theft rather than productive effort. He also had little use for Marxist concepts like class struggle, the labor theory of value, increasing misery of the working class, exploitation, and violent revolution. Instead, he is often associated with reform positions. While Veblen himself doubted that government was up to the task, many of his followers encouraged government action to regulate the scoundrels engaged in *industrial sabotage* and to offer some opportunity for their most unfortunate victims.

In *The Theory of Business Enterprise* (written in 1904), Veblen criticized the neoclassical notion of perfect competition, the tendency of many in business to seek monopoly power in their pricing policies, the wastefulness of advertising (which he once referred to as *creative psychiatry*), and the bureaucracies in giant corporations. In all of these areas, he anticipated the work of Edward Chamberlin and Joan Robinson on imperfect competition, which was not to appear for nearly three decades.

Veblen sought to unify the social sciences by drawing on the best approaches of economics, anthropology, sociology, psychology, and history. Although his books showed how knowledgeable he was in all of these areas, he left no grand vision or model on which his followers could logically build. In the conflict of forces between technology and institutions, for example, the outcome was never specified. A pattern of continual evolutionary change was all that was certain.

The reform impulse advocated by Veblen influenced Franklin Roosevelt's New Deal. Because several of Veblen's former students actually advised FDR at this time, many considered their role in the design of programs to combat the Great Depression to be the ultimate triumph of institutionalism in the policy area. To some extent, the multidisciplinary approach championed by Veblen has been used to study the problems of post–World War II developing nations and post–1990 socialist economies in transition.[23] In addition, Veblen's charge that neoclassical economists proposed theories without supporting data has prompted the profession to collect and analyze statistics on economic performance. One of Veblen's students, Wesley C. Mitchell, established the National Bureau of Economic Research in 1920 for that specific purpose.

In 1911, Veblen predicted a political revolution in Russia and a major war in Europe, both of which came to pass before the decade ended. During the 1920s, he also forecast a major depression, but he died just weeks before the 1929 stock market crash. Veblen strongly influenced a number of writers including Mitchell, John R. Commons, Clarence E. Ayres, Joseph Schumpeter, Gunnar Myrdal, and most importantly, John Kenneth Galbraith.

Despite Veblen's literary reputation as a critic and satirist (or maybe because of it), however, his ideas have generally not found their way into mainstream economic thought. The direct influence of institutionalism in the public policy arena has declined since the 1930s although the role of domestic social programs has remained strong since that time.

Nevertheless, many economists today recognize the importance of institutions and the evolutionary/historical approach in economic analysis. Veblen's interdisciplinary use of the social sciences has inspired many who teach to respect how other disciplines may have influenced their own. Finally, Veblen has encouraged aspiring writers in any field to develop their own unique style and to question dubious claims made even by their discipline's high priests.

Summary and Conclusions

By the middle of the nineteenth century, a number of classical economic concepts were being challenged by actual events. The time was ripe for the introduction of new economic theories. The most thorough critique of classical economics and capitalism was given by Karl Marx, who used several classical concepts to argue that capitalism would eventually fail. Marx adapted the dialectic of Hegel into what would become known as dialectical materialism: capitalism (the thesis) would be challenged by socialism (its antithesis) which would eventually give way to communism (the synthesis). Marx developed a stages theory of history in which he believed that capitalism represented the height of a class struggle between capitalist (bourgeoisie) and worker (proletariat).

Marx argued that Smith's division of labor gave rise to worker alienation because workers were divorced from the final product of their labor. Marx used the classical labor theory of value to argue that a product is sold for more than its labor value. The difference between the selling price or exchange value and labor value was surplus value, which capitalists tried to increase by lengthening the work day or by using more technology.

Marx studied business cycles and argued that, as each

downturn became more severe, the industrial reserve army or excess pool of labor would eventually revolt. Although Marx provided a perceptive model of class conflict, his prediction of the overthrow of capitalism has not come to pass for numerous reasons including the rise of a middle class, government intervention, and rising living standards for much of the population. The strongest defense of Marxism may be its claim that capitalist exploitation has shifted to poor countries whose discontented workers may yet attempt a social revolution.

In misapplying Darwin's theory of biological evolution to society, the Social Darwinists argued that government tampering in an otherwise laissez-faire economy would interfere with natural law. Despite publicly praising competition, many corporate executives consciously tried to eliminate it while accepting huge government handouts. During the Gilded Age, many robber barons stole from the public through financial manipulation and corruption. They succeeded, in other words, not because of "survival of the fittest" theories of the Social Darwinists but because of dubious business practices, many of which were illegal.

The marginalist school refined classical ideas, made them more theoretically precise, and offered ideological arguments that supported Social Darwinism and rejected socialism. Early marginalists used Bentham's diminishing marginal utility principle to explain why price and quantity demanded were inversely related, a relationship that became known as the law of demand. Later marginalists used Ricardo's law of diminishing returns to argue that workers were paid exactly what they deserved based on productivity. Ideas of both groups along with those of classical economists were synthesized by Alfred Marshall, who provided concepts such as supply and demand graphics and equilibrium, which are still widely used today. Marshall and his followers have come to be known as neoclassical economists.

American social critic Thorstein Veblen rejected the

invisible hand concept and distinguished between making money and making goods. Through financial manipulation, robber barons did the former and sabotaged the latter. Veblen rejected the neoclassical notion of equilibrium because it assumed as fixed those factors that changed and needed explanation. He also rejected hedonistic psychology in favor of instinct psychology and argued that three instincts (the parental bent, workmanship, and idle curiosity) clashed with a fourth (the acquisitive drive). The Veblen-Ayres dichotomy in institutionalist theory argues that two conflicting forces have dominated all cultures. The first is technology, which is dynamic, open to change, and forward looking. The second is institutions, which are static, resistant to change, and past binding.

Veblen satirized the idle rich in his classic *The Theory of the Leisure Class,* in which he coined such terms as conspicuous consumption and pecuniary emulation. Institutionalism has been important in influencing government programs during the Great Depression, in studying developing countries, and in encouraging collection and analysis of statistical data on economic performance. Institutionalist ideas, however, have largely remained outside the mainstream of economic thought.

Footnotes:

1. The literature on Marx is (more than) huge. Two of the better recent works are Justin P. Holt, *The Social Thought of Karl Marx*, (Los Angeles: Sage Publications, 2014) and Jonathan Sperber, *Karl Marx: A Nineteenth Century Life*, (New York: W. W. Norton, 2013). One of the most thorough books on the life of Marx was originally published in German in 1918. For an English version, see Franz Mehring, *Karl Marx: The Story of His Life*, (London: Routledge, 2003).

2. For a recent discussion of Marx's use of Hegel, see John P.

Burkett, "Marx's Concept of an Economic Law of Motion," *History of Political Economy,* 32, 2 (Summer 2000), pp. 381–394.

3. Adam Smith, *The Wealth of Nations,* Edwin Cannan (ed.) (New York: Modern Library, 1937 (1776)).

4. For recent applications of the thought of the Social Darwinists, see Steve J. Shone, "Cultural Relativism and the Savage: The Alleged Inconsistency of William Graham Sumner," *American Journal of Economics and Sociology,* 63, 3 (July 2004), pp. 697–716 and Rick Tilman, "Herbert Spencer and the Political Economy of Mean-Spiritedness Revived," *Journal of the History of Economic Thought,* 21, 2 (June 1999), pp. 137–144.

5. It was also the title of his 1873 book, co-authored with Charles Dudley Warner.

6. Sean Dennis Cashman, *America in the Gilded Age,* 3rd ed., (New York: New York University Press, 1993), especially pp. 30–35.

7. David A. Shannon, *Between the Wars: America, 1919–1941,* 2nd ed., (Boston: Houghton Mifflin Company, 1979), p. 79.

8. While his work has often been praised for its mathematical rigor and presumed objectivity, a recent study criticizes Gossen for the " obsessive presence of religious references" in his writing. See Philippe Steiner, "The Creator, Human Conduct and the Maximisation of Utility in Gossen's Economic Theory", *European Journal of the History of Economic Thought,* 18, 3 (2011), pp. 353-379.

9. T. C. Leonard, "A Certain Rude Honesty: John Bates Clark

as a Pioneering Neoclassical Economist," *History of Political Economy,* 35, 3 (September 2003), pp. 521–558 and John F. Henry, *John Bates Clark: The Making of a Neoclassical Economist,* (New York: Macmillan Press, 1995).

10. To appreciate how Marshall's thinking made the work of earlier classical and neoclassical economists more precise, see Tiziano Raffaelli, "Marshall's Metaphors on Method", *Journal of the History of Economic Thought*, 29, 2 (June 2007), pp. 135-152; Robert F. Hebert, "Marshall: A Professional Economist Guards the Purity of His Discipline," *American Journal of Economics and Sociology,* 62, 5 (October 2003), pp. 61–82; and Tom Warke, "Mathematical Fitness in the Evolution of the Utility Concept from Bentham to Jevons to Marshall," *Journal of the History of Economic Thought,* 22, 1 (March 2000), pp. 5–27. For wider views of Marshall, see Katia Caldari, "Alfred Marshall's Idea of Progress and Sustainable Development," *Journal of the History of Economic Thought,* 26, 4 (December 2004), pp. 519–536 and Patrik Aspers, "The Economic Sociology of Alfred Marshall: An Overview," *American Journal of Economics and Sociology,* 58, 4 (October 1999), pp. 651–667.

11. Peter Groenenwegen, *A Soaring Eagle: Alfred Marshall, 1842–1924,* (Brookfield, VT: Edward Elgar, 1995), pp. 260-262.

12. Groenenwegen, p. 502.

13. Groenenwegen, pp. 507-508, 526.

14. Groenenwegen, p. 225.

15. Recent scholarship has shown that Marshall did not invent supply and demand curves as well as several other concepts for which he is commonly given credit. Antoine-Augustin

Cournot, for example, actually used a similar graph as early as 1838. Other "Marshallian" ideas originated with Karl Rau, Jules Dupuit, Hans von Mangoldt, and Fleeming Jenkin. See, for example, Robert B. Ekelund Jr. and Robert F. Hebert, "Retrospectives: The Origins of Neoclassical Microeconomics," *Journal of Economic Perspectives,* 16, 3 (Summer 2002), pp. 197–216 and Thomas M. Humphrey, "Precursors of the Marshallian Cross," *The Margin,* (Spring 1993), p. 31. It should be pointed out that Marshall was most generous in crediting others whose work preceded his. The "error" in proper citation is more likely the fault of careless textbook authors than Marshall himself.

16. Stephen Pratten, "Marshall on Tendencies, Equilibrium, and the Statical Method," *History of Political Economy,* 30, 1 (Spring 1998), pp. 121–164.

17. This literature is discussed in E. Ray Canterbery, *A Brief History of Economics: Artful Approaches to the Dismal Science,* (Singapore: World Scientific Publishing Company, 2001), pp. 128–129.

18. For a comparison of the views of Veblen and post-1960 followers of Marx, see Joseph E. Pluta and Charles G. Leathers, "Veblen and Modern Radical Economics," *Journal of Economic Issues,* 12, 1 (March 1978), pp. 125–146.

19. Joseph Dorfman, *Thorstein Veblen and His America,* (New York: Viking Press, 1934), p. 319. For more on Veblen and religion, see Charles G. Leathers and J. Patrick Raines, "Natural Religion and 'Moral Capitalism': Insights from Adam Smith and Thorstein Veblen", *International Journal of Social Economics*, 38, 4 (2011), pp. 330-340.

The Dofrman book contains numerous insightful observations on the life and career of Veblen and for some 60 years was considered "the" authoritative biography. During the 1990s, however, Dorfman's private papers became publicly available. Using these papers and other sources, recent scholarship challenges Dorfman's claims that Veblen spoke English poorly when he first entered Carlton and was the victim of an impoverished and socially backward childhood, which contributed to his disdain for corporate America and the wealthy. See especially Stephen Edgell, "Rescuing Veblen from Valhalla: Deconstruction and Reconstruction of a Sociological Legend," *British Journal of Sociology,* 47, 4 (December 1996), pp. 627–642. Evidently, there was a touch of "Hollywood" in Dorfman, who bent the truth (maybe even not so) slightly for dramatic effect. For more on the inaccuracies in the work of this pseudo-scholar, see the Epilogue following chapter 14.

20. Dorfman, p. 57.

21. For recent surveys of this school, see Anne Mayhew, "Clarence Ayres, Technology, Pragmatism and Progress", *Cambridge Journal of Economics*, 34, 1 (January 2010), pp. 213-222; Pier Francesco Asso and Luca Fiorito, "Human Nature and Economic Institutions: Instinct Psychology, Behaviorism, and the Development of American Institutionalism," *Journal of the History of Economic Thought,* 26, 4 (December 2004), pp. 445–477; Malcolm Rutherford, "Institutional Economics: Then and Now," *Journal of Economic Perspectives,* 15, 3 (Summer 2001), pp. 173–194; Helge Peukert, "On the Origins of Modern Evolutionary Economics: The Veblen Legend After 100 Years," *Journal of Economic Issues,* 35, 3 (September 2001), pp. 543–556; and Marc R. Tool, *The Discretionary Economy: A Normative Theory of Political Economy,* (London: Transaction Publishing, 2001).

22. Richard L. Brinkman and June E. Brinkman, "Cultural

Lag: In the Tradition of Veblenian Economics," *Journal of Economic Issues,* 40, 4 (December 2006), pp. 1009–1028.

23. Agnieszka Ziomek, "Economic Performance and Institutional Economics in Poland After 1989", *American Journal of Economics and Sociology*, 69, 5 (November 2010), pp. 1553-1565.

Chapter Nine

Evolutionary Economics Today

I hope we shall crush in its birth the aristocracy of our moneyed corporations which dare already to challenge our government to a trial by strength and bid defiance to the laws of our country.

Thomas Jefferson

The thief or swindler who has gained great wealth by his delinquency has a better chance than the small thief of escaping the rigorous penalty of the law.

Thorstein Veblen

Rather than justice for all, we are evolving into a system of justice for those who can afford it. We have banks that are not only too big to fail but too big to be held accountable.

Joseph Stiglitz

We must guard against the acquisition of unwarranted influence, whether sought or unsought, by the military industrial complex.

Dwight D. Eisenhower

As recently as the late 1990s, any list of the most-successful and most-respected corporations in America would have included names like Enron, Arthur Andersen, JPMorgan Chase, World Com, Adelphia, Tyco, and Martha Stewart. By 2002, the CEOs and other top executives of several of these firms were taken into custody and handcuffed like common criminals. A number of these and other corporate giants were featured in news stories charging fraud, deceptive accounting practices, insider trading, obstruction of justice, and shredding of documents. By 2007, many of these CEOs and their underlings were convicted and were doing, or had done, time in federal prisons. As it turned out, this was just the tip of the iceberg.

In 2008, major banks and insurance companies were exposed for dubious behavior that created the greatest global economic crisis since the Great Depression. Numerous loans to borrowers with inadequate collateral resulted in thousands of mortgage foreclosures and hundreds of companies who quickly found themselves holding loan packages that were little more than worthless pieces of paper. Some firms such as Lehman Brothers quickly exited the scene while others (Bank of America and Chase, to name two of the largest) were labeled "too big to fail" and, after crawling to the federal government for help, were given multi-billion dollar bailout loans.

One insurance company (AIG) received over $100 billion in federal bailout money and then used portions of it to finance bonuses for many of their top executives (some of whom were also treated to luxurious weekend getaways at taxpayer expense) who drove the company to the brink of collapse. Several banks made similar use of government bailout money in a blatant display of arrogance and indifference toward their customers. Incompetently managed auto companies, General Motors and Chrysler, saw their CEOs fly to Washington in corporate jets to beg for government handouts without any plan for restructuring their companies so that solvency might be attained.

A culture of corporate greed has surfaced as excessive executive pay, weak leadership, complacent boards, corrupt analysts, and shockingly fraudulent accounting schemes have been exposed. Numerous corporate executives have broken laws, shaded the truth, and lined their own pockets with huge stock-option profits while stockholders have endured gigantic losses and employees have lost their life savings, their pensions, their jobs, and everything they have spent a lifetime working to achieve.

A number of corporate criminals in these firms have accomplished what Al Qaeda, ISIS, and other terrorist groups have only dreamed: the destruction of billions (!) of dollars of wealth earned by honest, hard-working Americans who believe in the market system and have staked their future on its success. The actions of these corporate lawbreakers have shattered public trust, given American capitalism itself a black eye, and followed a pattern predicted by Thorstein Veblen more than a century ago.

This chapter addresses various ways economists have attempted to account for and model strategic behavior in the world of big business. Despite recent mind-boggling corporate practices and similar behavior for more than 130 years, many Americans still cling to the hope that the vast majority of large firms do, in fact, conduct their business affairs both legally and ethically. Many do. A number of current CEOs and their top assistants bring to their pursuits credentials that include honesty along with business acumen.

Nevertheless, while this survey describes some aspects of corporate decision making, it also raises two important questions: 1) Is there something inherent in giant corporate structures that makes them more prone to disreputable behavior? 2) Might the writings of Veblen and other evolutionary economists provide greater insight into patterns of corporate conduct than mainstream economic theories do?

The Trend Toward Concentration

On the surface at least, corporate leaders have been praised as heroes at various points in American history. The 1920s, 1950s, and 1980s were three such periods. Led by entrepreneurs who delivered products that previously were only dreams of the most optimistic of visionaries, large U.S. corporations offered consumers automobiles, radio, television, jet travel, computers, and a host of household gadgets that made their lives not only more bearable but even pleasant. Competition from Europe and Japan eventually challenged U.S. innovative supremacy, but the end result was a higher standard of living in all of these regions, as well as in several other emerging economies.

One outcome of this rush to deliver the most advanced of technological wonders was huge shifts in market shares. Dominant among world auto producers just after World War II, General Motors saw its 46 percent market share in 1976 fall to under 25 percent by 2010. Foreign competition, especially from Japan, produced this result. Due to both merger and internal growth, many U.S. industries became highly concentrated. Today, four large manufacturers produce 99 percent of tobacco products made in the United States. The four largest breakfast cereal firms make about 80 percent of ready-to-eat cereals. The four largest airlines carry 70 percent of all passengers. There is even high concentration in the music industry. The top four producers of CDs (Universal/ Polygram, Sony, Time-Warner, and EMI) account for 74 percent of sales.[1]

Many U.S. industries, therefore, are dominated by a small number of very large firms. Economists use the term oligopoly to describe this wide variety of industries which are not monopolies but have substantial market power. In the discipline of political science, an *oligarchy* is a form of government in which people are governed by a select few. *Oligopoly,* a word of similar Greek origin, refers to a market structure in which there are only a few sellers.

Much of basic U.S. manufacturing activity fits the oligopoly model. So does food processing, the automobile and steel industries, aluminum producers, brewers, soft drink manufacturers, airlines, and long distance telephone service. Other examples of oligopoly include the industries that produce household appliances, greeting cards, cameras, soap, lawn equipment, electric light bulbs, motorcycles, coffee, tires, televisions, radios, and men's slacks. Oligopoly, therefore, describes the world of the large corporation whose role in both the U.S. and global economies is extremely important.

Mainstream Oligopoly Models

Numerous mainstream oligopoly models exist and all build on the concept of *mutual interdependence*, which means that what one firm does will often generate a response from rival firms. The most popular of these models today is *game theory*, a form of strategy that involves decision making under conditions of uncertainty, similar to a game of poker or chess.

Other mainstream oligopoly models include the cartel, dominant firm price leadership, price rigidity, and cost-plus pricing. A *cartel* is a formal written agreement which divides the market and fixes prices. Although illegal in interstate commerce within the U.S., two prominent examples include the Organization of Petroleum Exporting Countries (OPEC) and professional sports. The latter is exempt from antitrust prohibitions due to an absurdly reasoned Supreme Court decision in the 1920s which ruled that sports constituted entertainment and was not a big business.

When a cartel is formed, the result is the same as pure monopoly, at least as long as all firms abide by the agreed-upon rules. From the standpoint of society as a whole, the result is less output, higher prices, a distortion in the allocation of resources, inefficiency, and a tendency for firms to be deceptive with each other. The unimpressive history of cartels includes the dubious character of professional and amateur sports, the electrical equipment industry scandals of the 1950s, the price-fixing convictions in agricultural research in the late 1990s, the political soap opera of OPEC, and other tales of rule bending, fraud, and deception.

In other oligopolies, patterns of implicit collusion, such as *price leadership by a dominant firm*, arise. Compared to competitive industries, inefficiencies occur, prices are artificially high, behind the scenes behavior of questionable legality is commonplace and, worst of all, few incentives for innovation exist. The history of the steel and automobile industries documents these shortcomings. Once again, consumers suffer.

In yet other cases, no dominant firm emerges and the presence of a few roughly equal sized firms may elicit some hope for genuine competition. This is the case of *price rigidity* represented by the kinked demand curve. However, inefficiency again persists, the industry may become sluggish, prices are inflexible, firm output is unresponsive to changes in demand, little incentive to innovate is present, and collusion becomes likely as firms seek cooperation in the face of uncertainty. The airline industry, perhaps the best contrived example of kinked demand curve behavior, has teetered on the brink of collapse long before the terrorist attacks of 2001.

Cost-plus pricing, where instead of setting MR = MC, firms set P = ATC + target profit at normal capacity output, also results in uncompetitively high prices and tendencies toward collusion. This model may come closest to describing how actual firms set prices. Much oligopoly advertising, instead of being informative, contains messages of doubtful value to anyone, drives up prices to consumers, counters and therefore cancels the advertising of rivals, and creates anticompetitive barriers to entry.

In all of these models, mutual interdependence makes pricing according to some static rule, like maximizing profit where MR = MC, somewhat *less* likely. In all cases, the tendency toward some type of formal or informal collusion becomes *more* likely. And yet, none of these models provide insight into the illegal and otherwise dubious behavior that has so dominated the world of the giant corporation.

Three Evolutionary Perspectives

For more than a century, evolutionary economists have had much to say about the inadequacy of mainstream models in explaining corporate behavior. Presented here are three views: those of Thorstein Veblen, Kenneth Boulding, and John Kenneth Galbraith.

Veblen's Theory of Business Enterprise

In 1904, Veblen published his second major work, *The Theory of Business Enterprise.* Not only did this book appear nearly three decades before Edward Chamberlin and Joan Robinson published their theories on monopolistic/imperfect competition but it also predated all current theories of oligopoly. More importantly, evolutionary economists argue that Veblen's theory of business enterprise is more relevant and more insightful in explaining contemporary corporate behavior than any existing mainstream oligopoly model. During the past decade, there has been a renewed interest in Veblen's approach, no doubt in part because of recent corporate scandals and the total absence of mainstream explanations as to why they occur.

Veblen did not build formal market structures similar to the models of monopoly or oligopoly. He did, however, conceive of modern American business enterprise as an evolving process from a period of free competition in the eighteenth century to an era of trusts and giant corporations by the late nineteenth and early twentieth centuries. When free competition prevailed, government regulation of business was virtually nonexistent. Because firms were fairly small, bargaining power was rather evenly spread among: sellers who produced goods, employees who could still exhibit some amount of creativity in their work, middlemen who transported goods to final destinations, and consumers.[2] Producer/sellers used their own financial resources since lending activities of banks were not yet well developed. These entrepreneurs also engaged in considerable price competition by reducing costs and selling larger quantities whenever possible. When technological advances in manufacturing inevitably occurred, costs were lowered further, competition was enhanced, and prices fell along with profits.

Many manufacturing processes required large amounts of technologically advanced capital goods. Only larger firms with substantial financial resources could attempt these investments. The industrial corporation logically evolved and borrowed huge sums of money through issuing securities (stocks and bonds) and obtaining loans from banks, which were growing in size and becoming quite eager to help finance these promising large ventures. Smaller firms that produced fairly standard goods gradually gave way to the new behemoths that began marketing a wide array of diverse offerings to both domestic and foreign buyers. Having emerged in the mid-nineteenth century, this new form of business organization became dominant as the century drew to a close.

Although he acknowledged that such huge injections of new technology greatly increased potential productivity, Veblen saw the corporation as created by borrowed money and ultimately valued on the basis of its presumed earning capacity. Stocks, for example, were continually changing in value. When stock prices rose, the dollar value of the corporation's assets also rose, at least on paper. Buying more machinery on credit further inflated stock prices as the enterprise was perceived to be increasingly healthy. Anticipated earning capacity often drove stock prices to previously unexpected levels. *Saleability* of both the product and the company image began to take precedence over product quality itself. Put somewhat differently, salesmanship began to replace workmanship.

Veblen also saw the personal relationship between producer-sellers and their consumers vanishing because of increasing *absentee ownership*. The corporation was, and is, nominally owned by its stockholders who make fewer and fewer business decisions for the firm. These decisions are made instead by corporate managers. Unlike smaller firms where owner and manager were the same person who was always on site, the owners of corporations were absent from day-to-day operations and relegated executive decisions to professional managers. Rather than maximizing profit, managers of giant corporations became more interested in maximizing the value of the firm's common stock. Higher stock prices are appreciated by shareholders, but so is profitability, which contributes directly to dividends. Goals of managers (captains of industry) and stockholders (absentee owners), therefore, did not necessarily coincide.

Neither did the goals of management and the goals of the community at large, including consumers of the firm's products. Veblen believed that the manager pursuing his/her self-interest generally conflicted with community preferences for efficiently produced goods. Managerial manipulation of stock prices was risky to the health of large firms but not especially dangerous to managers themselves, who held limited amounts of the firm's stock and had the best advanced warning of when it might tank.[3] Further, financial data could sometimes be cleverly manipulated and massaged by the captains of finance to make conditions look better than they actually were. To ensure growth, acquisitions and mergers were pursued with a vengeance. When firms grew in this manner, their earnings expectations generally rose along with the value of their stock.

According to Veblen, the primary goal pursued in modern corporations is the creation of a stream of revenue. This may come from actually producing goods, from various types of financial manipulation (such as acquisitions and borrowing to inflate stock prices), or from industrial sabotage (restricting output and raising prices). To modern captains of finance, it is immaterial which of these three strategies is used.[4] In the late nineteenth century, cutthroat competition and price wars resulted in many corporate failures. In response, a key strategy eventually became the elimination of these costly price wars which had devastating effects on corporate profits.

To assure the steady flow of desired revenue, Veblen saw corporations resorting to two possible approaches.[5] The first was encouraging yet further types of conspicuous consumption through advertising. There was a limit to how far consumers could be persuaded to behave in this manner, however, and Veblen recognized this fact. In particular, he saw that this partial remedy was unlikely to stimulate firms operating with idle capacity to utilize fully their existing space.[6]

The second approach held greater potential and involved eliminating cutthroat competition through the formation of cartels and trusts. In this way, industrial sabotage could be achieved most effectively, as competing giant firms would now restrict output and raise prices *together* while avoiding price wars, special sales, and competing forms of investment. Through trusts and collusion, competitors evolved into collaborators.[7] The winners were the giant firms; the losers were consumers and any pretense of a concept called competition.

In Veblen's view, neoclassical economists oversimplified (and therefore erred in) their analysis by assuming that corporate executives, like all other people in business, always pursued ways to expand output, improve efficiency, and maximize profit for the firm. Instead, Veblen maintained, the modern corporation often exhibited a predatory side that subverted these traditionally assumed goals to achieve financial gain for a few at the top of the corporate hierarchy.[8]

The enormous salaries received by CEOs and other top executives may even be seen in some cases as part of an arranged payoff whereby large stockholders can capture billions of dollars fairly quickly as stock prices are temporarily driven upward by mergers, acquisitions, bank loans, and other expansionary efforts. Those on the inside of the arrangement are likely quite aware that the long-term effects of these manipulative strategies may prove devastating to the health of the enterprise and, therefore, its employees. The insiders, however, are protected from severe loss as long as they sell their stock options before the crisis begins.[9] Their handsome salaries, of course, also help. The negative publicity and even loss of their positions may be a fairly small price to pay if the financial gain achieved during the upswing was large enough.

So long as regulatory constraints are few or are laxly enforced, this process may occur across several industries more than merely a few times. When the day of reckoning inevitably arrives, loyal employees who were not privy to the inside information (outsiders) lose their jobs, pensions, and life savings while insiders have safely escaped serious financial (and in some cases even legal) consequences. Some even remain on company payrolls of the very firms they helped to dismember.

Recall that in the era of free competition, government involvement in business affairs was limited, in fact virtually nonexistent. Veblen saw government, however, as playing a crucial role in the era of giant corporations largely by intervening *on their behalf.* Veblen viewed a U.S. economy composed primarily of three sectors: finance, industry, and agriculture. Stock exchanges and banks[10] were examples of the first, a number of established industries made up the second, while farms of various sizes accounted for the third.[11] Within industry, Veblen saw two major market settings. The first was basically what would one day come to be called the dominant-firm price leadership version of oligopoly, where huge corporations dominated a number of firms in the competitive fringe. The second consisted of a large number of small and medium sized firms where no one was dominant and competition, therefore, still took place on a roughly equal footing.

In the first market setting, Veblen envisioned a key role to be played by government, *which was controlled largely by corporate giants to further their own interests.*[12] A pro-business foreign policy[13] including military adventures abroad protected corporate owned property there. Fringe firms in the first market setting and many owners of small and medium sized businesses in the second were fairly easily persuaded to support this role for government on grounds of protecting private property and business interests generally.

Even with this partnership between government and selected corporate conspirators, along with the absence of strict legal supervision, prosperity for a given large corporation eventually ends. Wages and prices of raw materials rise as both resources experience increased demand. This drives up costs and squeezes profits from below. Advances in technology force prices downward and squeeze profits from above. Instead of being sudden, the end is gradual as the firm behaves recklessly and continues to speculate despite falling profits.[14] The long-term effect on the overall economy, as well as on scores of individual families, is potentially devastating.

Parallels between Veblen's description of Gilded Age corporate excess and early twenty first-century scandals involving Enron, Arthur Andersen, Chase Bank, Tyco, AIG and others are concisely summarized as follows:

> As Veblen's theories demonstrated a century ago, these corporate meltdowns, resulting from unwise paper acquisitions, mergers, expansions, new stock issues, excessive borrowing, and executive over compensation, all designed to drive up share prices and eliminate competitors, are key ingredients in the current recession. Bankruptcies, precipitous declines in share prices, forced liquidations,

> major banking losses, and, of course, huge employee layoffs by the mismanaged corporations all helped to fuel the current economic crisis.[15]

The changing nature of business enterprise is indeed a dynamic process which is arguably more accurately captured by Veblen's description than by formal mainstream models. In Veblenian terms, the corporate crises both in his day and at the beginning of the twenty-first century were caused by the acquisitive drive dominating the instinct of workmanship.[16] In the technology versus institutions paradigm, workmanship is a positive force that stimulates the development of technology while the acquisitive drive is a predatory institution that has the capacity to slow economic progress. In seeking short-term pecuniary (financial) gain over long-term productivity, captains of finance lined their own pockets while destroying the firms they (mis)managed, inflicted irreparable harm on their employees and legitimate (mainly smaller) shareholders, and planted the seeds of a downward spiral in the overall economy. As Veblen might have said, two of the longest surviving imbecile institutions are that segment of the corporate system that allows these excesses and abuses to occur and mainstream economics that offers an apology for this behavior.

During the 1920s, Veblen went on to suggest that the forces this evolutionary process set in motion could conceivably lead to a continuing downward spiral and significant economic turmoil.[17] Many scholars see in his forecast an alternative explanation of the roots of the Great Depression which would paralyze global capitalism in the following decade. This is not meant to imply such a scenario would likely repeat itself today because, as evolutionary economists argue, each historical situation is unique with a logically unpredictable outcome. Similarities in the two time periods, however, suggest anything but a positive future development if the initial disturbance is left to run its course.

Given this sobering assessment, is there reason for optimism or pessimism about the future? The discouraging view has two components. The first is that efforts at reform come slowly and reluctantly. Stock options remain at the center of controversy. "(T)heir treatment in corporate accounting are something most neutral financial analysts regard as one of the main culprits in the current accounting and executive compensation scandals. . . . options encourage executives to try to increase short-term profits in order to increase the value of their options, at the expense of long-term growth and stability."[18] A comprehensive review of stock options and other forms of executive compensation is long overdue and would likely contribute much to understanding how creative financing schemes add to the abuse of power.[19] Even these arguments, however, provide an incomplete picture because there are accounting advantages to corporations at present that "the vested interests" are reluctant to disturb:

> The claim in favor of stock options is that they provide incentives for corporate executives to do well because their own fortunes are tied to those of the corporations they run. Less often mentioned is that stock options provide a cheap way of rewarding executives "off the books" because the options do not have to be treated as a corporate expense. But stock options generally have the effect of watering down the value of other shareholders' claims and can be used to overstate earnings when not treated as an expense. . . . This failure to count them as an expense inflates the book earnings of the corporation and can give a false impression of the corporation's profitability and financial health. They are, nonetheless, a

> liability for the corporation. The failure to expense them may serve to drive up the price of the stock and make the options more valuable. So far, the various lobbying groups opposed to changes in the use of stock options have had extraordinary success, and the corporate reform measures debated in Congress . . . (have) not mention(ed) stock options.[20]

The second discouraging component is that even those modest efforts at reform that have been attempted have been largely unsuccessful. To quote one observer, "each new reform seems to bring with it some new distortion, as savvy executives and their lawyers find new ways to bend the rules. . . . They have a strong incentive to do so, for they are rewarded handsomely by their boards of directors and even by their stockholders if they are successful in increasing the market price of the stock. To do this they must play the game of financial expansion, according to the dictates . . . described by Veblen."[21]

Perhaps the major (the lone?) reason for optimism is that many economists and the general public have both become fed up with traditional (mainstream) explanations that either justify corporate chicanery, label specific instances as minor exceptions to otherwise stellar behavior, or ignore the issue entirely. More people are beginning to realize the problem is more prevalent than the few cases that make headlines.[22] The loyal, hard-working employees of firms like Enron, Arthur Andersen, and numerous other corporate criminals today have nothing to show for their efforts, while various accomplices in ("alleged") illegal activity have either quietly retired to a life of luxury or busied themselves in less high profile occupations. Only in rare and extreme cases are jail sentences forthcoming. To address the problem, an interdisciplinary evolutionary approach appears to hold greater promise in identifying its critical dimensions than any oligopoly model offered by mainstream economics.

The Boulding Critique

Religious humanist, peace activist, and rogue economist Kenneth Boulding (1910–1993) has argued that potential threats to survival of the firm play a greater role in motivating managerial behavior than profit maximization.[23] Put somewhat differently, fear of loss inspires managers more than hope of gain. This view is consistent with biological evolution, which emphasizes the ability of organisms to adapt to unpredictable changes.[24] Boulding was similarly critical of game theory, believing it could lead to illusions of certainty about the future.[25] Once again, adaptability to unexpected change was considered to be more important than creating artificial expectations of minimal uncertainty.

Boulding rejected marginal productivity theory as an inadequate explanation of income distribution. He did not believe in a movement of prices toward a long-run equilibrium. He did, however, appreciate the harsh realities of diseconomies of scale and, therefore, did not trust large organizations, including corporations and socialist economic systems. He actually saw the two as quite similar, at least in terms of their inefficiency compared to smaller businesses in producing goods at low cost. In his view, both large corporations and socialist governments were bureaucratic dinosaurs. In other words, Boulding held great respect for those businesses that delivered goods efficiently but felt that many corporations were incapable of doing so.

Not only was Boulding critical of oligopoly performance, but he also questioned the ability of neoclassical economics to describe the industrial enterprise accurately. Instead of beginning production analysis with inputs like land, labor, and capital, Boulding believed the important inputs were knowhow (information), matter, and energy.[26] He rejected the labor theory of value (championed by Smith, Ricardo, and Marx) and argued that goods were not produced by labor but by human knowledge (knowhow), operating through institutions that enable this knowhow to capture energy and rearrange materials. In Boulding's evolutionary view, the history of human civilization has involved a succession of short-run equilibria, each of which is undermined by the cumulative, irreversible processes to which they must adapt.

Because of his interdisciplinary interests, Boulding founded a movement that uses *systems analysis* in an attempt to unify the social and natural sciences by seeking propositions that are valid in two or more disciplines.[27] The goal is better communication among specialists such as environmental economists, physical chemists, and water resource engineers. Instead of organizing knowledge and research along the lines of existing fragmented disciplines, Boulding proposed that professionals use the tools of their specialty to study common phenomena such as populations, growth, information, or the interaction between an individual and the environment. He also was a pioneer in peace research and the study of conflict resolution. Many of his diverse interests are surveyed in his 1968 collection of articles titled *Beyond Economics: Essays on Society, Religion, and Ethics.*[28]

Boulding's environmental concerns caused him to challenge the basic proposition that all economic growth was beneficial. Instead of the blind, reckless pursuit of consumption without limit, he cautioned that continued pollution of the environment and eventual exhaustion of natural resources would reduce, not increase, living standards. As an alternative to the *cowboy economy*, he substituted the term *spaceship earth* to suggest that we do not live on a mammoth prairie whose resources can be exploited indefinitely but, rather, on a finite planet or enclosed sphere where environmental disaster is possible. Ever-increasing growth and infinitely expanding consumption, both of which are considered positive outcomes in neoclassical microeconomics, are not possible in a finite world. When limited resources run out, a day of reckoning inevitably arrives.

Boulding was optimistic that the necessary adjustments could be made but warned that neither mainstream economic thinking nor traditional corporate behavior would likely be helpful. In his own words, "Anyone who believes exponential growth can go on forever in a finite world is either a madman or an economist."[29]

Large amounts of production and consumption are generally regarded as measures of economic success. Boulding proposed a different economic indicator: maintenance of a given capital stock. By this he meant not only the quantity and quality of physical capital (i.e., goods used to produce necessary consumer goods) but also the quantity and quality of human capital (i.e., human capabilities). Preoccupation with *flows* of goods and services has drawn attention away from maintaining sufficient *stocks* of what is needed to meet human needs. According to Boulding, relatively small, efficient producers are better able to achieve this goal than giant industrial enterprises whose very existence is based on the principle of growth.

The Galbraith Thesis

One of the most prominent economists of the twentieth century, John Kenneth Galbraith has presented an even more powerful attack against oligopoly and the large corporation.[30] In a landmark book entitled *The New Industrial State* and in subsequent writings, Galbraith has argued that, instead of producing what consumers want, large corporations have the power to create and manipulate consumer demand. Threatened by the uncertainty of future demand changes, large firms engage in long-term planning to stabilize demand. Their major vehicle is huge advertising expenses to sell what they can profitably produce instead of what consumers want to buy. Such promotional efforts reduce the risk of innovative new products spoiling the market for existing goods. As a result, *producer sovereignty has replaced consumer sovereignty.*

In addition, according to this view, corporations minimize government interference in their activities by co-opting or corrupting government agencies that possess the legal authority to regulate corporate excess. Instead of serving the public interest, government has become the servant of the corporation. Through its huge political contributions, large and powerful firms are able to undermine public institutions from regulatory agencies to universities. Government, as a result, supplies corporate America with workers educated in its image, funds research that large firms deem too risky, responds with tax breaks and subsidies as needed, and initiates tariffs and import quotas to protect U.S. firms from foreign competition.

Galbraith argues further that separation of ownership and control has created a ruling elite capable of furthering its own interests over those of the public and manipulating federal domestic as well as foreign policy. Large corporations are theoretically owned by their stockholders, who make fewer and fewer decisions about corporate strategy. Those decisions are now made by technically trained managers who are part of an increasingly powerful *technostructure.* This elite group is able to use large corporate profits to further its own agenda over that of a diverse group of investors, as long as those stockholders remain satisfied with an adequate rate of return.

More seriously, Galbraith charges, these industrial technocrats join forces with the military to form a *military-industrial complex.* In this joint effort, corporate managers jump between private sector jobs and prestigious positions in government where they help make policies beneficial to corporate interests. Such policies include the waging of war to protect corporate investments abroad and lax enforcement of environmental regulations to enhance corporate profits at home.

This devastating critique of corporate America has many advocates and much evidence to support its major arguments. Corporate power is significant by any measure. One writer, for example, proposes several measures of corporate power, the two most workable of which are: (1) the percentage of total government revenue derived from taxes on corporate profits; and (2) the percentage of the labor force that is unionized. When either declines, corporate power increases. Both have fallen dramatically since the 1950s, the first by more than half.[31]

The separation of ownership and control is a fact whose consequences have not always been beneficial to either investors or consumers. Corporate research teams do invent gadgets that advertisers then try to convince consumers will make their lives more complete. Highly profitable corporations are major campaign contributors who obviously expect and receive government favors in return. Former corporate executives turned government policy makers have played key roles in American military ventures in the Middle East and elsewhere as well as in a wide range of domestic programs, including some that have harmed the environment.

Critics counter that even the most powerful of corporations have not been sheltered from market forces and changing consumer tastes. Most leading American firms a century ago no longer exist. Many others have struggled to survive and are less influential than they once were. Horse-drawn carriage manufacturers have disappeared, critics argue, because consumers *prefer* automobiles. While such arguments state the obvious, they conveniently ignore the fact that many established large firms remained on the scene longer than they would have in a more open competitive environment.

Even critics admit that advertising influences consumer demand. Most, however, place more faith in the informational value of advertising than recent ads deliver. Critics also point out that, despite government efforts on behalf of business, government also has limited corporate power in several instances. A key example is government warnings about the hazards of cigarette smoking and restrictions on tobacco company advertising, despite political contributions from the tobacco industry. Such arguments downplay the lengthy struggle that was required to eventually win government support for such positions versus how quickly and easily corporations win government favor with its giant payoffs.

An even weaker critique is that, in addition to the influence of big business, government also receives contributions from labor unions, farmers groups, consumer groups, and small businesses. In the halls of government, money talks, and corporations still have more of it than anyone else.

Especially in light of the corporate scandals in the energy, banking, and accounting industries early in the twenty-first century, the Galbraith thesis has become a particularly perceptive corporate critique. The collusion, corruption, incentives to cheat, fraud, and inefficiency so evident in contemporary corporate America stand in sharp contrast to the record of smaller competitive firms in delivering the goods consumers want at reasonable prices.

The Pattern of Recent Events

So much of what has happened in the corporate world in recent years can be explained far more accurately by analyses rooted in the tradition of Veblen and Galbraith than by any mainstream oligopoly model. The latter primarily point out a tendency toward collusion before stopping short of further explanation other than litigation which always seems to be several steps behind the next round of corporate aggressiveness. There is so much more that needs to be addressed. One particularly insightful view has recently been offered:

> An economic system that facilitates the privatisation of gains in the hands of ever smaller elites while also socialising risk (losses) in an anarchic manner to the detriment of the many is not politically viable in the long run. This is the case, in particular, if a core element of this system's legitimacy is its claim to promote democracy at home and around the world based on principles of transparency and accountability. Both the global financial crisis and the Deepwater Horizon oil spill have already attained the status of 'watershed' events mainly because the social, economic and environmental risks inflicted by private actors on very large groups of people were extraordinary and the causes of failure to manage these risks were systemic rather than accidental.[32]

Put bluntly, banking conglomerates have become even bigger after the most recent wave of mergers. These giant firms are capable of earning higher profits than smaller banks because they can assume greater risks due to an "implicit bailout guarantee" funded by unwilling taxpayers. Some of these "ordinary citizens" have lost retirement savings due to corporate mismanagement of their accounts. Others have even lost their jobs or means of livelihood. In effect, it is organized and systematized robbery without the use of a gun.

The most asinine argument for federal bailout is the "too big to fail" cliché and the most ridiculous federal policy is bailout of these behemoths which inevitably makes them even bigger. When they cause the next financial crisis just a few years down the road, the cliché will again be recited despite few if any guarantees the first round of money found its way into channels that might have fixed, or even addressed, the initial problem.

Federal dollars that end up as corporate bonuses to inept executives responsible for the crisis in the first place instead of as loans to consumers potentially capable of investing in new small business ventures are infinitely less productive than dollars given to thousands of impoverished public assistance recipients. Federal money given, or even loaned, to corporations that then increase investment but outsource jobs does little or nothing to alleviate unemployment problems. The stimulus value of such dollars is quite small while the distribution of income becomes increasingly skewed. Any call for government assistance to the new ranks of the jobless is met with its traditional scorn.

It appears reasonable that, in the interest of a more competitive environment, huge banks be broken up into smaller entities, much as government did with AT&T in the early 1980s. Equally logical would be the re-separation of commercial and investment banking.[33]

The first of these would enhance, and in some cases simply create, competition that would benefit consumers, eliminate the "too big to fail"[34] nonsense, and reduce the need for huge federal bailouts in the future. Further, it would encourage more responsible lending practices, internalize risks to the banks themselves, and reduce both the economic and political power currently wielded by megabanks. Alleged economies of scale in banking have proven to be overstated. The benefits of size are clearly smaller than the potential costs large banks impose on the public.

The second of these was initially enacted because banks played the stock market with the money of depositors during the 1920s. Such speculation contributed to the Great Crash of 1929 and the more than decade long depression that followed. Repealing the 1933 law that separated commercial and investment banking was arguably one of the most shortsighted appeals to special interests this country has ever seen.

If commercial and investment banking are again separated, commercial banks could return to the "boring and simple" tasks of accepting deposits and making standard loans. Under this proposal, bailout of gambling casino institutions like investment banks would be strictly prohibited. In the free market, such firms would be free to succeed or fail. Those that became profitable would attract additional clients while those that lost money would exit from the industry. Sadly, because of the strength of the "vested interests", neither proposal is likely to be undertaken any time soon.

Pressure to deregulate financial markets in the last two decades of the 20th century recreated an only slightly modernized version of pre-Great Depression banking.[35] For those who had learned from history, chaotic results were predictable. Imagine what might have happened if social security had been privatized before 2007, as many in the financial sector had hoped. Enormous fortunes would have morphed into the hands of unscrupulous money managers while most Americans would have seen their retirement savings stolen from them.

The experience of JPMorgan Chase Bank is most instructive. After "allegedly" underwriting a substantial portion of the Enron financial scam and paying $2.2 billion to avoid prosecution of the charge,[36] the bank has consistently been involved in lawsuits claiming fraud, racial discrimination in lending practices, and numerous other charges.[37] When federal bailout money came its way, some of the cash was awarded as bonuses to top executives and mergers have made the firm more powerful than ever. Chase routinely contributes to the political campaigns of those who sit on prestigious Congressional banking committees. Is the competitive invisible hand of the marketplace working effectively in the Chase case?

Despite repeated instances of corporate misbehavior, the view somehow persists that unregulated megafirms will automatically produce results that are both ethical and beneficial to all.[38] Until that view disappears or is at least substantially modified, repeated financial crises, each successive one more severe in magnitude, may not be inevitable but certainly are highly plausible.

Footnotes:

1. Joseph E. Pluta, *Small Trees in the Large Forest,* (Redding, CA: CAT Publishing, 2006), Ch. 7.

2. Tuna Baskoy, "Thorstein Veblen's Theory of Business Competition," *Journal of Economic Issues,* 37, 4 (December 2003), p. 1124.

3. William T. Ganley, "The Theory of Business Enterprise and Veblen's Neglected Theory of Corporation Finance," *Journal of Economic Issues,* 38, 2 (June 2004), p. 399. See also Lino Sau, "Instability and Crisis in Financial Complex Systems", *Review of Political Economy*, 25, 3 (July 2013), pp. 496-511 and Cristina Peicuti, "Securitization and the Subprime Mortgage Crisis", *Journal of Post Keynesian Economics*, 35, 3 (April 2013), pp. 443-456.

4. James V. Cornehls, "Veblen's Theory of Finance Capitalism and Contemporary Corporate America," *Journal of Economic Issues,* 38, 1 (March 2004), pp. 29–58, especially p. 34. See also Jeremy Green and Colin Hay, "Towards a New Political Economy of the Crisis: Getting What Went Wrong Right", *New Political Economy*, 20, 3 (2015), pp. 331-341 and Malcolm Sawyer, "What is Financialization?" *International Journal of Political Economy*, 42, 4 (2013), pp. 5-18.

5. Baskoy, pp. 1128–1129.

6. Thorstein Veblen, *The Theory of Business Enterprise,* (New York: Charles Scribners Sons, 1904), p. 255.

7. Thorstein Veblen, *The Engineers and the Price System,* (New York: Viking Press, 1921), p. 127 quoted in Baskoy, p. 1129. See also Kees Van Der Pijl and Yuliya Yurchenko, "Neoliberal Retrenchment of North Atlantic Capital: From Corporate Self-Regulation to State Capture", *New Political Economy*, 20, 4 (2015), pp. 495-517 and William Redmond, "Evolution of Corporate Governance Principles Among U. S. Firms", *Journal of Economic Issues*, 44, 3 (2010), pp. 615-627.

8. Veblen, 1904, p. 20. See also Cornehls, p. 35. The overall movement of the economy toward financial concerns has recently been described in Tae-Hee Jo and John F. Henry, "The Business Enterprise in an Age of Money Market Capitalism", *Journal of Economic Issues*, 49, 1 (March 2015), pp. 23-46.

9. Antoon Spithoven and Piet Keizer, "Markets and Rules: The Case of the Global Credit Crunch", *Journal of Economic Issues*, 45, 2 (June 2011), pp. 391-400. See also Donald C. Wellington and Sourushe Zandvakili, "Globalization and Inequality According to Veblen," *International Journal of Social Economics,* 31, 11-12 (2004), pp. 1061–1070.

10. J. Patrick Raines and Charles G. Leathers, "Veblenian Stock Markets and the Efficient Markets Hypothesis," *Journal of Post Keynesian Economics,* 19, 1 (Fall 1996), pp. 137–151 and J. Patrick Raines and Charles G. Leathers, "Financial Innovations and Veblen's Theory of Financial Markets," *Journal of Economic Issues,* 26, 2 (June 1992), pp. 433–440.

11. Baskoy, p. 1130.

12. Baskoy, pp. 1130–1131.

13. Joseph E. Pluta and Charles G. Leathers, "Veblen and Modern Radical Economics," *Journal of Economic Issues,* 12, 1 (March 1978), pp. 129–130.

14. Veblen, 1904, pp. 195–196, as quoted in Baskoy, p. 1131.

15. Cornehls, p. 43.

16. Philip Anthony O'Hara, "The Contemporary Relevance of Thorstein Veblen's Institutional-Evolutionary Political Economy," *History of Economics Review,* 35 (Winter 2002), p. 92.

17. Veblen, *Absentee Ownership and Business Enterprise in Recent Times,* (New York: B. W. Heubsch, 1923), pp. 418–445.

18. Cornehls, pp. 47–48.

19. Irwin M. Stelzer, "The Corporate Scandals and American Capitalism," *The Public Interest,* no. 154, (Winter 2004), pp. 19-31; John Vickers, "Abuse of Market Power," *Economic Journal,* 115, 504 (June 2005), pp. 244–261; Stephen M. Renas and Richard J. Cebula, "Enron, Herding, and the Deterrent Effect of Disclosure of Improprieties," *American Journal of Economics and Sociology,* 64, 3 (July 2005), pp. 743–757; and Joseph E. Pluta, "Evolutionary Economic Explanations of Corporate Scandals", *Perspectives in Business* 5, 2 (Fall 2008), pp. 23-29.

20. Cornehls, p. 48; Brian J. Hall and Kevin J. Murphy, "The Trouble With Stock Options", *Journal of Economic Perspectives*, 17, 3 (Summer 2003), pp. 49-70; Marianne Bertrand and Sendhil Mullainathan, "Are CEOs Paid for Luck? The Ones Without Principals Are", *Quarterly Journal of Economics,* 116, 3 (August 2001), pp. 901-932; and John

Abowd and David Kaplan, "Executive Compensation: Six Questions That Need Answering", *Journal of Economic Perspectives*, 13, 4 (Fall 1999), pp. 145-168.

21. Cornehls, p. 45.

22. John Grahl, "The Professors and the Banks: U. S. Views on the Subprime Crisis", *International Review of Applied Economics*, 28, 3 (May 2014), pp. 383-400; Brian Fahey, "A Critical Review of Neoclassical Modeling Techniques in Structured Finance", *Journal of Post Keynesian Economics*, 35, 3 (April 2013), pp. 319-340; and A. Larry Elliot and Richard J. Schroth, *How Companies Lie: Why Enron Is Just the Tip of the Iceberg,* (New York: Crown Business, 2002).

23. Kenneth E. Boulding, *The Organizational Revolution: A Study in the Ethics of Economic Organization,* (New York: Harper, 1953).

24. Kenneth E. Boulding, *Evolutionary Economics,* (Beverly Hills, CA: Sage Publications, 1981) and Vladislav Valentinov, "Kenneth Boulding's Theories of Evolutionary Economics and Organizational Change: A Reconstruction", *Journal of Economic Issues*, 49, 1 (March 2015), pp. 71-88.

25. Kenneth E. Boulding, "Social Risk, Political Uncertainty, and the Legitimacy of Private Profit," in R. H. Howard, ed., *Risk and Regulated Firms,* (East Lansing: Michigan State University Graduate School of Business Administration, 1973).

26. Robert Waters, "What Happened to Boulding's Evolutionary Economics?" *Journal of Economic Issues,* 40, 2 (June 2006), pp. 465–471.

27. Joseph E. Pluta, "Kenneth Boulding's Skeleton of Science

and Contemporary General Systems Theory", in Wilfred Dolfsma and Stefan Kesting, eds., *Interdisciplinary Economics: Kenneth E. Boulding's Engagement in the Sciences*, (London: Routledge, 2013), pp. 48-60.

28. Kenneth E. Boulding, *Beyond Economics: Essays in Society, Religion, and Ethics,* (Ann Arbor: University of Michigan Press, 1968).

29. Quoted in R. P. Beilock, *Beasts, Ballads, and Bouldingisms: A Collection of Writings by Kenneth E. Boulding,* (New Brunswick, NJ: Transaction Books, 1980).

30. For a concise collection of Galbraith's most important arguments, see John Kenneth Galbraith, *The Essential Galbraith,* (Boston: Houghton Mifflin, 2001). For a recent summary of many of Galbraith's positions, see Steven P. Dunn and Stephen Pressman, "The Economic Contributions of John Kenneth Galbraith," *Review of Political Economy,* 17, 2 (April 2005), pp. 161–209.

31. Randy R. Grant, "Measuring Corporate Power: Assessing the Options," *Journal of Economic Issues,* 31, 2 (June 1997), pp. 453–460.

32. Stephanie Blankenburg, Dan Plesch, and Frank Wilkinson, "Limited Liability and the Modern Corporation in Theory and in Practice", *Cambridge Journal of Economics*, 34, 5 (September 2010), pp. 821-836.

33. Both of these proposals as well as several others are made by Helge Peukert, "The Financial Crisis: Origins and Remedies in a Critical Institutionalist Perspective", *Journal of Economic Issues*, 44, 3 (September 2010), pp. 830-838.

34. Andrew Ross Sorkin, *Too Big to Fail*, (New York: Viking

Press, 2009).

35. William Van Lear and James Sisk, "Financial Crisis and Economic Stability: A Comparison Between Finance Capitalism and Money Manager Capitalism", *Journal of Economic Issues*, 44, 3 (September 2010), pp. 779-793.

36. Joseph E. Pluta, "The Role of Chase Bank in the Enron Scandal", in Daniel Fireside and Amy Gluckman, *Real World Banking and Finance*, 6th ed., (Boston: Economic Affairs Bureau, 2010).

37. Joseph E. Pluta, "Chase: A Bank for the New Century?", *Dollars and Sense*, No. 270, (Spring 2007), pp. 24-27, 35.

38. Joseph E. Pluta, "The Libertarian Fantasy of an Ethical Market", *Research in the History of Economic Thought and Methodology*, 25-A, (2007), pp. 13-23.

Epilogue

Recent Research on the Life of Veblen

Facts about the background and personal life of Thorstein Veblen have been severely distorted by a character defamation effort that lasted *for more than six decades.* Academic administrators who resented positions Veblen took, rivals jealous of his success, biographers interested in furthering their own careers by adding unsubstantiated lurid details, and sloppy scholarship have all contributed to an image that is not only inaccurate but in many cases blatantly false.

The most egregious fallacious claims include an alleged poverty and cultural backwardness of Veblen's family, his supposed limited facility with the English language until he entered college, his overly eccentric personality traits that caused him to be alienated from society, and his presumed numerous extramarital affairs. Research beginning in the 1990s has proven these and other claims to be based on hearsay and to be purely fictional.*

According to the 1870 census, Thomas and Kari Veblen were the richest farmers in Cato Township. The family was prosperous enough that it did not have to borrow money to send several of the twelve children to a private college where they did not even have to apply for scholarships. Thorstein spoke both English and Norwegian by the age of five and eventually became fluent in more than twenty languages. While he possessed numerous eccentricities, including his distaste for proper dress and an often biting wit, he was much beloved among a wide circle of friends who possessed similar dissident viewpoints.

A Columbia University graduate student in his twenties composed a biography of Veblen as his doctoral dissertation. *Thorstein Veblen and His America* published by Joseph Dorfman in 1934 became "*the* definitive work" on Veblen until its author's private papers were released after his death in 1991. Those papers and other research including interviews with Veblen's stepdaughter revealed that much of the biography was fabricated and based on unproven anecdotes. Among other things, the papers contained correspondence between Dorfman and Veblen's older brother, Andrew, who found the manuscript filled with so many factual errors that he threatened to block its publication.

Dorfman's mentor who supervised the project was an economist named Alvin Johnson, a rival of Veblen who resented the success he achieved and the public wit he often displayed. Johnson was fond of storytelling and apparently filled Dorfman with numerous invented tales that his student used freely in his writing. Subsequent scholars have often quoted these stories while doing nothing to document their veracity. As a result, Veblen's "backward" rural upbringing in a Norwegian community, his personality, and his marital problems have become the folklore of invented legend. Presumably, the motivation was that, if Veblen's background and behavior could be portrayed as erratic, his ideas could more easily be discredited as well.

The most serious character assassination his legacy has had to endure concerns his alleged philandering and insatiable sexual appetite. Over the years, various accounts have claimed that no one was safe from his wandering eye. His "licentious womanizing" was supposedly directed toward young students and faculty wives. Derogatory statements he made in jest that he found faculty wives to be undesirable and a trip he made to Europe no doubt fueled the latter claim.

When Veblen was critical of corporate funding of higher education, University of Chicago President William Rainey Harper manufactured a story that Veblen travelled to Europe accompanied by the wife of a faculty colleague. Unwilling to participate in this libelous account, Chicago newspapers refused to print the story. Its contents, however, were leaked and repeated by numerous later writers whose careless retelling of the incident ultimately gave it an air of credibility. In fact, Veblen travelled to Europe with a colleague (English professor Oscar Triggs), the colleague's wife (Laura McAdoo Triggs), and their child. Since Veblen remained friends with the family for many years after the trip, the likelihood of an extramarital affair in this instance is remote at best.

The charge of affairs with students demands closer inspection. In the late nineteenth century, relatively few women attended universities. Even fewer became graduate students in economics. In a male-dominated discipline, scholarly interaction between men and women was rare. Its occurrence naturally prompted unfounded wild speculation.

When Veblen taught at the University of Chicago, one of his most gifted graduate students was a young lady named Sarah (Sadie) Hardy. Their professor-student relationship eventually grew into a friendship and later a professional colleague status. Veblen actively sought Miss Hardy's comments on his work including the manuscript that was to become his best selling and classic first book. Upon leaving the U of C, Sadie became an instructor at Wellesley College.

Throughout their association, Veblen was married to his first wife, Ellen, although their marriage was a troubled one and included several separations. There is no evidence whatsoever that Veblen and Sadie ever engaged in physical intimacy. The number of times they were seen on walks together, however, no doubt contributed ample fodder to the rumor mill. It is true that Veblen was extremely fond of her and did consider a future relationship with her. When Sadie announced her plans to marry a San Francisco attorney, Veblen was disappointed, professed in writing his love for her and his intention to seek a divorce, but eventually stepped aside and offered his congratulations. They maintained a professional relationship after her marriage and later Veblen was even a guest at the couple's home in California. Ellen Veblen obviously resented her husband's attraction to Sadie, although his actions were clearly within accepted Victorian standards.

While living in Chicago and not yet legally divorced, Veblen did begin an intimate relationship with another of his graduate students, the woman who was to become his second wife. Separated from her husband but not yet formally divorced, Ann Fessenden ("Babe") Bradley was a free-thinking socialist with two young daughters. She eventually followed Veblen to California and enrolled in graduate school at UC Berkeley. When Veblen taught at Stanford and lived (separated from Ellen) in a place called Cedro Cottage, he and Ann met frequently. There are carelessly concocted stories of young women coming and going from the home where Veblen then resided with three male students. Most likely, Babe was the only woman who visited and stayed with him. After Ellen finally granted the divorce he had requested some fifteen years earlier, Veblen married Babe and adopted her two daughters, Becky and Ann.

After Ellen died in 1926, an autopsy revealed that her female organs were not fully developed. Pregnancy and even sexual relations were determined to have been impossible. While this "terrible secret" had been kept from public knowledge throughout her lifetime, it no doubt contributed to a less than satisfactory marriage.

During the time Veblen spent married to Babe, he was more content than at any previous point in his life. The two conceived a child but the little boy was stillborn seven months into the pregnancy. Veblen loved her daughters as his own and spent considerable time with his new family. Accounts of their time together suggest anything but a lothario seeking to engage in mischief. In fact, given the circumstances of his first marriage, it is distinctly possible that, during his entire lifetime, Veblen may have had sexual relations with only one woman.

While she generally shared the political and philosophical views of her husband, Ellen Veblen often exhibited both overly jealous and outright neurotic behavior. She complained to the presidents of both Stanford and Chicago that Veblen was engaging in extramarital affairs, claims that neither man could independently verify. Correspondence Ellen sent to Veblen after their divorce suggests a troubled mind filled with loose associations among several unrelated events as well as a profound interest in a religious cult. She clearly attempted to use difficulties in her marriage in an effort to ruin the career of her husband. To a significant degree, she succeeded.

Subsequent Veblen biographers have described Ann Veblen in less than flattering terms. Some have even implied that the name "Babe" was somehow indicative of dubious moral character and that her institutionalization late in life was related to a long history of serious mental issues. Both claims were targeted at establishing a link between the company Veblen kept and his "radical" ideas.

In fact, Ann was known as "Babe" since early childhood because she was the youngest member of her family. Of course, mental illness was treated far less sympathetically in the 1920s than in recent times. More seriously, it has been documented that, upon learning of her intention to marry Veblen, Ann's brother-in-law, Wallace Atwood, struck her on the side of her head with the butt of his rifle causing her to fall to the floor. Both he and Ann's sister, Harriet, then shouted at her as she lay near motionless and in obvious pain. Mr. and Mrs. Wallace were both fearful that their family would be disgraced if Ann married a man with views that were offensive to "civilized society". Ann's 13-year-old daughter, Becky, had been present and observed what had happened. Her mother later told her never to relate this incident to anyone.

In the months that followed, Ann began to undergo severe head pain and eventually swelling of the brain, a condition that worsened over time and resulted in her placement in an institution. She died in the fall of 1920 after experiencing symptoms of madness and borderline insanity. Although the official Massachusetts death certificate and statement of a UCLA cancer specialist list different (and conflicting!) causes of Ann's death, Becky Veblen has stated in interviews and in writing that her mother died from the head injury inflicted by Atwood. While her conclusion was based on neither medical competence nor professional evaluation of an autopsy, it does come from the person most knowledgeable of her mother's mental state over the last years of her life.

Apparently, Veblen never knew of the physical assault on his soon-to-be wife.

There is no doubt that women were attracted to Veblen. Some of his biographers have argued the reason had more to do with his progressive views on women's rights than any physical characteristics. Such views were so counter to established Victorian thinking that they provided yet another reason for his critics to smear his character. An unhappy first marriage that resulted in divorce and an openness to equal rights for women were simply not tolerable in a culture that accepted neither.

---

* See, for example, Russell H. Bartley and Sylvia Erickson Bartley, "Stigmatizing Thorstein Veblen: A Study in the Confection of Academic Reputations", *International Journal of Politics, Culture and Society*, 14, 2 (2000), pp. 363-400; Elizabeth Watkins Jorgensen and Henry Irvin Jorgensen, *Thorstein Veblen: Victorian Firebrand*, (Armonk, NY: M. E. Sharpe, 1999); Russell H. Bartley and Sylvia Erickson Bartley, "In Search of Thorstein Veblen: Further Inquiries Into His Life and Work", *International Journal of Politics, Culture and Society*, 11, 1 (1997), pp. 129-173; Stephen Edgell, "Rescuing Veblen From Valhalla: Deconstruction and

Reconstruction of a Sociological Legend", *British Journal of Sociology*, 47, 4 (1996), pp. 627-642; Russell H. Bartley and Sylvia E. Yoneda, "Thorstein Veblen on Washington Island: Traces of a Life", *International Journal of Politics, Culture and Society*, 7, 4 (1994), pp. 589-613; and Rick Tilman, *Thorstein Veblen and His Critics, 1891-1963*, (Princeton, NJ: Princeton University Press, 1992), especially chapter 1.

www.ingramcontent.com/pod-product-compliance
Lightning Source LLC
Chambersburg PA
CBHW051443170526
45166CB00001B/93

* 9 7 8 1 5 1 9 3 1 5 8 1 6 *